Tourism Development and Local Participation in Latin America

Edited by
Heidi Dahles
and
Lou Keune

COGNIZANT COMMUNICATION CORPORATION
New York • Sydney • Tokyo
www.cognizantcommunication.com

Tourism Development and Local Participation in Latin America

Cognizant Communication Offices:

U.S.A.   3 Hartsdale Road, Elmsford, New York 10523-3701
Australia   P.O. Box 352 Cammeray, NWS, 2062
Japan   c/o OBS T's Bldg. 3F, 1-38-11 Matsubara, Setagaya-ku, Tokyo

Library of Congress Cataloging-in-Publication Data

Tourism development and local participation in Latin America / edited by Heidi Dahles and Lou Keune.
    p. cm. — (Tourism dynamics)
    Includes bibliographical references and index
    ISBN 1-882345-42-8 (alk. paper) — ISBN 1-882345-43-6 (soft bound : alk. paper)
    1. Tourism — Latin America. 2. Tourism — Caribbean Area. 3. Community
development — Latin America. 4. Community development — Caribbean Area. 5.
Tourism — Social aspects — Latin America. 6. Tourism — Social aspects — Caribbean Area. I.
Dahles, Heidi. II. Keune, Lou. III. Series.

G155.L3 T66 2002
338.4'7918—dc21

                                                                      2002041022

Printed in the United States of America

Printing: 1 2 3 4 5 6 7 8 9 10 Year: 1 2 3 4 5 6 7 8 9 10

Contents

Chapter 9. The (Missing) Gender Dimension: A Review of   130
Tourism Literature on Latin America and the Caribbean
Anne-Marie Van Broeck

Chapter 10. Future Prospects and Perspectives of   153
Latin American and Caribbean Tourism Policies
Lou Keune and Heidi Dahles

List of Figures

List of Tables

Preface

Most chapters of this book are based on empirical research conducted in major tourist areas in a number of Latin American and Caribbean countries. The case studies as presented in Chapters 5, 6, and 8 were conducted by graduate students of the Department of Leisure Studies of the faculty of Social Sciences of Tilburg University on behalf of their MA thesis. Chapter 7 is based on an MA thesis produced at the University of Amsterdam in cooperation with Tilburg University. The other chapters are based on either fieldwork (Chapter 4) or elaborate statistical (Chapter 2) or literature analysis (Chapters 3 and 9). All the authors who contribute to this volume have first-hand research experience in Latin American or Caribbean countries.

All the field research on which this book is based was conducted in 1995–1997. The graduate projects were conducted during a 4-month fieldwork period. The projects basically apply a multidisciplinary approach. Given the nature of the research population and the conditions under which the research was conducted, the emphasis is on qualitative methodology, centering around anthropological fieldwork and ethnographical interviewing. In addition, surveys and secondary analysis were applied where appropriate.

The editors would like to acknowledge the support of the following persons and institutions:

- The Departments of Leisure Studies and Sociology of the faculty of Social Sciences of Tilburg University (Netherlands) for providing the institutional conditions to develop the research and compose this book.
- The Department of Culture, Organization and Management of the faculty of Social Studies of Vrije University of Amsterdam for generously allocating time and money to one of the editors to finalize this volume.
- The Talencentrum of Tilburg University, and in particular Hildegard Penn, for the editing of some of our English texts.

The editors would like to express their gratitude to Anne-Marie van Schaardenburgh, graduate student and student-assistant of the Department of Leisure Studies of Tilburg University, who compiled an annotated bibliography on small entrepreneurs and local participation in tourism on behalf of this volume.

Paul Wilkinson, professor of Environmental Studies at York University (Ontario, Canada), took great pains reading and editing the first draft of this volume. His critical approach based on his vast expertise in tourism in the geographical area central to this book is greatly appreciated. The editors also wish to acknowledge Valene Smith, Professor of Anthropology at California State University in Chico, for her ongoing support throughout this project.

Finally, the editors want to thank Piet den Blanken for the excellent photographs.

Heidi Dahles
Lou Keune

Chapter 1

Introduction

Heidi Dahles and Lou Keune

After World War II, tourism became an asset to contribute to the fast recovery of the devastated economies of many Latin American and Caribbean countries. Governments decided to incorporate tourism either as an economic alternative to achieve growth or as a supplementary aspect of other economic activities. Tourism development implemented after the 1950s was designed to create leisure resorts for residents of industrialized countries. In accordance with the cultural link with Spain, the Spanish tourist boom set the tone for tourism development in many Latin American countries. Therefore, the characteristics of tourism development were decided by the industrialized countries and were accepted without hesitation by countries in Latin America and the Caribbean, where tourism was seen as the magic solution to all their problems. As in so many other developing countries, tourism was regarded as an engine of modernization and industrialization. At present, tourism is an extremely diverse phenomenon in Latin America and the Caribbean. Its organization, impact, and significance vary across different national economies; similarly, sharp differences can also be found within the national borders of each individual country. This is related partly to the colonial past, when borders were arbitrarily drawn, and partly to geographical differences, which impacted on the cultural occupation of the territory (Chant, 1992; Schlüter, 1994).

Three basic themes can be distinguished in the tourist product of Latin America. First, there is mass tourism based on the "three Ss" (sun, sand, and sea), generating resort beach tourism (e.g., Cancún in Mexico, Puerto Plata in Dominican Republic, and Varadero in Cuba). Second, there is cultural/folkloric tourism, focusing on the archaeological remains of the three major pre-Columbian cultures (i.e., the Aztecs in Mexico, the Mayas in Mexico, and the Incas in Peru and Bolivia). Other cultural attractions exploited for tourism are the colonial Spanish architecture and contemporary handicraft industries and markets. Third, there is environmental/ecotourism that is nature based and appeals to those Latin American countries that lack attractive beaches. Costa Rica, for example, has become the ecotourist destination par excellence in Latin America. Other famous "eco" destinations are the Galapagos Islands (Ecuador) and, to a lesser degree, the Bariloche area in Argentina (Schlüter, 1994).

The volume of, and benefits from, tourism vary widely among countries in Latin America and the Caribbean. Mexico receives not only the largest number of foreign visitors in the region, but also the largest benefits. On the other hand, the small island economies in the Caribbean, such as the Bahamas, Barbados, St. Lucia, and others, are totally dependent on tourism (cf. Wilkinson, 1997). In countries such as Honduras, El Salvador, Suriname, and the Guyanas, on the other hand, the contribution of tourism to the national economy is negligible (Chant, 1992). In general, tourism in South America is largely dependent on regional tourists (i.e., Latin Americans). Countries such as Argentina and Uruguay rely heavily on domestic and regional tourism, while travelers from Colombia, Chile, and Paraguay establish the bulk of all international arrivals in the region (Chant, 1992). International arrivals from outside the region have increased since the postwar period above the world average growth rate. However, the share of the world total of international tourists is still very small (only 3.8% in 1990 compared with 3.2% in 1950) (Chant, 1992). And the growth of tourism receipts in Latin America lags behind worldwide growth, which means that the growth of average tourist expenditure in Latin America lags behind that on other continents. (For a more elaborate presentation of these figures, refer to Chapter 2.)

In contrast to developing countries in Africa and Southeast Asia, which are experiencing large-scale tourism developments, many Latin American countries have established or are in the process of establishing policies that give priority to forms of tourism that may be described as "community-based" tourism with a strong emphasis on the natural environment (ecotourism, "green" tourism) and cultural integrity ("responsible," "appropriate," or "soft" tourism). In particular, those countries lacking the three Ss put much effort into developing ecotourism in order to benefit from the concern about the deterioration of the environment. National governments have all been heavily involved in investments in large-scale tourism resorts as well as in planning processes for ecotourism. While in some areas the resorts have come to dominate the landscape, only a few ecotourist projects have left the launching pad. Schlüter (1994) relates this failure to the intertwining of tourism planning with political favoritism, as a consequence of which executives are appointed for political reasons and not for their expertise and know-how. Projects that have materialized are mostly the result of foreign initiatives and funding by the industrialized countries (Schlüter, 1994).

In many Latin American countries, community-based forms of tourism are emerging that are mediated by nongovernmental organizations (NGOs). These new forms of tourism come to exist side by side or in overt competition and even conflict with existing or newly planned resorts of a mass tourism character. These new forms of tourism have to position themselves in a market that is driven by commercial forces under conditions of structural inequality between a tourism sector that originates in the developed, metropolitan countries on the one hand and destination areas in the developing or less developed world on the other (cf. Britton, 1989). Therefore, this volume focuses on the issue of community-based tourism. Questions that will be raised are:

- To what extent and under which conditions does community-based tourism emerge and operate in Latin American and Caribbean countries?

- How does community-based tourism relate to mass tourism organizations and which opportunities and restrictions does mass tourism constitute?
- To what extent does community-based tourism contribute to sustainable developments?
- What opportunities does tourism offer to local people to make a living in a sustainable way?
- To what extent does tourism stimulate local entrepreneurship?
- What kinds of tourism need to be developed to meet the objectives of sustainability?
- What social and political structures need to be established to generate and monitor community-based tourism projects? How do NGOs fit in?
- What economic, ecological, political, social, and cultural conditions are necessary to successfully establish and maintain community-based tourism?

These questions revolve around concepts such as community, local participation, and sustainability, which will be used as key concepts throughout this volume. Therefore, before venturing into descriptions and analyses of tourism developments in specific Latin American and Caribbean countries, a closer look at the significance of these concepts is needed for the discussion about the future of tourism in developing countries.

The Organization of International Tourism

Tourism is expanding at a global level and this expansion is interrelated with processes of globalization. An important aspect of this development is the organization of mass tourism travel to large-scale tourism resorts involving national governments and large multinational investors. Many governments in developing countries give priority to large-scale investments in tourism as they expect this sector to contribute significantly to national income and employment, and therefore constitute an effective strategy of modernization and development. However, large-scale multinational enterprises are often not as effective as originally believed in increasing foreign exchange earnings and job opportunities, because there is significant economic leakage due to the purchase of foreign goods and labor and to the channeling of profits out of the developing countries (see Chapter 2).

The economic and political implications of promoting development strategies that favor large-scale developments and foreign participation are but part of a still wider problem: the unequal relationship between large-scale and small-scale businesses in the tourism sector. Dependist theorists like Britton (1989) point out that the tourism sector is part of the set of unbalanced linkages between developed and developing countries, the core and the periphery. The economic organization and associated political institutions of developing countries can be identified as a distinct type of social formation—that of a peripheral capitalist economy (Britton, 1989). This scenario applies where a capitalist sector, consisting of oligopolistic firms, is deeply integrated in an economy and linked to a variety of noncapitalist ("traditional") sectors. The resulting linkages between the two sectors are primarily a response to the needs and pace of expansion of the capitalist sector: peripheral capitalist economies are characterized and defined by a combination of capitalist and noncapitalist forms of production under the domination of the former. As governments in the periphery are dependent on the dominant sectors for the economic development of the state and for their own political legitimacy, the operation and expansion of these capitalist interests are given free reign. The allocation of financial aid, the provision of infrastructure, the orientation of administrative services, and the passing of licensing, labor, and marketing regulations all proceed in accordance with the requirements of the dominant sectors.

Because foreign companies are most important in defining what constitutes a tourism product, tourism services in a peripheral destination are likely to be owned and provided by these firms. The role that local-level economic activities are assigned in this dependist scenario is rather limited, as "external" forces largely determine their success and failure. The nature of the international tourism system and the marginal niche that local people are filling seem to support the idea of the local economy operating in a "traditionalist" way and representing the underdeveloped and stagnant part of society. Developmental organizations strongly reflect this image. Tourism was and still is largely rejected as a development strategy because it is regarded as a neocolonial instrument enforcing inequality and exploitation through the international tourism industry (Van der Duim, 1997). And as far as developmental organizations initiate tourism projects at all, they are NGO led and oriented towards community development or nature conservation. Multinational, as well as local business, strategies and practices to develop tourism were and still are considered detrimental to these goals.

Sustainability

The increasing concern for the environment in the 1980s set the stage for a critical assessment of tourism and, in particular, for the view that "in some cases the economic benefits of tourism are more than outweighed by the environmental and social costs of tourism" (Archer & Cooper, 1994, p. 74). In this light, the growth scenarios linked to rapid mass tourism development came under fire—the more so as the tourism boom slowed down in the 1980s and 1990s and the detrimental environmental and social impacts of mass tourism became visible. In response, the concept of "sustainable tourism development" came to be used as the basis of tourism planning and management. This concept, which is derived from the field of resource management, gained much prominence after publication of the Brundtland Report, *Our Common Future*, where sustainable development is defined simply as "meeting the needs of the present without compromising the ability of future generations to meet their own needs" (cf. Archer & Cooper, 1994, p. 87). Although this concept has come to be criticized for being abused as a marketing instrument to satisfy consumer demand, tourism consumption is not purely the outcome of manipulation by the image makers of the tourism sector. Consumer demand and consumer ideas about the ethics of consumption also change. Such reactions are illustrated by the emergence of the critical consumer demanding, as Krippendorf explained, a soft and humane tourism for which the common goal must be to develop and promote new forms of tourism, which will bring the greatest possible benefit to all participants—travelers, the host population, and the tourist business—without causing intolerable ecological and social damage (Krippendorf, cited in Shaw & Williams, 1994, p. 246).

The concept of sustainable tourism development is based on the goal of renewable economic, social, and cultural benefits to the community and its environment (Richards & Hall, 2000a). Behind this definition, complex issues lie hidden. As Archer and Cooper (1994) point out, strategies of "hardening" the environment, zoning, and concentration of visitors allow the accommodation of large numbers of tourists in an area without violating the environment to an unacceptable degree. But these strategies do not necessarily contribute to economic benefits for local communities and may even be detrimental in social and cultural respects. Therefore, Archer and Cooper (1994) emphasize that the central question of sustainable tourism development is: "tourism management—for whom?" (p. 74). After all, tourism planning and management involves different stakeholders—tourists, developers, planners, environmentalists, the related industries, and local communities—among whom conflicts and tensions about the scale and scope of tourism development easily flare up.

These different stakeholders are not "equal" partners in this debate; unequal power relations define their position. Often, tourism ranges under the economic departments of national and regional governments, yet the impacts of these policies are felt at local community levels. Equally so, decisions taken in the board rooms of multinational (tourism) companies in Tokyo, Singapore, and New York may affect the success or failure of national policies in, for example, Latin American countries. For the past 30 years, the benefits from tourism were almost exclusively measured in terms of tourist expenditures and, therefore, the planning and marketing of tourism have been primarily oriented towards the needs of the (foreign) tourist and the provision of attractive tourist experiences (Archer & Cooper, 1994). As the concept of sustainable tourism development is exerting more and more influence on tourism planning, the perspective of politicians and planners is slowly shifting to the long-term consequences of tourism expansion. This shift of perspective brings the role of local communities as important providers of tourist experiences and beneficiaries from tourism development into the picture.

Community

The debate on sustainability has related tourism development to local needs. The concept of community-based tourism has broadened the scope of the term of sustainability to integrate a wide range of issues, including local participation and democracy (Richards & Hall, 2000b). An increasing number of publications indicate the need to involve local communities in the process of sustainable tourism development (cf. Bramwell et al., 1998; Murphy, 1985; Richards & Hall, 2000a). In this vein, the local community has become the appropriate context for the development of sustainable tourism. In many developing countries, a more appropriately planned tourism development process is needed that would spread its costs and benefits more equitable and that would be more sensitive to its social and cultural impacts. Hence, the goal is that a large proportion of the local population should benefit from tourism rather than merely bearing the burden of its costs. As destinations are essentially communities, a community-based approach to tourism development, which considers the needs and interests of the popular majority alongside the benefits of economic growth, should be adopted. Community-based tourism would seek to strengthen institutions designed to enhance local participation and promote the economic, social, and cultural well-being of local people. It would also seek to strike a balanced approach to development that would stress considerations such as:

- the compatibility of various forms of tourism with other components of the local economy (i.e., backward linkages);
- the quality of development, both culturally and environmentally;
- the divergent needs, interests, and potentials of the community and its inhabitants.

At the local community level, a holistic concept of sustainability is applied that integrates environmental, economic, political, social, and cultural aspects. The local community becomes the arena where actions are taken to preserve the immediate environment, where entrepreneurship among local people is encouraged, local decision-making power is facilitated, social measures are designed, and the integrity of local culture is safeguarded.

The intertwining of strategies for sustainable development and for community development raises questions about the nature and significance of the community itself. "Community-led sustainable development requires an understanding not just of the relationship between local communities and their environment, but also of the political, economic and cultural tensions within communities" (Richards & Hall, 2000b, p. 6). Many experts seeking sustainable solutions for tourism-related problems view communities as homogeneous and harmonious. However, the interests of those living in local communities seldom coincide. Plans to generate tourism often arouse debate and conflict among local residents. Benefits from tourism are not shared equally by all. Moreover, many communities are multicultural as a consequence of either colonialism or processes of economic globalization or both. Multiculturalism produces a complex response to tourism in communities (Jafari, 1989), as will be discussed in a number of contributions to this volume.

One important arena where there is marked intracommunity inequality in participation in and benefits from tourism is in gender relations. Analyzing gender relations in the tourism labor market, Richter (1994) points out that "women have the majority of jobs at the base of the tourism employment hierarchy; men have almost all of the jobs at the middle and top" (p. 149). Men dominate the tourism sector in financial terms as well as in terms of policy making and decision making. Men control the political arena and government organizations where tourism policies are designed and implemented. Men also dominate those sectors where big money is generated, such as the airlines, railroads, major destination resorts, hotel chains, car rental companies, and travel magazines. Often, women owners and managers can be found in the smaller enterprises such as in the tour and travel agencies.

Turning to developing countries in particular, the tourism sector is first of all dominated by foreigners and secondly by men. Female ownership or management is generally negligible here. Women are the majority at the bottom of the hierarchy in tourism employment: chambermaids, restaurant helpers, and laundresses.

They get few tips and have the least dignified positions (Enloe, 1989). While women have been particularly perceived as appropriate for "frontline" tourism positions because they are assumed to be more hospitable than men (Richter, 1994), these positions are taken by males if one moves up the hierarchy of tourism establishments. Women may work as cooks and waitresses in local restaurants, but men take their place in star-rated restaurants. The jobs in the tourism sector that are accessible to women are often seasonal, part-time, or minimum wage. The status of these jobs reflects the status of the travel labor market, which is the least organized sector in the labor market in general.

The unequal distribution of benefits and burdens from tourism creates a niche for the "third sector" or grass-roots organizations, NGOs, and other organized groups that operate outside institutionalized frameworks (Richards & Hall, 2000a, p. 7). Increased popular participation in tourism requires institutional reform to provide possibilities for various groups to organize, represent themselves, and exert influence over decision making. Hierarchical institutional structures should be replaced by more democratic, two-way planning processes that empower people to design policies in their own interests and build on their own resources. The institutional design of tourism planning should facilitate the participation of various social groups that represent the diverse interests of the broader community. To prevent undemocratic, top-down decision making, the possible role of intermediaries (e.g., NGOs) between state and local community becomes more prominent. NGOs may facilitate local tourism development in a way that the state-versus-market dichotomy is surpassed. Empowerment being paramount to most versions of sustainable tourism, any top-down approach to tourism planning should be challenged by the need for local participation in all aspects of tourism planning and implementation.

Local Entrepreneurship

The new forms of tourism that are required to contribute to sustainable development consist of smaller-scale, dispersed, and low-density tourism development located in and organized by communities where it is hoped they will foster more meaningful interaction between tourists and local residents (Brohman, 1996). Financial subsidies alone are insufficient to guarantee involvement of local actors in the community. Instead, local entrepreneurial development is required. New forms of tourism depend on ownership patterns, which are in favor of local, often family-owned, relatively small-scale businesses rather than foreign-owned transnationals and other outside capital. By stressing the participation of local entrepreneurs, it is anticipated that tourism will increase multiplier and spread effects within the local community and avoid problems of excessive foreign exchange leakages. Local ownership implies that economic success for the entrepreneur results in benefits to the local economy.

Such developments are much more likely to rely on local sources of supplies and labor and are much less likely to produce negative sociocultural effects associated with foreign ownership. Local tolerance to tourism activities is significantly enhanced if opportunities exist for active resident involvement in the ownership and operation of facilities. Small-scale operations can also respond more effectively to changes in the marketplace and fill gaps overlooked by larger, more bureaucratic organizations. The problems in the majority of developing countries are that the private sector is small and entrepreneurial experience in many areas, including tourism, is lacking. The success or failure of small-scale entrepreneurs, however, largely depends on a number of conditions of which a supportive government and a local organizing capacity are the most important factors (cf. Dahles & Bras, 1999). Without government control that is stimulating instead of stifling, local tourism cannot develop in a sustainable way; this applies to the individual enterprise as well as the community as whole.

Policy Planning Management

Local participation—or rather its failure—is a problem of power relationships within the community as much as between the community and the provincial and national governments. Involving the community in decision-making processes "requires a free flow of appropriate intelligible and useable information within that community" (Richards & Hall 2000b, p. 299) and between communal and provincial and national government levels.

Whereas national governments in many developing countries promote tourism as a passport to development, the role that these governments attribute to the participation of small entrepreneurs in this development is highly limited. Government policies towards the local tourism sector vary widely, and there is no consensus regarding the ways in which tourism should be developed and the major objectives that this development should pursue. State involvement in community development can range from an overtly antiparticipatory to a participatory mode (Midgley, 1986). Where state bureaucracies expect tourism to contribute significantly to national development, tourism policy is directed towards large-scale investments in cooperation with transnational enterprises and project developers.

According to the classical economic definition, entrepreneurs are instruments for transforming and improving the economy and society, as entrepreneurs are regarded as innovators and risk takers pursuing progressive change (Go, 1997). Liberal market theorists believe that prosperity is the outcome of successful individual entrepreneurship (Mazumdar, 1989). While in the modernization paradigm small entrepreneurship may flourish in the early stages of capitalist development, it will soon be absorbed by large-scale business agglomerations. Small-scale businesses surviving under these circumstances are regarded as an obstacle rather than a vigorous force in tourism development. In that case, governments are characterized by an overtly antiparticipatory attitude: local participation in general and business initiatives of small-scale entrepreneurs in particular do not meet with supportive policies. Instead, governments often counter deregulatory measures at the top with more regulation and control below (cf. Dahles & Bras, 1999). While deregulation facilitates large-scale and transnational investments, the petty business sector is subdued to rules.

About This Book

The contributions to this book reflect the diversity in Latin American and Caribbean tourism. Referring to the three different categories of tourism as distinguished by Chant and Schlüter, the emphasis in this volume is on cultural/folkloric and ecotourism.

Some chapters in this book are based on extensive statistical analysis (Chapter 2) or on a thorough review of the literature on tourism impacts in a number of selected Latin American and Caribbean countries (Chapters 3 and 9). Chapter 4 combines the use of empirical data with an investigation of government plans and reports. The remaining chapters in this book are based on sociological and anthropological fieldwork. The authors lived in local communities in Costa Rica, El Salvador, Belize, and Ecuador that can be classified either as popular tourist areas offering cultural attractions (e.g., Cahuita in Costa Rica, San Ignacio in Belize, and Otavalo in Ecuador) or as emerging ecotourist destinations (e.g., San Carlos Lempa in El Salvador and Misahuallí in Ecuador). Through the choice of these field sites, the authors were able to observe and participate in the practice of tourism. Field data were obtained through informal and structured interviews with different actors in the local tourism industry and by recording life histories of a number of local key informants.

Where relevant, the authors participated in local tourist events and excursions. These excursions and events, combined with taking up temporary residence in local accommodations, formed the arena for the examination of the interaction between the local community and tourists. Although the research projects did not focus on tourist behavior, the authors considered it of importance to observe the local actors "on the job," giving information about the attractions, telling tales, and interacting with tourists. The information generated by participant observation was supplemented by interviews with government representatives and respondents working in the tourism sector and in NGOs. Additionally, secondary data, statistics, and case studies were obtained from government agencies, educational institutions, and consultancies.

The chapters are arranged as follows. Based on an assessment of social and economic developments in Latin America and the Caribbean in general, Keune and Vugts argue in Chapter 2 that tourism is considered an important potential growth sector that could contribute to solve persisting problems of economic imbalance, poverty and inequality, and environmental degradation. To make this happen, governments have to be aware of the leakages that diminish the income drawn from tourism. The extent to which governments can control these leakages depends, among other things, on the size of the economy. As this chapter shows, the possibilities of drastically limiting leakages are few. As is often the case in small countries with a strong dependence of foreign investment, it is highly doubtful whether a country should stake a high proportion of its resources on growth of the tourist sector. Especially in combination with such factors as low attractiveness for tourists and unstable political circumstances, tourism development can become a threat instead of an opportunity for the countries involved.

In Chapter 3, Groen addresses the advantages and disadvantages of ecotourism vis-à-vis mass tourism. This comparison is based on an analysis of tourism developments in Jamaica, Costa Rica, and Cuba. In these countries, tourism is one of the main sources of income. Private interests or bureaucratic barriers exist that hamper an efficient management of nature, tourism, and nature conservation. The governments of these countries cannot manage on their own to create and maintain ecotourism; rather, they need the support of the international community. Therefore, the author advocates stricter international guidelines and the intervention of organizations that contribute to the realization of conventions and that watch over the outcome of them—organizations that also have the power to pursue their goal of creating a more sustainable world.

Chapter 4 raises the question of how "eco" Costa Rica's ecotourism actually is. The analysis of Van der Duim and Philipsen focuses primarily on ways in which tourism contributes to nature conservation, in a material as well as symbolic way. On the one hand, it cannot be denied that tourism provides a very significant financial contribution to maintaining both national parks and private nature reserves in Costa Rica. Ecotourism has motivated the private sector to conserve or even restore natural environments. On the other hand, tourism development in the immediate vicinity of these nature reserves has led to negative impacts on nature and the environment and has given rise to serious concern. These impacts cannot be adequately countered because of a lack of planning and legislation. Moreover, the income derived from ecotourism does not benefit local people sufficiently, and the tourism sector is still to a very large extent in the hands of foreign businesses.

Local participation implies that local people benefit from and are given opportunities to participate actively—not only in decision-making processes but also in the initiation and implementation of tourist projects. This is the focus of Van Schaardenburgh in Chapter 5. The structures of influence and the mechanisms of control and dependence are crucial factors in the empowerment of people and are discussed in this case study of local participation in tourism development in a beach destination on the Caribbean coast of Costa Rica. Questions are raised concerning the opportunities that tourism offers the local community and the role of the national government to facilitate the participation of local people in tourism. Special attention is paid to the role of ethnicity in tourism-related local entrepreneurship as foreigners still constitute the most successful entrepreneurs, even in small-scale businesses.

Recently, El Salvador has devoted a lot of attention to promoting international tourism. As Brouwer shows in Chapter 6, a number of NGOs and small private enterprises have taken up the challenge to develop small tourism projects and build new hotels, looking for new development alternatives and a new source of income and employment. Among the NGOs is the CORDES Foundation (Fundación Para La Cooperación Y El Desarrollo Comunal De El Salvador), which, in the area of San Carlos Lempa located in the southern part of the country, promotes the *Sistema Economico Social* (SES), a form of organizing economic and social activity in such a way that decision making is in the hands of the local people. The aim is to achieve sustainable self-management. In search of new development alternatives, the idea was created to develop an ecotourism project. The central question raised in this chapter, therefore, addresses the conditions that need to be satisfied to develop a tourism attraction system that contributes to the sustainable development in the region.

The effects that the tourism policy of Belize's national government is exerting at a local level are investigated by Volker and Soree in Chapter 7. Interestingly, this tourism policy is positioned in a framework of sustainable economic development. Based on anthropological fieldwork the authors focus their attention on local business life in the tourism sector of San Ignacio, in the Cayo district of the country. By means of network analysis that centers on two key players in the local tourism sector, they show how the strategic use of economic, social, and cultural capital enhances opportunities, while cleverly applying the new regulations issued by the government in their attempt to enforce sustainable tourism development strengthens the position of some entrepreneurs at the cost of others and fuels tensions and conflicts at the local level.

Unlike in many other developing countries, tourism in Ecuador is usually initiated at a local level, as De Bont and Janssen point out in Chapter 8. However, only few initiatives have been undertaken and government support is generally lacking. There are no properly defined policy guidelines for state intervention in tourism projects, although once the state recognizes a place as a tourist resort, it usually will promote this place. How this unplanned government approach affects local tourism destinations is analyzed by means of two case studies. Considered as economically unprofitable and unimportant as a tourism destination, Misahuallí, a village in the Amazon rainforest, is ignored by the government. However, places that develop successfully do not enjoy government support either. Nevertheless, some places do extremely well in terms of tourism development, as are illustrated by the case of Otavalo, a market town north of the capital city of Quito. Considering the role that may be played by nongovernmental intervention, the authors issue a warning addressed to those Western researchers and planners who think they may be able to bring about tourism development in still un(der)developed Ecuadorian areas. In contrast to "Western" popular wisdom, indigenous people do not let themselves be overruled when decisions regarding their involvement in tourism have to be taken.

In Chapter 9, Van Broeck investigates gender issues in Latin American tourism from the perspective of women. Based on an extensive review of literature, questions are raised and answers are traced regarding the ways in which women participate in tourism in Latin America and the Caribbean—the ways they are involved in the construction of tourism. Their position in tourism employment and the kind of jobs available to them in the tourist sector are submitted to close scrutiny, as is their role in image building and as promotion and marketing instrument. Explanations are sought in the way in which aspects of gender are linked to socially and culturally constructed gender roles and relationships.

Finally, in Chapter 10, Keune and Dahles summarize and evaluate the eight contributions to this volume in light of the key concepts developed in this first chapter. The future prospects and perspectives of sustainable tourism development in Latin America are discussed against the background of socioeconomic and political aspects of the region.

Chapter 2

The Economic Significance of Tourism in Latin America

Lou Keune and Jan Vugts

Introduction

After World War II, international tourism increased dramatically in Latin America (including the Caribbean). In 1950, 1.3 million tourists traveled to these regions; in 1997, this figure had risen to 53 million. Such dramatic growth is not consistent with all developments in Latin America since World War II. In general, this period can be regarded as one of growth and progress, but also of increasing imbalance.

Both national governments and international organizations see tourism as an important vehicle towards economic development. There seems to be a general agreement of opinion that the sector can contribute considerably to the alleviation of many existing problems, such as poverty, unemployment, and balance of payment shortages. Yet, since the 1980s, there has been a growing concern about this assumption. Mowforth and Munt (1998), for example, develop the argument that tourism can endanger the possibilities of sustainable development: ecological, social, cultural, and economic. And Tosun (2000) formulates severe doubts about the opportunities with regard to participation of local people in the benefits of and the decision making about tourism. These opportunities depend, among others, on the contribution of the tourism sector to economic development, and on its power structure.

This chapter focuses on the possible economic significance of tourism for Latin America. The first section describes in a general way the process of uneven development in Latin America since World War II. The second section gives a picture of the growth of international tourism towards Latin America, both at the level of the region as a whole and at that of individual countries. As will be shown, there are great differences, both absolute and relative, with respect to the magnitude of the presence of tourism within countries. The third section is dedicated to the main question of the potential economic contribution of tourism. This section concentrates on the issue of leakages, which may explain to a large extent the difference between the gross and the net proceeds of foreign tourism. Finally, in the last section some policy conclusions are formulated.

Postwar Latin American Socioeconomic Development: Growth and Imbalance

Demographic Development

Latin America is a region with a fast-growing population. In 1969, there were around 210 million inhabitants (United Nations Development Program [UNDP], 1990, p. 174); in 1970 the population rose to 289.4 million, and in 1995 to 486.9 million (UNDP, 1998, p. 209). It is expected that this figure will rise to 624.9 million by 2015 (UNDP 2000, p. 226). It would seem that the rate of growth is steadily decreasing. Between 1950 and 1959, the growth rate was 2.8% per year on average; in the period 1960–1969 it was 2.9%, while the next decade saw a growth rate that decreased to 2.5% per year, and consequently to as low as 2.1% in the 1980s and 1.8% between 1990 and 1997 (calculations based on Economic Commission for Latin America and the Caribbean [ECLAC], 1998, pp. 346, 350, 355, 360, 365). It is expected to be 1.3% during 1998–2015 (UNDP, 2000, p. 226). Relatively speaking, however, and despite this steady decrease, the population figures for this region, compared with countries in the north, have remained high. In comparison to other developing countries, with the exception of Eastern Asia (including China), they have remained relatively low. In addition, Latin America is undergoing the same process of fast urbanization that has become so widespread in practically all the developing countries (Table 2.1).

Latin America makes up a large region in the world in terms of total population as well as size. There are enormous differences between the countries in this region. With respect to total population, two countries dominate: Brazil with its population of 165.9 million in 1998, and Mexico with 95.8 million inhabitants (UNDP, 2000, p. 224). In contrast, a number of countries in the Caribbean have a population of less than half a million, including very small countries like St. Kitts and Nevis with 38,819 inhabitants (Central Intelligence Agency [CIA], 2001). And with regard to size, Brazil is 8.5 million square kilometers, while Mexico is 2 million square kilometers, and St. Kitts and Nevis are 261 square kilometers (CIA, 2001).

Economic Growth

Economic development is generally seen as the first step towards wiping out poverty. From the perspective of economic development, Latin America has certainly seen progress (Table 2.2).

The figures in Table 2.2 reflect postwar economic development. Until the 1980s the region had seen a spectacular economic growth. This growth was balanced, to a certain extent, by an increase in the population, but, nevertheless, this period in history saw significant growth per capita. It was accompanied by an inflation rate that was significant compared with that in the countries in the OECD. In addition, the growth in GDP was comparable to the increase in foreign trade, although import figures clearly increased more significantly than export figures in the 1970s. However, in the early 1980s, the region was subjected to a serious economic crisis. The clearest manifestations were the dramatic decrease in the growth of GDP (GDP per capita even went down) and a high rate of inflation that was unprec-

Table 2.1. Some Demographic Indicators: World Regions

	Sub-Saharan Africa	Arab States	South Asia	East Asia	Southeast Asia and the Pacific	Latin America	Industrial Countries	World
Estimated population (millions, 1995)	543	242	1293	1296	487	472	1233	5627
Population growth rate 1970–95 (%)	2.9	2.8	2.3	1.6	2.1	2.1	0.7	1.7
Crude birth rate (%)	43.1	31.9	28.2	17.2	25.4	23.9	12.6	23.2
Crude death rate (%)	14.9	7.7	9.2	7.1	7.7	6.5	10.1	9.0
Urban population (as % of total)								
1970	19	39	20	19	20	57	67	37
1995	32	54	28	33	33	73	74	45

Source: UNDP (1998, p. 209).

edented. During the next decade, the situation improved to a certain extent, but growth figures never again equaled those attained in the preceding decades.

In Latin America, too, political and economic policy was geared to encouraging economic development. In the 1940s and 1950s, the point of departure for such policy was the concept of "supply economy" and its underlying ideas. A clear at-

Table 2.2. Latin America: Main Economic Indicators 1950–1997 (Annual Rates of Variation)

	1950–59	1960–69	1970–79	1980–89	1990–97
Growth (%)					
Overall	4.9	5.7	5.6	1.7	3.2
Per capita	2.1	2.8	3.1	−0.4	1.4
Inflation (%)	17.8	21.6	37.9	203.4	160.7
Foreign trade (%)					
Exports	4.0	4.5	2.6	5.4	9.1
Imports	3.2	4.1	7.8	0.0	14.2

Source: ECLAC (1998, pp. 346, 350, 355, 360, 365).

tempt was made to develop an inward-oriented industrialization process that aimed at import substitution. Industrialization was regarded as the engine of economic development that included protection of domestic production through tariffs and other import barriers. The investment capital that was needed was generated by introducing greater internal economic measures but also by exports, and by foreign investment contracts and loans. Also, policy makers were by no means averse to monetary expansion, as was reflected in a relatively high rate of inflation. Gradually, these measures only served to increase the existing imbalance, at both an internal level (inflation became increasingly difficult to control) and an external level. The reason for this was that the policy of accelerated industrialization produced increased demand for imported capital goods, technology, and certain raw materials. In the 1960s, policy was geared more towards a large number of internal economic reforms, including land reform and regional economic integration. In addition, higher priority was given to the acquisition of foreign capital, including foreign aid, which was stimulated by the fact that the United Nations had declared the 1960s as the decade of development. The world market was expected to play an even greater role in economic development. In reality, however, these policies had only limited effect.

Import substitution policy became the subject of increasing criticism; one of the reasons was the fact that the policy had worsened rather than resolved problems relating to trade and payment. In addition, this type of policy is relatively useless in smaller countries, particularly when further regional, economic integration is not encouraged. Orientation on the world market was intensified in the 1970s. At the same time, there was an enormous influx of foreign capital. This only served to increase the external imbalance that already existed: there was an enormous shortage in the balance of trade and foreign debt was increasing dramatically. In the 1980s, economic policy was dominated by neoliberal attitudes, influenced by, among others, the International Monetary Fund (IMF) and the World Bank. This led to a policy of economic adjustment: cutbacks, decentralization, and further liberalization of trade and investment. Although this policy did improve the countries' financial health, it also led to greater imbalance characterized by growing poverty and inequality, hyperinflation, and even a net transfer of resources from Latin America to other countries, because Latin American investors began investing more and more capital in

OECD countries. Foreign loans had to be paid back with increasing interest; and more and more private investments were being made, leading to profit transfers. ECLAC would later refer to this period as the "lost decade."

In the 1990s, there were initiatives to mitigate the policy of economic adjustment and to once again assign a more prominent role to the government. However, as a consequence of international aid, investments, and trade, the increased international dependence of the region with respect to the world economy appears to have made it vulnerable. The Asia crisis of 1997, for instance, had a far-reaching influence on the Latin American economies (ECLAC, 1998, pp. 366–368). Moreover, foreign debt generally takes up a fair share of the available means. In 1988, this debt had risen in magnitude to approximately half the GDP (49.1%) of Latin America. In 1996, this figure had gone down to 33.7% (Inter-American Development Bank [IDB], 1999, p. 247). Debt services (interest and repayment), meanwhile, placed a heavy burden on export earnings: 40.1% in 1988, 26.5% in 1990, and 37.6% in 1996 (IDB, 1999, p. 248).

Human Development

In the postwar period, major improvements in living standards in Latin America have been realized in various ways. Average life expectancy has risen sharply and infant mortality has gone down considerably. Access to safe water has improved, as has literacy and participation in education, though less spectacularly than improvements in the state of public health. Per capita income has once again risen dramatically. Taking other regions in the world into account, progress is actually worldwide. In some regions, progress for certain indicators (such as income) is even more pronounced than in Latin America (Table 2.3). All in all, the Latin American region belongs to the more developed parts of the world, though it is still a long way behind the industrialized countries. This becomes clear when the various regions are compared on the basis of the human development index (HDI)[1] (Table 2.3).

In the context of the world in its entirety, the Latin American region is not doing badly in terms of average human development. However, there are major differences within the region. This is illustrated by Table 2.4, which includes Canada, the most developed country in the world in 1998, for comparison.

The table shows even more clearly the big differences between the Latin American countries. Some countries, particularly Argentina, Honduras, and Bolivia, have made a great leap forward of more than 0.120 point in a relatively short time span, viz. 23 years. Nevertheless, the differences between the countries are rather large. The UNDP classifies Argentina, Chile, and Uruguay as high human development countries, Haiti as one of the low human development countries, and the other countries as medium human development countries. The table also shows that countries with the highest HDI do not also have the highest GDP per capita. Costa Rica, Panama, and Ecuador have markedly higher HDI than the GDP per capita would expect. This shows once again that a higher income does not say everything about people's well-being; other factors, especially health care and education, play an equally important role. It is quite plain that different countries prioritize different elements of human development.

Table 2.3. Some Indicators of Human Development: World Regions

	Sub-Saharan Africa	Arab States	South Asia	East Asia	Southeast Asia and Pacific	Latin America	Industrial Countries	World
Life expectancy (years)								
1960	39.9	45.5	43.9	47.5	45.3	55.3	68.6	50.2
1995	50.6	63.5	61.8	69.3	64.7	69.2	74.2	63.6
Infant mortality rate								
1960	166	166	163	146	127	107	39	129
1996	104	55	74	37	48	35	13	60
Access to safe water								
1975–80						60		
1990–96						77		
Adult literacy rate (%)								
1970	31	31	32	53	66	74		
1995	57	56	51	82	87	87	99	78
Gross enrollment for all levels (% age 6–23)								
1980	39	47	37	51	51	59		
1995	42	58	52	65	61	69	83	62
Real GDP per capita (PPP$)								
1960	996		698	729	732	2137		
1995	1407	4454	1724	3359	3852	5982	16337	5990
Human development index	0.386	0.636	0.462	0.676	0.683	0.831	0.911	0.722

Source: UNDP (1998, p. 206).

Table 2.4. Human Development Index 1975–1998, and Gross Domestic Product per Capita 1998 in Selected Countries

	Human Development Index Value					HDI Rank 1998	GDP per Capita 1998
	1975	1980	1985	1990	1998		
Canada	0.865	0.880	0.902	0.925	0.935	1	20458
Argentina	0.781	0.795	0.801	0.804	0.837	35	8475
Chile	0.702	0.736	0.753	0.780	0.826	38	4784
Uruguay	0.753	0.773	0.777	0.797	0.825	39	6029
Costa Rica	0.732	0.756	0.756	0.775	0.797	48	2800
Mexico	0.687	0.731	0.749	0.757	0.784	55	4459
Panama	0.707	0.726	0.740	0.741	0.776	59	3200
Venezuela	0.714	0.729	0.736	0.755	0.770	65	3499
Colombia	0.657	0.687	0.700	0.720	0.764	68	2392
Brazil	0.639	0.674	0.687	0.706	0.747	74	4509
Peru	0.635	0.664	0.686	0.698	0.737	80	2611
Paraguay	0.660	0.695	0.701	0.713	0.736	81	1781
Dominican Republic	0.611	0.648	0.678	0.686	0.729	87	1799
Ecuador	0.620	0.665	0.686	0.696	0.722	91	1562
El Salvador	0.581	0.581	0.604	0.642	0.696	104	1716
Honduras	0.520	0.569	0.601	0.624	0.653	113	722
Bolivia	0.512	0.546	0.571	0.595	0.643	114	964
Nicaragua	0.569	0.580	0.588	0.597	0.631	116	452
Haiti				0.436	0.440	150	370

Source UNDP (2000, pp. 178–181).

Poverty

Despite all postwar human development efforts, poverty remains an immense problem. Poverty here should be taken to mean income poverty. According to the 1998 human development report (UNDP, 1998, p. 206), 23.8% of the entire Latin American population had an income below the poverty line, as established by the United Nations, of $1 a day, and are therefore regarded to be "extremely poor" and leading an undignified existence. As Table 2.5 suggests, despite improvements in living conditions, poverty is not a problem that will soon disappear.

The table shows that, in absolute numbers, the problem of poverty increased in the 1970-1990 period. In relative terms (i.e., the proportion of poor in the total population of Latin America), it has not decreased and there are some indications that it has in fact increased slightly. Although in 1970 poverty was mainly a problem among the rural population, at present it is increasingly becoming an urban problem, without it decreasing in rural areas. This is all the more remarkable as it is the poverty in rural areas that is generally considered one of the causes of accelerated urbanization in Latin America. These data are at odds with the progress in human development noted above. It is with respect to income, in particular, that poverty is apparently a structural problem.

Table 2.5. Latin America: Extent of Poverty 1970–1990 (19 Countries)

	1970		1980		1986		1990	
	%	Total Persons (Millions)	%	Total Persons (Millions)	%	Total Persons (Millions)	%	Total Persons (Millions)
Poverty								
Urban	29	44.2	30	62.9	36	94.4	39	115.5
Rural	67	75.6	60	73.0	60	75.8	61	80.4
Total	45	119.8	41	135.9	43	170.2	46	195.9
Extreme poverty								
Urban	13	19.9	11	22.5	14	35.8	15	44.9
Rural	20	43.8	33	39.9	36	45.6	37	48.6
Total	14	63.7	19	62.4	21	81.4	22	93.5

Source: UCLA (1976, 1984, 1996, p. 431).

The phenomenon of the persistence of poverty in Latin America is related to a number of factors. One of these is income inequality. Globally, the wage gap appears to have widened since the 1960s. According to the 1992 human development report (UNDP, 1992, p. 34), the countries with the poorest 20% of the population received 2.3% of the world's income in 1960; in 1989, this share had decreased to 1.4%; and according to the 1998 report (UNDP, 1998, p. 2), it had gone down even further in 1995 to 1.3%. On the other hand, the share of those countries with the richest 20% of the population rose from 70.2% in 1960 to 82.7% in 1989, and to 86% in 1995. In terms of mutual relations, this means that inequality rose from 1:31 to 1:59 to 1:66, and therefore more than doubled.

Added to this is the income inequality within Latin American. According to the IDB, the region has the greatest disparities in income distribution in the world. A quarter of all national income is received by a mere 5% of the population, and the top 10% of the population receive 40% of the income. The poorest 30% of the population receive only 7.5% of total income, less than anywhere else in the world. On top of this, it turns out that, in as far as data are available and with the exception of Jamaica, all countries in the region show an income distribution that is more unequal than the world average (IDB, 1999, p. 11). It would be reasonable to assume that inequality would have to be greatest in those countries with the lowest levels of economic development. However, this is not true for Latin America: the countries in the region belong to the more prosperous countries in the developing world. Within the region, countries such as Chile and Brazil are both more developed and more unequal (IDB, 1999, p. 13). Another remarkable fact is that incomes deconcentrated in the 1970–1982 period. Since 1982, however, the trend has turned around again to reach levels higher than those of 1972 (IDB, 1999, p. 15).

The Environment

In ecological respects, too, postwar developments have clearly left their mark. The United Nations Environment Program (UNEP) paints a gloomy picture. First of all, it should be acknowledged that it is hard to make generalizations about a continent as large as this. The region still possesses a wealth of natural resources. However, it seems that this wealth is increasingly being eroded. Of all farmland currently in use in the southern part of Latin America, 72.7% suffer from moderate to extreme degradation; some 47% of the soils in grazing lands have become infertile. This land degradation includes erosion, soil degradation in hillsides and mountain areas and in tropical pasture lands, desertification brought on by overgrazing, and salanization and alkalization of irrigated soils (UNEP, 1997, p. 80). Although the region still possesses the biggest stretches of original virgin forests (particularly in the Amazon area), large-scale deforestation is in progress. Since 1980, 0.8% of the forests have vanished each year; in 1990, 7.4 million hectares disappeared. Only 2% of the original tropical forests in Central America are still intact (UNEP, 1997, p. 81).

Far-reaching damage to biodiversity is imminent. It is expected that 100,000–400,000 species will be threatened with extinction in the next 40 years (UNEP, 1997, p. 83). The quality of much of the water supply is under pressure from toxic contamination from industry, waste disposal, and human sewage. The bacterial pollution of water supplies in the region is a continuing problem that adversely affects human health. In the Caribbean Sea, there is clear evidence of elevated levels of phosphorus, nitrates, potassium, pesticides such as DDT, and organic effluents. Twenty-six percent of the Latin American coastline is under high potential threat of degradation and a further 24% is under moderate potential threat due to coastal development (including tourism and infrastructural works), discharge of sediments, wastes, and contaminants from urban and industrial areas, sewage, industrial pollution, and oil spills (UNEP, 1997, p. 85). More than 50% of the mangroves have been degraded (UNEP, 1997, p. 86). The southern latitudes of South America are the areas closest to the seasonal ozone hole that opens up over Antarctica each spring and summer (UNEP, 1997, p. 88). Air pollution is a constant problem for 81 million urban residents, causing an estimated 2.3 million cases of chronic respiratory illness among children each year (UNEP, 1997, p. 89).

The outlook is rather pessimistic with regard to the immediate future of the region. According to UNEP, the causes of these ecological risks include the growth of the population, urbanization, a strong emphasis on promoting export of agricultural and other raw materials and foods (which involves large-scale use of pesticides and defoliants and pushes back the green frontier), the lack of financial means, which is partly due to the high debt serving, liberalization of the economy, and the governments' general lack of interest in these problems. However, the rapidly growing involvement of environmentally active NGOs in these issues is encouraging (UNEP, 1997, pp. 90–93). As a matter of fact, it is the poor who suffer most from the consequences of environmental degradation (UNDP, 1998).

It is hard to estimate the economic value of ecological deterioration. Some case studies have been done to establish realistic estimates. "In Costa Rica, the accumulated depreciation of its forests, soils and fisheries amounted to more than $4.6 billion (in 1989 dollars) between 1970 and 1990—about 6 per cent of its total GDP in that period" (Pronk & Haq, 1992, p. 9).

The Growth of International Tourism in Latin America

Arrivals and Receipts in Latin America

Worldwide, tourism is a booming sector: in 1950, there were some 25 million arrivals of tourists[2]; in 1997, this had gone up to 611 million. In Latin America (including the Caribbean), relative growth was even more spectacular: it went up from 1.3 million in 1950 to 53 million in 1997 (Figure 2.1) (World Tourism Organization [WTO], 1997, 1999). This growth is still going upwards, a trend stronger than others. For example, in 1950 there were 10.05 trips per thousand of world population; in 1992 it was 87.49 per thousand. In 1950, the international tourism receipts were 2.7% of world imports and in 1992 they were 7.3% (Easton, 1998, pp. 525-526).

In Latin America, growth in the tourism sector was evident in all countries. Nevertheless, on the world list of top tourist destinations, the Latin American countries do not do as well as countries in other continents: Mexico is in 8th place, followed by Argentina in the 28th position (WTO, 1999). In looking at the various groups of countries (Table 2.6), there are clear regional differences. Most tourists head for the countries to the north of the Panama Canal. Mexico heads the field, followed by the Caribbean. Growth is strongest in Central America (Figure 2.2).

Considering the receipts[3] foreign tourists generate in the receiving countries, even more spectacular developments can be seen. Worldwide, tourists generated US$2.1 billion in 1950 and US$436 billion in 1997. These are nominal amounts

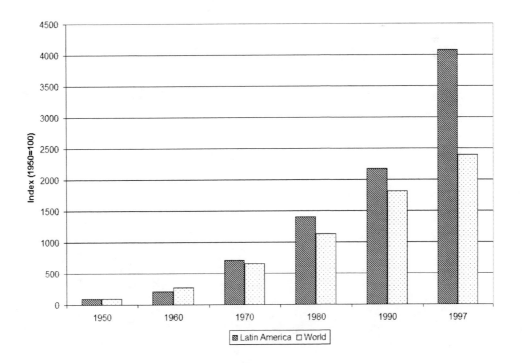

Figure 2.1. Arrivals of tourists Latin America and the world.

Table 2.6. Arrivals of Tourists (×1000) in Latin America by Region: 1950–1997

Year	Central America[a]	Mexico	South America	The Caribbean	Total
1950			410	504	1305
1960	59	690	426	1530	2705
1970	669	2250	2422	3907	9248
1980	1507	4144	5767	6908	18327
1990	1881	17176	8604	11498	28376
1997	2937	19351	15868	15286	53442

[a]Central America includes Honduras, El Salvador, Guatemala, Nicaragua, Costa Rica, and Panama.
Sources: Holder (1979); UCLA (1976, 1984, 1996); WTO (1992, 1996, 1999).

that do not take inflation into account. In the matter of receipts, Latin America also witnessed enormous growth, from nearly US$400 million in 1950 to US$37 billion in 1997. In relative terms, growth in Latin America lags behind worldwide growth (Figure 2.3), which means that the growth of average tourist expenditure in Latin America lags behind that of other continents. Within Latin America itself, tourist expenditure also appears to be growing at different rates (Table 2.7).

The increase in receipts from tourism is highest in the Caribbean, in both absolute figures (Table 2.7) and relative figures (Figure 2.4), even though this region

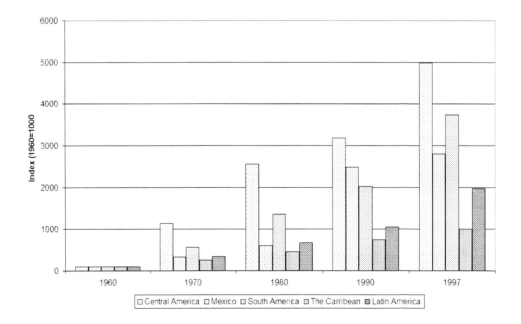

Figure 2.2. Arrivals of tourists by region.

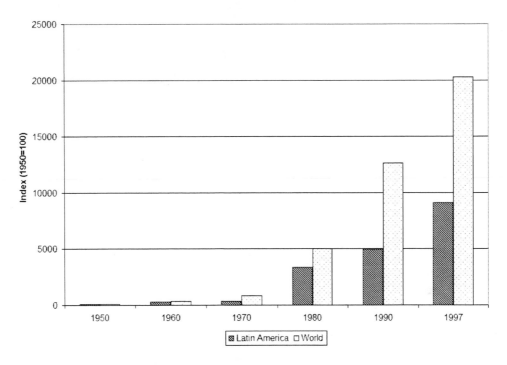

Figure 2.3. Tourism receipts in Latin America and the world.

has the lowest growth level in numbers of arrivals. It could be concluded from the evidence that, within Latin America, it is in the Caribbean that expenditure per tourist has risen sharply. However, passengers from cruise ships have not been counted as tourists, while this is a particularly important growth market for the Caribbean islands. According to Wood (2000, pp. 347–348), cruise tourism has been growing at an annual rate of 8% since 1980, increasing at almost twice the rate of

Table 2.7. Tourism Receipts (US$ Million) in Latin America by Region: 1950–1997

Year	Central America[a]	Mexico	South America	The Caribbean	Total
1950			223	66	392
1960	68	704	212	158	1064
1970	138	1454	321	435	1281
1980	493	1671	3784	3486	13163
1990	737	5467	4674	8710	19536
1997	1800	7594	13559	13776	36729

[a]Central America includes Honduras, El Salvador, Guatemala, Nicaragua, Costa Rica, and Panama.
Sources: Holder (1979); UCLA (1976, 1984, 1996); WTO (1992, 1996, 1999).

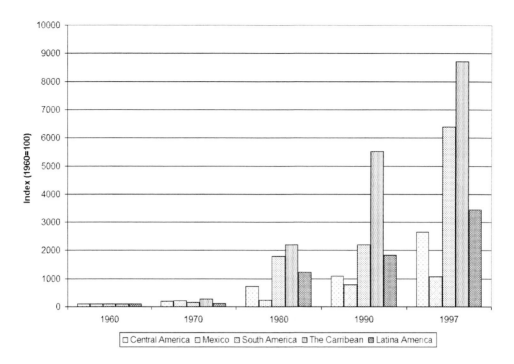

Figure 2.4. Tourism receipts by region.

tourism overall. The North American market, including the Caribbean, is the dominant one, although this market share has been declining. In 1997, cruise ships accounted for roughly 10 million tourist arrivals at ports in the Caribbean islands; in 1990, a number of islands received more cruise than stopover tourists.

The gross receipts presented in Table 2.7 only provide a partial picture of the money flows involved in tourism. The definition of receipts used by the WTO does not include receipts from international transport. For the growing group of European travelers visiting Latin America in particular, transport expenses take up a sizeable share of their total budget. These expenses generally end up with American or European airlines (Sinclair, 1998, pp. 14–17). For the Caribbean region, Pattullo (1996) writes that:

> In 1992, foreign airlines controlled nearly three-quarters of the seats to the region, with American Airlines alone picking up more than half of those seats. American Airlines, KLM, British Airways, Air France (the last three reflecting old colonial links), and foreign-owned charter companies dominate the Caribbean skies. In contrast, regional airlines get a tiny slice of the schedules. In 1991, nine regional airways (Air Aruba, ALM, Air Jamaica, Bahamas air, BWIA, Cayman Airways, Guyana Airways, LIAT and Surinam Airways) scrambled around for just 29 per cent of seats from the USA, 19 per cent of seats from Canada and 15 per cent from Europe. These small, under-equipped, state-owned regional airlines are not only outclassed by the international carriers but, in their struggle to survive, they lose phenomenal amounts of money. (p. 16)

As will be seen below, developing countries will have to make major investments in the construction and maintenance of airports to enable tourists to visit the country by plane. The receipts from these air journeys, however, will tend to go largely to foreign airline companies.

The figures presented above disguise major differences between the various countries, not only in terms of the scale and development of tourism, but also in the nature of tourism. In some countries, tourism was and is insignificant in terms of both the number of tourists visiting the country and the economic significance of tourism for the country. This is the case for countries such as El Salvador, Honduras, Bolivia, and Peru. Motives for tourists to visit certain countries are also widely divergent. A rough distinction can be made between tourists in search of sun, sea, and beach (predominantly the Caribbean), those looking for natural scenery (e.g., Costa Rica), and those in search of culture and folklore (e.g., Guatemala). The largest numbers of tourists visiting Latin America do so for sun-sea-beach reasons. Particularly in South America and some countries in Central America, tourism from neighboring countries is also considerably large scale. Visits to relatives probably play an important role here. A combination of these various forms of tourism is in evidence in many countries (such as Mexico). Many countries show a strong regional concentration (certain beach areas, for instance). The presence of certain natural elements plays a role here, but also the opening up of such regions by means of infrastructural facilities. The development of Varadero in Cuba or Cancún in Mexico as tourist destinations, for example, is largely the result of government policy.

Differences per Country

In order to illustrate the importance of tourism at the level of individual countries, longitudinal data on nine countries in Latin America were collected. These countries were: Mexico, the Bahamas, the Dominican Republic, Bermuda, St. Lucia, Guatemala, Costa Rica, Argentina, and Uruguay (Figure 2.5). This choice of countries was made on the basis of a combination of the following criteria:

1. distribution over the regions (the Caribbean, Central America, and South America);
2. absolute number of tourists visiting the country (high and low);
3. gross receipts from tourism compared with receipts from exports (high and low);
4. number of tourists compared with the size of the national population (high and low);
5. number of tourists per square kilometer.

For the Caribbean Region, two larger countries (the Bahamas and the Dominican Republic) and two smaller ones (Bermuda and St. Lucia) have been selected.

As far as the number of arrivals is concerned (Table 2.8), Mexico receives the greatest number of tourists by far. Argentina comes second, which is something of a surprise as, certainly in Europe, it is virtually unknown as a tourist destination. In absolute numbers, the growth in the total number of arrivals per year is highest in Mexico. In a relative sense, the increase is biggest in the Dominican Republic (Figure 2.5). All countries except Bermuda are witnessing an enormous growth in the

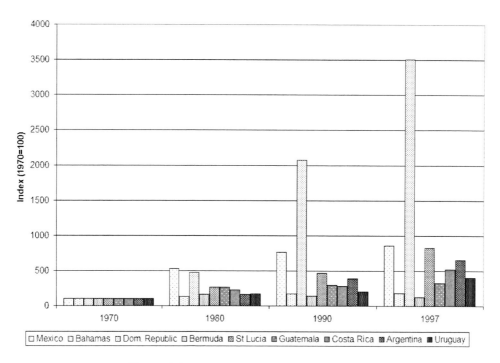

Figure 2.5. Arrivals of tourists by country.

number of tourists. Tourism to Bermuda goes back to as far as the 19th century, and the islands have always been a popular resort for affluent, elderly, American tourists. The decline in the number of tourists can be explained by the increased competition from other Caribbean islands and by government policies aimed at decreasing tourist pressure on the island.

Table 2.8. Arrivals of Tourists (×1000) in Selected Countries: 1970–1997

Country	1970	1980	1990	1997
Mexico	2250	11945	17176	19351
The Caribbean				
Bahamas	891	1181	1562	1592
Dominican Republic	63	301	1305	2211
Bermuda	302	492	435	380
St. Lucia	30	80	141	248
Guatemala	174	466	509	576
Central America				
Costa Rica	155	345	435	811
South America				
Argentina	695	1120	2728	4540
Uruguay	615	1067	1267	2317

Sources: Holder (1979); UCLA (1984); WTO (1992, 1996, 1999).

Although the various growth rhythms vary, Mexico is the undisputed number one in absolute numbers. This picture changes, however, when the number of arrivals is compared with the number of inhabitants, the so-called tourist intensity rate (TIR).[4] As shown in Table 2.9, the pressure that tourism exerts on a country's population is highly diverse.

Mexico belongs to those countries that have the lowest tourist intensity, and the Mexican population, consequently, has very little to do with tourism, particularly in comparison with countries such as Bermuda and the Bahamas, or even St. Lucia, which are veritable tourist countries in this respect. It should be observed that these figures are, in actual fact, only fairly rough indicators: pressure on the population may vary significantly per region or period. Yet, they provide an interesting indication of the rate of pressure. Especially in St. Lucia this rate is increasing, whereas it has been going down in Bermuda since 1980.

The pressure of tourism on a society can also be visualized in relation to its surface area (Table 2.10). In this respect, too, Bermuda is in the lead with the highest degree of tourist intensity by far, even if it is now somewhat on the decrease. The position of St. Lucia is remarkable, as its tourist intensity, in both absolute and relative terms, has increased enormously. Mexico again turns out to be one of the low-intensity countries. Naturally, there may be significant differences in intensity per region within a country. All the same, the intensity figure in a country like Bermuda is exceptionally high.

Looking at the total amount of tourism receipts (Table 2.11), it turns out that Argentina comes second, after Mexico. Unfortunately, data from a number of countries are unavailable. In as far as comparisons across time can be made (Figure 2.6), the Dominican Republic appears to be experiencing a very rapid growth in tourism. Argentina is also one of the fastest growers. Mexico, once again, shows slightly disappointing figures here.

Table 2.9. Arrivals of Tourists per 1000 Inhabitants in Selected Countries: 1970–1997

Country	1970	1980	1990	1997
Mexico	44	172	199	201
The Caribbean				
Bahamas	524	5623	6125	5509
Dominican Republic	16	55	182	273
Bermuda	6040	9111	7131	6333
St. Lucia	300	667	1062	1699
Central America				
Guatemala	33	67	55	55
Costa Rica	89	154	155	234
South America				
Argentina	29		84	127
Uruguay	213	367	410	719

Sources: see Table 2.8; UNO (1979, 1984, 1994, 1997).

Table 2.10. Arrivals of Tourists per Square Kilometer in Selected Countries: 1970–1997

Country	1970	1980	1990	1997
Mexico	1.2	6.1	8.8	9.9
The Caribbean				
Bahamas	64.2	85.1	112.6	114.7
Dominican Republic	1.3	6.2	26.8	45.6
Bermuda	5698.1	9283.0	8207.6	7169.8
St. Lucia	48.2	128.6	226.7	398.7
Central America				
Guatemala	1.6	4.3	4.7	5.3
Costa Rica	3.0	6.8	8.5	15.9
South America				
Argentina	0.3	0.4	1.0	1.6
Uruguay	3.5	6.0	7.1	13.2

Sources: See Table 2.8; UNO (1979, 1984, 1994, 1997).

In terms of possible profits from tourism, mean expenditure per tourist serves as an indicator. As Table 2.12 shows, the figures per country differ. In Mexico, Guatemala, and Uruguay, tourists are apparently of the frugal kind. On the small Caribbean islands and in Argentina, on the other hand, mean spending is highest.

As regards receipts, it would be interesting to take a look at the relative importance of the tourist sector (e.g., the relation between gross receipts from tourism and receipts from exports) (Table 2.13). In interpreting Table 2.13, one must take into account not only the problem of missing data, but also the fact that these receipts are expressed in gross figures. The figures, therefore, do not represent the added value generated in the sector. Moreover, the export data are limited to the

Table 2.11. Tourism Receipts (US$ Million) in Selected Countries: 1970–1997

Country	1970	1980	1990	1997
Mexico	1454	1670	5467	7594
The Caribbean				
Bahamas			1333	1416
Dominican Republic	16	168	890	2107
Bermuda			490	474
St. Lucia			154	282
Central America				
Guatemala	12	183	185	325
Costa Rica	22	87	275	719
South America				
Argentina	74	344	1976	5069
Uruguay	41	298	238	759

Sources: Holder (1979); UCLA (1984); WTO (1992, 1996, 1999).

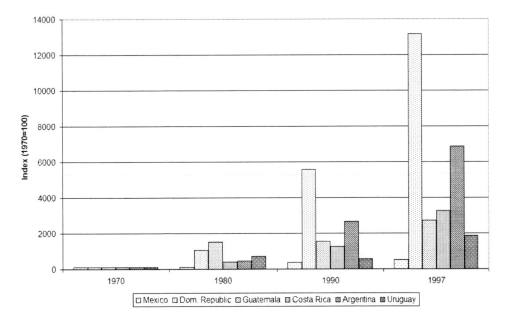

Figure 2.6. Tourism receipts by country.

export of goods. They are but very rough indicators. All the same, it is striking that some of the Caribbean islands in particular are highly dependent on tourism. These countries generally lack a diversified economy; and their dependence on tourism, therefore, is much greater than in other countries investigated in this study. For many Caribbean islands, dependence on tourism has come to replace dependence

Table 2.12. Tourism Receipts per Tourist Stay-Over Arrival in Selected Countries: 1997

Country	1997
Mexico	392
The Caribbean	
Bahamas	889
Dominican Republic	953
Bermuda	1247
St. Lucia	1137
Central America	
Guatemala	564
Costa Rica	887
South America	
Argentina	1117
Uruguay	328

Sources: Calculated on Tables 2.8 and 2.11.

Table 2.13. Tourism Receipts/Export of Goods Earnings in Selected Countries: 1970–1997

Country	1970	1980	1990	1997
Mexico	1.0	0.1	0.2	0.1
The Caribbean				
Bahamas			4.3	4.8
Dominican Republic	0.1	0.2	1.2	0.5
St. Lucia			1.2	3.1[a]
Central America				
Guatemala	0.04	0.1	0.2	0.1
Costa Rica	0.1	0.1	0.2	0.2
South America				
Argentina	0.04	0.04	0.2	0.2
Uruguay	0.2	0.3	0.1	0.3

[a]1996.
Sources: See Table 2.11; IMF (1990, 1995, 1998).

on an agricultural end product like sugar or bananas. Six Caribbean countries earned more from tourism in 1992 as a share of exports than they did from all other sectors. These were Antigua (65.1%), the Bahamas (72%), Barbados (59.3%), Grenada (54.3%), St. Kitts-Nevis (58.4%), and the Dominican Republic (50.9%) (Pattullo, 1996, p. 12).

McElroy and Albuquerque (1998) have made an effort to calculate a "tourism penetration index" for small Caribbean islands. In this index they combine the tourism indicators "visitors," "visitors spending," and "hotel rooms" with the country indicators "population" and "area." Doing so, they demonstrate that out of 20 islands, St. Maarten is by far the number one, Bermuda taking the third position, and St. Lucia number 14. These authors stress the importance of developing a policy towards the threats of tourism for sustainability (McElroy & Albuquerque, 1998, p. 145-168).

The Potential Economic Contribution of Tourism

Preconditions for the Growth of Tourism

As noted above, in the development literature tourism is generally looked upon as an important potential growth sector, with development potential for society as a whole. According to Theuns[5] (1989, pp. 97-102), a number of conditions have to be met for tourism to get off the ground. Once these conditions have been met, the question whether or not foreign visitors will indeed be attracted hinges on a large number of things. The good climate, the presence of beaches, and the geographical position vis-à-vis the US are undoubtedly the main factors contributing to the growth of tourism in especially the Caribbean and Mexico. Although developments in aviation have also opened the continent for tourists from Europe, the vast majority of tourists, as far as coming from "rich" countries, is still from the US

(Table 2.14). This certainly does not go for Argentina, which is mainly visited by tourists from neighboring countries.

The number of tourists visiting Latin America has in various periods undoubtedly been influenced by the absence of legal security and political stability, two of the preconditions mentioned by Theuns (1989). This is also true for the image of the situation in a country as created by the media in the US, and the measures taken against a country by the US government. A clear example of the latter is the boycott imposed by the US on Cuba in 1961 that made it illegal for US citizens to spend money in Cuba, which in practice added up to a ban on visiting Cuba. When in 1977 this ban was lifted partially by President Carter, the number of visitors to Cuba quadrupled. In 1982, the ban was reimposed by President Reagan. In 1991, only 2.6% of the total number of tourists to Cuba came from the US, a considerably lower percentage than those for Caribbean islands given in Table 2.14. In her study of tourism to Mexico and Costa Rica, Chant (1992) goes so far as to state that, "Indeed, political stability is viewed as one of the major reasons for the popularity of holidays here compared with other Latin-American destinations" (p. 88).

Besides the conditions mentioned by Theuns, the opinion of national and international organizations about the potential meaning of tourism is also of considerable importance, the more so because many countries (have to) rely on international donors and foreign investors for the development of the necessary infrastructure. Various international organizations and national governments have emphasized the expected favorable effects of tourism. In 1969, the World Bank decided to found a Tourism Projects Department.

Table 2.14. Arrivals of Tourists by Country of Destination and Region of Origin (%): 1998

Country of Destination	Country or Region of Origin	
	United States	Europe
Mexico	93.9	1.8
The Caribbean		
Bahamas	81.8	7.7
Dominican Republic	18.75	45.6
Bermuda	78.6	10.1
St. Lucia[a]	32.2	35.1
Central America		
Guatemala[b]	26.5	18.1
Costa Rica[c]	36.9	14.0
South America		
Argentina[d]	8.9[e]	11.5

[a]24.5% from the Caribbeans.
[b]34.6% from Central America.
[c]31% from Central America.
[d]72.8% from South America.
[e]North America.
Sources: Calculated from WTO (2000).

> [I]n view of its growing importance as a source of foreign exchange earnings for a number of developing countries, a new Tourism Projects Department was set up during the year with the specific task of identifying, preparing and implementing projects in this field. . . . The availability of adequate facilities for visitors provides a stimulus not only to earnings directly associated with tourist traffic, but also to general economic development by encouraging potential foreign investors to visit developing countries. (World Bank, 1969, p. 18)

In 1967, an OECD publication appeared in which tourism was described as a promising source of economic development; almost 30 years later, the Caribbean Tourism Organization announced that the region's tourism industry would grow by 6.3% annually over the next 16 years, at "almost twice the projected 3.6 per cent world tourism growth rate" (Pattullo, 1996, p. 6).

Also, in countries where so far tourism has not been economically significant, possibilities are being detected. In a study of tourism possibilities in an El Salvador region, Brouwer (1996) states,

> Tourism has recently been receiving more attention from the government sector and the media. As coffee-yields are decreasing, tourism is seen as the only option. . . . Central aims are now the building of five-star hotels and extension of the airport. For international tourism, a new organization has been founded: CORSATUR, which tries to attract foreign investment on favorable conditions. . . . The first glimpses of policy-making can be observed: in 1984, a national tourism strategy was formulated, on the basis of which six large-scale projects have been outlined. (pp. 63–64)

Costs and Benefits of Tourism

As stated in the first section of this chapter, Latin America, including the Caribbean, is in urgent need of new sources to alleviate the many problems of uneven development and poverty. That is one of the reasons why so many governments in the region are looking for possibilities to stimulate the sector. The question remains, however, whether that is a wise policy.

One of the reasons to doubt this argument is the far-reaching concentration (both horizontal and vertical) of control by international companies in the subsectors of transportation, tour operators, travel agents, and hotel accommodations. The larger part of the world tourism industries is under control by a relatively small number of enterprises of North American or European origin (see, e.g., Mowforth & Munt, 1998; Sinclair, 1998). Mowforth and Munt (1998, p. 49) use the term "neo-colonialism" to characterize the state of affairs. The implication of this concentration of power is that, generally speaking, the major part of the possible gains of international tourism will neither stay nor arrive in the countries of destination. Another implication is that the opportunities of Latin American citizens and enterprises to develop forms of local participation and ownership are constantly under pressure by foreign companies that in many ways are far more effective in exploiting the potentials of international tourism. These companies are in a good position to take advantage of domestic sources of capital and supply expertise. "Hence, as in other sectors of the economy, the effect of foreign participation in the host country may be minimising rather than growth-enhancing, particularly if local firms are forced out of business" (Sinclair, 1998, p. 21). So, the potential positive effects of the sector for the economies of Latin America are in many cases limited to the spending and behavior of the tourists in the areas they are visiting.

As Sinclair (1998, p. 2) states, tourism expansion involves considerable costs, including the provision and maintenance of infrastructure (roads, airports, water, sanitation, energy), and investment in human capital (skilled labor). Expenditure by foreign tourists may alter domestic consumption patterns via the demonstration effect and can be inflationary. Land acquisition for tourism construction has repercussions on the domestic distribution of wealth, while tourism expansion may deplete the country's natural resource base. On the other hand, of course, tourism can bring benefits. Among them are alleviation of the problems of the balance of payments, employment effects, increases in gross national product and in personal incomes, and tax revenues for the government. After a survey of the literature on tourism and economic development, Sinclair (1998) concludes: "At first sight, tourism appears an attractive option for developing countries with few alternatives. . . . None the less, the question remains as to whether developing countries are obtaining an optimal return from tourism" (p. 38).

There are more studies indicating that the balance of costs and benefits of tourism is insecure. Demeritte (1998), for example, has studied the impact of foreign capital flows in Bahamian tourism. This flow followed the policy of the government after 1993 to divest itself of the state-owned hotels by selling them to foreign investors. Until then, the sector suffered from severe overstaffing and from pressures on potential profits. A general impact of this influx of private capital was the enhanced international competitiveness of the sector. Other positive effects were the stimulation of the construction sector and significant impacts on many locally produced products and services, both directly and indirectly. Nevertheless, negative implications have to be noted, too, such as the lowering of employment in the formerly state-owned hotels, lost revenues of the government (leading to a reduction in the provision of goods and services), the weakening of the position of hotel workers (lower remuneration and longer worker weeks), and a loss of control: the national destiny became more determined by foreigners "who may not be sensitive to national needs and overall development goals" (Demeritte, 1998, pp. 103–110).

With regard to the costs and benefits of cruise tourism, Dwyer and Forsyth (1998) are even more doubtful. According to them, this issue has received "scant attention" (p. 393). After developing a framework for assessing the economic impacts of cruise tourism, and based on a case study undertaken in Australia, they conclude, among others: "It would not be worth promoting in a market that might require $10 million of promotion to generate $50 million of additional expenditure but only $2.5 million of additional benefits" (p. 409).

Leakages

Tourism may be considered, by many, a potentially important sector of economic development, in that it creates income and employment, and brings in foreign exchange. Nevertheless, it remains to be seen to what extent tourism does indeed have positive economic effects. Much depends on the extent to which the above-mentioned gross proceeds are actually put to economic use in the country itself.

As far as field researches are undertaken on this subject, they mostly discuss cases of the Caribbean. Calculating the net proceeds from tourism is difficult. The difference between gross and net receipts is called "leakage." Seward and Spinrad (1982) describe this as

> [T]he loss of tourism foreign exchange caused, in large part, by the need to import goods and services required by the tourist industry. . . . First-round leakages: foreign exchange earnings flowing out of the tourist destination almost immediately upon receipt. A large portion of these leakages is due to the import of goods such as foods and liquor required by hotels, restaurants, and other subsectors of the tourism industry. Generally, purchases of imported goods from local intermediaries are included. Second-round leakages: foreign-exchange earnings that circulate at least once through the economy of the tourist destination before flowing out. (p. 21)

Calculating leakages is very difficult because of a lack of statistical information and methodological problems. Tourism as such is not a separate category in statistics. To determine leakages, one needs a detailed insight into the input–output relationships in the national economy, from which it must be possible to separate the tourism activities. In the International Standard Industrial Classification of All Economic Activities (ISIC), component parts of the tourist product are spread over various major divisions and, within those, over various groups (United Nations Organization [UNO], 1990). Besides this multitude of classifications, there is also the problem that the output of some companies is intended both for international and domestic tourists, and for the local population. A comparison of results often is not really feasible because it is not always the case that the same items leading to leakages of foreign exchange are included in the calculations.

In studies of the economic effects of tourism, attention is often also paid to the multiplier effect. This refers to the phenomenon that, upon entering the country, foreign currency starts to circulate, is consumed or invested, and thus has a positive influence on the national economy. In this chapter, this will not be elaborated any further; suffice it to say that studies generally show that the multiplier effect is stronger as the leakages are less.

Leakages mainly result from:

- repatriation of profits earned by foreigners;
- imports of construction material and equipment;
- imports of consumable goods (e.g., food, drinks);
- repatriation of income earned by foreigners;
- interest paid on foreign loans;
- overseas promotional expenditures.

Repatriation of Profits Earned by Foreigners

The remittance of capital abroad mainly concerns the transfer of profit accruing from direct foreign private investments. In principle, four ways can be distinguished in which multinational hotel chains participate in the Third World hotel

sector: (de facto) ownership, association through a management contract, a leasing agreement, and a franchise agreement. The last two occur only rarely in the
Third World. "The WTO estimates that 40 to 75 per cent of the gross income of a
hotel leaves the third-world country if the hotel is run by a multinational hotel
chain either via straight ownership or via a 'management contract' " (Van Hout,
1984, pp. 61–62).

The situation in which only independent hotel chains make these investments
has long ceased to exist. Concentration in the tourist sector is taking place in
three ways:

1. horizontally (i.e., mergers between enterprises in the same tourist sector);
2. vertically (i.e., mergers between enterprises that are all part of the same
   production process);
3. takeovers of (parts of) the tourist sector by "all round" multinationals.
   (Van Hout, 1984, p. 57)

The most important form of concentration is the second. The vertical integration in the production of tourist services (travel agent, tour operator, airlines company, hotel enterprise) leads to a mutual tailoring of capacities in the various
branches of the company and to a stronger market position of the separate branches.
The developing countries can prosper by using the services of vertically integrated companies, because this can lead to a higher and more stable occupancy in
hotels and other tourist facilities. The other side of the coin, however, is that the
ownership of vertically integrated companies lies elsewhere. Inherent in the power
wielded by these vertically integrated, multinational enterprises is the possibility
of tax evasion. By using fictitious clearance prices, they can create profits or losses
in any particular country at will. The loss of foreign currency resulting from leakages abroad is often facilitated by the receiving countries themselves via the creation of fiscal facilities ("tax holidays") for the benefit of foreign private investors.

It is also through other measures that governments try to make things easier for
foreign companies. "The formula created for joint ventures by the Cuban government was very beneficial for foreign companies. For example, the expenditure for
the infrastructure was defrayed by the Cuban government, and drastic changes
were made to labor law. Henceforth, joint ventures were allowed to hire and fire
staff at will, something that is illegal in Cuban trade and industry" (Langen, 1996,
pp. 53–54).

Pattullo (1996) gives the following examples of vertical integration:

> The British company Airtours plc is not only a tour operator, but is also an
> airline, a travel agent and a cruise line. Now the world's third largest holiday
> company with profits of 75.8 million (pound) in 1994, started as a tour opera-
> tor in 1978 offering holidays at the cheaper end of the market. First selling
> Caribbean holidays in 1987, it bought an up-market tour operator, Tradewinds,
> in 1993 to complement its Air-tours programs. By then it had also bought two
> travel agents, which were renamed Going Places, now with 625 high-streets
> outlets. In 1991 it launched its own airline, Airtours International, with a fleet
> of 20 leased aircraft, including two 767s for long-haul flights. In 1995, it also

started up its first "Caribbean Calypso" cruise. Airtours, then, can provide every sort of Caribbean holiday and can look after the tourist from start to finish. . . . Another example of such vertical integration is KLM, the Dutch airline. Besides owning 40 per cent of the regional airline ALM, it has a financial interest in Golden Tulips, the Dutch hotel group operating in Curacao, Trinidad, Bonaire and Aruba. It also has agreements with another major hotel group and a tour operator which buy seats from KLM. Thomson Travel Group, one of the largest of the UK's tour operators, also owns the charter airline Britannia Airways. The link works the other way for British Airways, one of only two scheduled airlines flying to the Caribbean from the UK; it also owns a tour operator, British Airways Holidays. (pp. 15–16)

In several studies mention is made, with respect to various countries, of the share of the available accommodation that is in the hands of foreigners:

- Over 80% of all tourist accommodations in the Bahamas are foreign owned (World Bank, 1986).
- Almost 90% of the over 3000 hotel rooms available in the Paradise Islands resort area are managed and/or owned by only five companies: Resorts International, Holiday Inn, Club Med, Sheraton, and Loews (Debbage, 1990, p. 518).
- In 1989 around 63% of the (Caribbean) region's rooms were owned by foreigners. In some countries, the percentage was even higher: St. Maarten, Anguilla, and the Caymans (82%); Antigua (87%) and Aruba (88%) (Pattullo, 1996, p. 20).
- More than 90% of the hotels and eco-lodges in Costa Rica is foreign owned (Van der Duim & Philipsen, 1996, p. 67).
- In the last 5 years, the number of rooms in Manuel Antonio Quepos (Costa Rica) has doubled to about 1200. An estimated 60% to 70% of the hotels, etc., are now foreign owned, especially by Italians (Van der Duim, 1997, p. 47).

Imports of Construction Materials and Equipment
The quantity of the imports of goods and services consumed by foreign visitors and of capital goods for the tourist sector depends on the extent to which the need for these goods and services can be met domestically. In other words, it depends on the extent of diversification in the domestic production structure and the flexibility of domestic supply.

The most important thing about these imports is especially that the country takes care of the basic technical infrastructure for tourism (i.e., roads, airfields, electricity, water supply, sewerage, etc.) and of the building of hotels. It may be the case that both the technical infrastructure and the hotels are exclusively intended for the (foreign) tourists. On the other hand, it may also be the case that they can be used by the local population. It is therefore very difficult to indicate to what extent the construction, etc., costs should be looked upon as belonging to the leakages of tourism. In many cases, however, it can be confidently stated that the construction, etc., was realized in the first place to attract foreign tourists. In most cases, this leads to large sums being borrowed abroad to make the arrival of foreign tourists possible. The Mexican government realized the complete technical infrastructure of the hyper-modern tourism center Cancún. For this, two big loans were necessary: a 300 million peso one, from the Inter-American Development Bank, and a $92 million one from a consortium of North American financial institutions. In 1976, the first hotel in Cancún was opened. In 1990, no fewer than 2 million tourists landed at Cancún airport. The investment in this airport can therefore be considered profitable. In Grenada, however, the situation is different. Here, an international airport was built at a total cost of US$85 million; in 1995, however, only three international flights on average arrived per day. In all probability, the governments of Cuba and the US did not take the construction costs on themselves entirely as a gift. Maintenance costs will probably have to be met by the Grenada government anyway.

Even if a certain industry is present in the area, there is no guarantee that it will profit from the building of hotels. "When Fidel Castro opened the first joint venture hotel at Varadero Beach, he noted that glass, copper and other necessary metalware imports were very expensive, and that although Cuba had an elevator factory, the quality of its output was not yet good enough for four- and five-star hotels" (Harrison & Husbands, 1996, pp. 116–117).

Imports of Consumable Goods (e.g., Food, Drinks)

"But not only foodstuffs are imported: also building materials, hotel equipment, film equipment, films, beach chairs, parasols, yes, even suntan oil" (Van Hout, 1984, pp. 62–63). This quotation concerning tourism in the African ministate Gambia indicates the great import need of small countries.

Belisle has drawn up a list of explanations for the fact that hotels decide not to use more locally produced agrarian produce.

> The reasons include tourists' preference for similar foods to those found in their own countries: imported food may be cheaper; hotels are willing to pay more for imports to ensure quality and/or a reliable supply; the quality of local food is not as good as imports (especially hygienic quality); hotel entrepreneurs may not be aware of the types and qualities of local foods available; farmers want to maintain their traditional crops and are not able to increase their production; farmers lack information about food requirements of hotels; hotels and farmers are inhibited from dealing with each other; and farmers or intermediaries are unreliable in maintaining a regular supply of local products or fulfilling contract agreements. (cited in Telfer & Wall, 1996, p. 640)

Other authors argue that the organizational structure of the international tourism industry itself acts as a barrier to domestic suppliers. Hotels that are foreign owned, or operated, may have strong links to overseas food suppliers and, as a result, may have a tendency to rely on them rather than on local suppliers (Telfer & Wall, 1996, p. 640).

> Yet in the dining rooms of many Caribbean hotels, where millions of meals are consumed daily, the tourists do not eat the mangoes and breadfruit, citrus and bananas of every Caribbean yard. They drink orange juice from Florida, eat a banana from Colombia or stab at pineapple chunks from Hawaii. Only

perhaps in countries like Jamaica, or perhaps for different reasons Dominica, can it be reasonably claimed that local products dominate tourist dining tables. There is now more traditional Jamaican food in hotels than ever before. (Pattullo, 1996, p. 39)

The situation in Jamaica is attributed to an initiative of the Manley government, which set up the Agricultural Marketing Corporation to help the farmers find local markets for their produce. Initiatives like this were the exception. After many decades in which farmers were trained to concentrate on growing crops for export, the ties between agriculture and the tourist sector are generally weak. A study conducted by the Caribbean Tourism Research Center (CTRC) in Grenada, St. Vincent, and St. Lucia shows that 54% of the food, 62.5% of the beverages, 70% of the meat, between 20% and 25% of the fruit and vegetables, and almost all the dairy products, consumed by tourists, were imported (Thomas, 1988, p. 160). Since then, Caribbean Islands have been focusing more on the local production of foodstuffs for the tourism sector.

In bigger countries such as Mexico, a large proportion of the necessary foodstuffs is often homegrown. Vellas and Becherel (1995, p. 243) mention a proportion of only 5% of the "tourism consumption" that has to be imported. In many countries, however, the smaller hotels serve more local products than the four- or five-star hotels, where the guests set more store by the food and drink and the quality that they are accustomed to.

Repatriation of Income Earned by Foreigners

For many developing countries, investing in tourism is also important with a view to the employment thus created. Tourism provides not only direct employment in hotels, casinos, restaurants, shops, and transport, but also indirect employment in the services generated by the industry. It also fuels a peripheral "informal" economic sector where the poor and unskilled attempt to earn an income (Pattullo, 1996, p. 52).

> Throughout the Caribbean up to one of six workers finds direct employment in tourism, more than in any other region of the world according to the World Travel and Tourism Council. Accurate figures are hard to come by, but the Caribbean Tourism Organization estimates that in 1994 tourism provided direct employment for 216,000 people in the region, with some 580,000 gaining indirect employment from the industry (Pattullo, 1996, p. 53).

Few figures are available, but in many studies it is pointed out that especially the higher positions in hotels are filled with foreigners. This is said to be related to the insufficient local availability of qualified workers, or to the tradition in international hotel chains to man top positions (at the management level) via an international turn-taking system (Theuns, 1989). Attempts are being made to reduce the deployment of foreign workers and of the attendant transfers of salaries by the creation of, for example, hotel schools.

Interest Paid on Foreign Loans

Above, the loans raised by Mexico and Grenada, respectively, were discussed. In 1969, the World Bank decided to found a Tourism Department, and, in subsequent years, many loans were made for tourism projects. Unfortunately, these loans cannot be traced in the Bank's annual reports. Because in other big financial institutions, such as the Inter-American Development Bank, loans for touristic projects have not been included under this title either, it is impossible to make an estimate of the size of the loans taken out by the governments for investments for or in the tourist sector.

Overseas Promotional Expenditures

Although the majority of the expenses made for promotion are defrayed by tour operators, countries sometimes take their promotion into their own hands. When, in the early 1990s, the dependence of the Caribbean on the American market became painfully clear because the tourist flow from America began to stagnate, the governments of 28 Caribbean countries decided to pool their resources for a concerted promotion campaign. This, incidentally, was their first action together, because previously everybody had been looking after their own interests.

> The US$12 million cost was financed by the private sector (hotels, airlines, cruise lines, tour operators and so on) and the member states of the Caribbean Tourism Organization (CTO). Twenty-eight member countries participated (only three countries of the CTO's membership were absent). The campaign was launched in 1993 with a 60-second TV commercial . . ., followed up with a 260-page glossy book, Caribbean Vacation Planner. . . . American travel agents were also targeted in the attempt to regenerate the US market. In 1994, some 3.000 agents signed up for individual city training programs to become Caribbean specialists and so more effectively advise their customers. The result of this Caribbean assault on the US market had already begun to take effect in 1993 when a 10.4 per cent growth rate over 1992 was reported. The advertisement worked. There's nothing else to explain it. The US market had been stagnant for 10 years. (Pattullo, 1996, pp. 147–148)

The Caribbean countries also began to target Europe. In 1993, a 3-year tourism development program costing US$10 million was launched. What the campaign aimed to achieve was for 90,000 extra European tourists to pay a visit to the Caribbean per year (Patullo, 1996, p. 148). Between 1993 and 1997, the number of stay-over arrivals grew with 67,000 (WTO, 1999, p. 45). "The Dominican Republic, a major tourism destination, is unique in leaving the private sector to shoulder all the promotional side of the industry. In 1993, it spent less than US$100,000 on promotion, compared to US$15 million in Jamaica and US$25 million in the Bahamas" (WTO, 1999, p. 151).

General Leakages

Given the various problems discussed above, it stands to reason that studies in which leakages have been calculated are not frequent and arrive at mutually quite different results. In most of the Caribbean, the level of what are known as leakages is very high, averaging at around 70%. In the Bahamas, a senior tourism official suggested in 1994 that the leakages for that country might be as high as 90%. More diversified economies such as Jamaica's have been more successful in blocking the leakages. The Organization of American States assessed Jamaica's leakage at 37% in 1994, a far more respectable figure than is usual in the region (Pattullo, 1996, pp. 38–39).

Wheatcroft (1994, p. 43) gives the following percentages for a number of Caribbean islands: St. Lucia 45%, Aruba 41%, Jamaica 40%, US Virgin Islands 36%, and Antigua 25%.

Earlier, the future expectations with respect to cruise tourism were sketched. J. A. Hall and Braithwaite (1990, p. 343) come to the conclusion that the leakage effect for cruise ships is lower than for stay-over tourists, because the guests on board cruise ships do not make use of touristic elements that have high a "leakage" value (e.g., accommodation), but do make relatively intensive use of sectors from which fewer dollars leak away, such as tourist attractions, sightseeing, and arts and crafts products. In the final analysis, however, a country will be worse off with cruise ship tourists than with stay-over tourists, because the net receipts from the former, given their very brief presence in the country, are probably much lower than those from the latter.

Conclusions

The main conclusion from the foregoing is that tourism in Latin America has become an important (and in some cases even very important) source of revenue. Both arrivals and receipts have grown spectacularly. This does not mean that the development must be qualified as favorable in every respect. First of all, the receipts are noted in current dollar values rather than constant values, which is of course important because of inflationary tendencies. So, the used receipt indicator is a rough one. In some countries and regions, it has put the country and people under considerable pressure, in addition to which there is the threat of a one-sided economic dependence on this source of revenue.

With regard to the opportunities for participation of local people one must have severe doubts about tourism. First, as has been shown, it is not clear whether the sector offers a positive balance of net receipts. On the contrary, there are indications showing that in many cases these receipts may be negative or at least very limited. In case of positive net proceeds, one cannot be sure that locals in general are in the position to take part in those benefits. Tosun (2000) has argued that in many developing countries the benefits of tourism go to either the international tourism companies or to local elite. Besides that, the overwhelming power of the international enterprises is by definition a limiting factor for local participation.

Nevertheless, it is a fact that tourism as a sector of economic activity is there to stay. It is easy to understand, therefore, that Latin American countries are assigning a central position in their policy plans to tourism. It remains to be seen, however, whether such a policy is sensible in every respect.

The first condition a country has to meet is that is has something to offer to tourists: sun-sea-sand, and/or natural beauty, and/or an interesting culture. Of course, the attractiveness of a country can be strongly enhanced, for example, by opening up certain areas and by improving the infrastructure. But if the latter requires considerable investment, a country should be very careful in weighing the pros and cons. On more than one occasion, large investment has led to sizeable foreign debt, without leading to matching revenue from tourism.

In addition, the political circumstances must be such that the tourist can visit the country in question without needing to worry about them. Inasmuch as the political circumstances concern internal political relations, they can be considered to be the business of the country itself. The external circumstances, however, can only be controlled up to a point, as is clear from an example like Cuba. Once more, it will be clear that it is not wise to depend too one-sidedly on the proceeds of tourism.

It should also be determined to what extent the potential economic advantages of the sector benefit the countries themselves. It is far from simple to chart the possible leakages. Tourism is a blanket concept, covering a large number of divergent activities. The extent to which governments can diminish leakages depends, among other things, on the size of the economy. For small economies, it often does not make sense to set up an import-replacing industry, and a large measure of dependence will continue to exist, for example, as far as the building of infrastructure and hotels is concerned. For the many Caribbean islands, closer mutual cooperation could possibly be a solution. If the possibilities of drastically limiting leakages are few, it is highly doubtful whether a country should invest a high proportion of its resources in the tourism sector, because this strategy, especially in combination with factors as low attractiveness for tourists and unstable political circumstances, can land the country from the frying pan into the fire.

Finally, with respect to the issue of local participation, one must be very cautious in promoting too many expectations. As Tosun (2000) has stated, "implementation of participatory tourism development approach requires a total change in socio-political, legal and economic structure of developing countries" (p. 628).

Notes

[1]The human development index is composed of data regarding health, education, and income per capita of the population.

[2]Tourist: Temporary visitors who spend more than 24 hours in destinations other than their normal plane of residence, whose journey is for the purpose of holiday-making, recreation, health, study, religion, sport, visiting family or friends, business or meetings (Sinclair, 1998, p. 4).

[3]Travel receipts are defined by the International Monetary Fund to include receipts for goods and services provided to foreigners visiting the reporting country, including transportation within that country. Includes funds spent by tourists, business travelers, students, patients undergoing medical treatment, military personnel on leave, and traveling government officials. In many cases, comparable data for a national series are not available throughout the period covered by the table, and also, close comparisons between countries are often rendered difficult by the lack of uniformity in definitions and scope. These data exclude receipts and expenditure of international transport (UCLA, 1984).

[4]In the literature we also find references to the tourist penetration rate (TPR) and the tourist density ratio (TDR) to single out the significance of tourism. TPR: average length of stay × number of tourists/365 × 1988 population. TDR: average length of stay × number of tourists/365 × area in square kilometers.

[5] Theuns (1989) distinguishes first of all primary and secondary conditions. Primary: a potential of tourist attractions is available (pleasant climate, beaches, tourist sites). Secondary: appropriate accommodations are available like hotels, bed and breakfast, holiday resorts, and camping grounds; and moreover restaurants, sport and recreation facilities, and major roads. Once both conditions are met, it depends on the following criteria whether foreign visitors will be attracted: the availability of tourist transport and the geographic location; tourist promotion and marketing; tourist demands from affluent consumer groups; the relative cost levels; the realization of basic facilities. In the case of developing countries these are: a) the standard of living; b) knowledge and skills; c) tourism mindedness; d) health conditions; e) legal security and stability.

Chapter 3

Tourists and Other People: Governments, Institutions, and Entrepreneurs in Jamaica, Cuba, and Costa Rica

Bea Groen

Introduction

While tourism is often seen in many developing countries as negatively affecting landscape, morals, rising prices, and increased crime and pollution increase, it is nevertheless one of the most important economic sectors for development in late 20th and early 21st century. While tourism is promoted for its expected economic benefits by many countries, it must not be forgotten that tourism is not a purely economic phenomenon. Tourism is always embedded in multiple institutions, government measures, entrepreneurial developments, and tourist (i.e., consumer) trends. This applies also to the area under scrutiny in this book. Many countries in Latin America and the Caribbean aim at tourism as a sector that is relatively clean and easy to promote for economic development. The impacts of this sector, however, are far reaching, affecting the societies in the destination area as a whole. In this chapter, common assumptions about tourism will be critically reviewed and the backgrounds, settings, history, and future of tourism in selected Latin American and Caribbean countries will be examined. The focus is on three examples of well-known holiday destinations: Costa Rica, Jamaica, and Cuba.

Costa Rica has built up quite a reputation for nature protection and reforestation, which attract many tourists. At the same time, the large numbers of tourists that have visited Costa Rica have impacted the country, leading to new developments in which local population and government play modest and not very convincing roles, with the government especially lacking strength in setting nature before money. The country's image, however, is "green," and Costa Rica is regarded as an ecotourist destination par excellence. Jamaica has quite a long history as a tourist destination with government—as owner of the majority of the large hotels on the island—playing a major role in the development of tourism. Cuba is an island with special social, economic, and political connotations, with government being the all-important—and, actually since the 1950s, the only—true actor on the scene.

This chapter is structured as follows. First, based on a literature review, the opportunities and problems of tourism in the three countries will be explored. Second, the role of governments and entrepreneurs in (eco)tourism in the three countries will be analyzed in more detail. In the concluding section, the future of tourism and, especially, ecotourism in Costa Rica, Jamaica, and Cuba will be discussed.

In summary, this chapter raises the following questions:

- How is tourism being controlled and guided by governments, institutions, and entrepreneurs?
- What does the concept of ecotourism imply in these three countries and to what extent does ecotourism figure as an alternative for conventional (i.e., beach) tourism in these countries?
- How should ecotourism develop in the future?

A Definition

According to Butler (1991, p. 201), tourism is the activity of people when traveling and sightseeing under the headings of "leisure" and "recreation." For sustainable tourism he adds a condition with far-reaching consequences: the same amount and quality of "leisure" and "recreation" must be available for the next generations. D. Wilson (1996) defines sustainable tourism development in terms of "exploitation without exhaustion of tourism resources" (p. 75). Tourism resources are assets for travel and sightseeing that Butler (1991, p. 202) identifies as historical and/or natural heritage, local people, and customs. These "tourist resources" are to be exploited as well as preserved for the benefit of both the tourists and the people earning an income from these resources. Focusing on the "sustainability" of ecotourism, Brohman (1996) adds the words "ecologically sound" (p. 64). With that in mind, the definition of ecotourism is as follows:

> Ecotourism is the type of tourism that makes use of local resources, environmentally friendly and ecologically sound materials and infrastructure, and that aims at the sustainability of itself and of its resources, respecting the local population with its culture and traditions.

In the literature, there are many definitions of ecotourism highlighting aspects like small-scale enterprises, low-density developments, importance of nature as a resource, importance of local heritage, importance of local population as owners and managers, community participation in planning, and importance of tourists adapting to local traditions. These aspects are reshuffled in different combinations to define concepts related to sustainable tourism, like "alternative tourism," "indigenous and integrated tourism," "nature tourism," or "green tourism" and "ecotourism." In this chapter the term ecotourism is given preference to other terms, as the ecological soundness of tourism development in the three countries with their vast nature-based potential will be emphasized.

Tourists, Tourist Organizations, and Tourist Industries

The tourist attractions in Costa Rica, Jamaica, and Cuba are mainly nature based. Tourist brochures feature wide beaches with palms, scenic rocky coasts, dramatic mountain ranges, rainforests, tropical wildlife, sun-sea-fun, national parks, waterfalls, etc. Until a decade ago, the tourism industry in the Caribbean used to boast of the ways it served and coddled tourists in its beach resorts. More recently, without giving up this image of sea-sun-sand pleasures, tourists are also encouraged to be active and get involved in hiking, rafting, swimming, and discovering. In this respect, the Caribbean tourist industry seems to imitate Costa Rica's image of a destination for the active tourists who want a survival trip in the jungle. The Caribbean also adds culture and history in the form of restored colonial buildings, and reggae as a musical tradition to its tourist product. Cuba in particular attracts tourists with historic buildings and poses as a cultural tourism destination. Nevertheless, tourism to the Caribbean, and in particular Cuba, is organized as package trips to be booked with tour operators. Backpackers are virtually absent in Caribbean destinations.

Costa Rica is generally associated with "adventure" and "discovery" trips with a certain amount of danger for the daring ones. With the aid of a travel agency or via the Internet travelers compose their own holiday consisting of different "modules." These can be a 2- or 3-day raft experience on the Río Reventazón, boat trips through the canals of rainy, Caribbean-sided Tortuguero, a canoe trip in the Golfo Dulce, and a hiking trail through the Peninsula of Osa on the Pacific side. National parks, covering 13% of the total area, are the most popular destinations for both individuals and groups who love nature. Apart from national parks, a number of private parks/reserves or enterprises exist that are labeled "eco." Beach holidays are offered at Costa Rica's Pacific coast where surfing is increasingly becoming more popular.

In the 1980s, tour operators in the Caribbean started a new phenomenon: the all-inclusive resort. Tourists book and pay everything in advance: their room, food, alcoholic drinks, and occasional excursions. Entertainment and shopping (the buys, however, are not inclusive) are also provided within the resort. The tourist need not go out, but can relax completely and remain in the all-inclusive hotel. For a few active people staying in the resort, national parks with nature trails as well as historic heritage sites (with reference to the plantation epoch and slavery) may provide a change of scenery. The all-inclusives in Jamaica have gained a firm foothold alongside smaller hotels and guesthouses, just as they have in Cuba. In Costa Rica, however, resorts do not play a prominent role, most probably due to the different type of tourist—adventurous, more independent—that the country attracts with its "green" image. While Costa Rica offers national parks and reserves, the Caribbean has for decades been known for its holidays with a languid and luxurious image, inviting people looking for lazy, relaxed holidays.

Turning to the organizational structure of tourism, institutions at different levels of governance are involved in tourism planning, policy making, and implementation. First of all, there is the WTO, which issued guidelines for governments in tourist destination areas to comply with in order to develop more sustainable forms of tourism. The report titled *National and Regional Tourism Planning Methodologies* (WTO, 1994) proposes measures to be taken by governments when developing and promoting tourism. The emphasis is on control of social and environmental impacts. Planning should involve institutional and organizational elements, like establishing a national tourist administration or organization (NTA or NTO), for instance, in the form of a Department of Tourism. Items on the WTO environmental list are: the establishment of systems of water supply, electricity supply, sewage, solid waste disposal, and drainage; the construction of adequate road and transport (e.g., electric shuttles for tourists) and proper maintenance of these while managing flows of tourists. Governments are also expected to provide open spaces, environmentally suitable land use and site planning principles, zoning regulations, standards, and architectural designs (WTO, 1994, p. 34). National tourism organizations should be entrusted with marketing and promotion, statistics and research, education and training, and tourism advisory services (WTO, 1994, pp. 40-41).

At regional levels, tourist organizations support the implementation of WTO guidelines. A good example is the Comité Especial de Turismo de la Asociación de Estados del Caribe (AEC), within which a working group is established to develop an agreement on a sustainable tourism zone, in which public and private sectors are supposed to participate. This organization applies the Costa Rican system as the term of reference for its categorization of sustainable tourism. In Costa Rica, the national tourism organization, the Instituto Costarricense de Turismo, claims to be the "responsible" institution for the development of tourism. In fact, their official task is limited to establishing tourist statistics and promoting Costa Rica as a tourist destination. However, the improvement of, for instance, the road from Aeropuerto Juan Santamaria to San José—essential for tourist transportation—is the task of the Ministry of Public Works and Transportation. Like in many other countries, tourism-related matters are scattered over different ministries, even in Costa Rica, a country that has been widely praised for its tourism policy.

Turning to the entrepreneurial structure of tourism, the basic characteristic of the tourism industry is its being a service industry. Coupled with the fact that entrepreneurs run businesses with the purpose of making a profit, tourism entrepreneurs in particular have to be demand oriented. Pearce (1992) writes about "matching markets and products with the notion of consumer satisfaction," which he explains as "to satisfy the needs and wants of chosen consumer groups at a profit" (p. 7). In order to be a successful entrepreneur, people in the tourism industry require not only economic capital to invest in their business, but also practical and social skills to provide good services and knowledge of the developments in tourism. This implies relevant training to access information and make knowledge operational for the business, and a vast social network. As these resources are scarce—in particular in developing countries—it is not unusual to find entrepreneurs (in tourism as well as in other sectors) among the (local) elite. Often, these elite establish a separate class and inequality may increase as a consequence of successful entrepreneurship among the local population (Brohman, 1996, p. 60). Local and/or national elite are also better connected with potential investors abroad, which facilitate large-scale investments as required in building resorts. These large tourist projects find easy support among many governments in developing countries as they promise large profits and tax revenues. In Costa Rica, Canatur, the national organization of tourism entrepreneurs, represents only a very small part of the bigger tourism entrepreneurs.

In addition, many foreigners set up tourism enterprises in Costa Rica and the Caribbean, as they have better (access to) knowledge, more practical skills, and easier access to money. Especially when it comes to performing host functions to tourists from their own countries of origin, they possess better and more appropriate knowledge and skills to satisfy these tourists' needs. Another point to their advantage is that local governments welcome their investments, often eager to attract foreign money as well as employment opportunities for the local population.

Economic Opportunities From Tourism for Government and Entrepreneurs: Three Case Studies

In this section tourism development in Jamaica, Cuba, and Costa Rica will be submitted to closer examination. The emphasis will be on the ways in which national governments and local population develop, exploit, and experience tourism, and how the interests of both actors sometimes converge but often conflict.

Jamaica

Tourism in Jamaica started around 1900. In *To Hell With Paradise*, Taylor (1993, p. 119) describes those early days of tourism in terms of decay: the streets were swarming with beggars, vendors selling liquorice seeds and postcards, and informal tour guides who "harassed" the tourists. In order to get a grip on this situation, the government supplied extra police and fined harassment (Taylor, 1993, p. 119). The local population looked at tourism with distrust: they felt it was the big storekeepers in Kingston who were getting the tourist money. The tourists would only laugh and take their pictures and it would be only the whites to benefit (Taylor, 1993, p. 110). But over the decades tourism was booming. In the 1990s, Jamaica was the fourth most popular destination in the Caribbean with more than 1.2 million tourist arrivals in 1999 (WTO, 2001, p. 402). Only the Dominican Republic and the Bahamas receive more tourists (Pattullo, 1996, p. 11). Eight percent of the Jamaican labor force works in the tourist industry (Pattullo, 1996, p. 53), and tourism contributes over 13% to the GDP (Pattullo, 1996, p. 47). Out of a total budget of US$60 million (in 1992), half went to the Ministry of Tourism to support the work of the Jamaica Tourist Board; another US$15.7 million went to maintaining and improving sewerage, city upgrading, water supply, roads, and other infrastructure on the island (Pattullo, 1996, pp. 32–33). In contrast to many other Caribbean countries, the majority of hotels (75%) are owned by locals nowadays. Strikingly, only 31% of the hotels are locally managed (Pattullo, 1996, p. 23). It is widely acknowledged that foreign managers are preferred in the tourism industry in many developing countries, as it is presumed that they are better equipped to establish the much desired contacts with foreign airlines and tour operators to bring in tourists (Pattullo, 1996, p. 24).

The case of the Negril, in west Jamaica, as described by Cater (1995), gives a more detailed picture of the impacts of tourism in a Jamaican tourist destination. In 1971, the Negril area was inhabited by farmers and fishermen, and mobility was confined to foot, bicycle, and an occasional bus. There were two hotels and five lodges offering hospitality. Roads were unpaved, there was no electricity, and water flowed from a pipe from a reservoir further east. Sewage was simple: a hole was dug until contact with the sea directly beneath was established. A foreigner could buy an acre of land by the sea for US$7000. In 1989 the same acre cost US$500,000. By 1992, there were 128 small, large, and all-inclusive hotels, villas, cottages, cabins, and restaurants in the same area. There were 2436 rooms and 2837 toilets, and 166,720 tourists were accommodated per year. These data were collected in the "Negril Environment Survey," carried out by the Negril Coral Reef Preservation Society (NCPRS). This organization was founded in 1990 by diving operators and instructors who noticed the reef deteriorating and who were losing some of their clientele due to infectious diseases caused by swimming in the sea. The NCPRS then launched an awareness campaign: "Reefsavers do it without touching." But there was more to marine pollution than a diver's touch.

In the early 1990s, the Negril Chamber of Commerce was still dealing with the old case of tourist harassment by vendors: "pushing back the pushers." The Chamber created the Negril Itinerant Vendors Association and the Negril Hairbraiders Association, provided the police with more means of transport, and initiated educational programs on the subject (Cater, 1995). In the meantime, the area was suffering under problems of a more serious kind. In 1992 some 3 million gallons of water were wasted by flushing toilets only, without a sign of proper sewage treatment. A new sewage system was under construction, financed with a loan from the European Union, but contribution of US$1000 as required from the small local hotel owners, lodge owners, and subsistence farmers met with difficulties. The NCPRS also created the Negril Environment Protection Trust (NEPT) (funded by USAID) as a coordinating agency for all local committees that were working on environment protection projects. NCPRS and NEPT and the National Resource Conservation were to manage the Marine Park. An example of these initiatives is the Mooring Buoy Project—to prevent damaging the reef by anchoring. Another initiative to protect the reef was the plan for a swimming lane and a water ski and ski jet area. Together with the Fishermen's Cooperative, the NCRPS developed a marine cash crop: Irish moss that could be sold locally at a good profit. Other marine culture projects were under way. Many NCPRS suggestions with an environmental background were implemented, such as the use of energy-saving light bulbs and water-saving showers. Especially the larger hotels bought these in order to save considerably on water and electricity bills. The condition of the water was more problematic. While many local people had hardly any access to piped water, the hotels close to the water reservoir used drinking water to maintain their lawns. Hotel tanks were filled at night and the smaller lodges and properties at the end of the pipe were cut off from the water supply during evenings and nights.

The protective measures were initiated by the NCPRS, a NGO. This raises the question what the Jamaican government had been doing all these years. In the Caribbean quite a number of politicians have a shrewd eye for their own private profits but show little regard as to what is good for their countries. Hotels, drugs, and Mafia connections contribute considerably to their income and, at the same time, enhance their problems to keep public and private interests separated (Pattullo, 1996, pp. 108– 109). The Jamaican government, however, contrasted favorably with these practices. Decades ago, when tourism was low, the government purchased hotels in order to maintain employment opportunities for the Jamaican citizens. If the government had not intervened, the Jamaican economy would have collapsed and the IMF would have taken over the country. At times, the Jamaican government owned about 90% of the hotel beds on the island. But after years of ownership and leasing out management, the Jamaican government decided to sell its properties. This sale was not confined to hotels, but extended also to land. Until then, there was no market for land. Creating a land market turned out to be a very profitable undertaking. The government's Urban Development Corporation started to develop large-scale property projects and leases and sells land to the highest bidders.

Large-scale property development shows little sensitivity towards environmental issues, as the Negril case testifies. There was a last stretch of wilderness along the beach and local organizations were developing plans to turn it into a national park, as a "pristine" location and buffer in between hotels to attract and divert tourists and conserve some of the original Jamaican jungle. Government decided otherwise; it sacrificed the wilderness to the building of the new, large "Beaches Hotel" and only a very small token bit remained unharmed (Cater, 1995, p. 26). The government was well aware of the (lack of) water supply in 1993 and they placed a moratorium on development until the system was upgraded, but they were only too willing to sell beach land at enormous profit and allow the construction of a 225-room hotel that would offer 350 jobs (Cater, 1995, p. 26). Contrasting with the 1970s, when the Jamaican government was in a very positive way involved with tourism, trying to save enterprises (hotels) and employment, the 1990s showed a different role played by the government. As the economy and tourism regained their strength, government took its chances and turned its former beneficial actions to its own advantage, presumably supporting other less viable activities with tourism money in the way many governments fill up holes with the leftovers from others. In short, the Jamaican government complies very much with the picture that Hudson (1996) paints in "Paradise lost": a lamentable failing in setting rules and guidelines for any development—and keeping to these. As such, the Jamaican government did not comply with the rules given by the WTO (see above).

In 1978 members of the local Town and Country Planners Association insisted on the establishment of a comprehensive development plan that would be supported by the local population. But the Jamaican government was satisfied with a development order only, focusing on quick hotel development and intensification of linear development along the coast (Hudson, 1996, p. 25). Their obsession with sheer numbers of (tourist) arrivals did the rest (Pattullo, 1996, p. 35). Their attention was focused on tourist development in the narrow sense, whereas infrastructure was neglected, like the sewage processing plant that soon proved too small and caused marine pollution (Pattullo, 1996, p. 23). As mentioned above, infectious disease scared away tourists as a consequence.

Figure 3.1. A Dominican woman on the beach of Boca Chica (Dominican Republic) giving a massage to a tourist.

Ecotourism is gaining an interest throughout the Caribbean, offering an opportunity "to create an image of political responsibility while supporting marketing strategy aimed at expanding tourism" (D. Wilson, 1996, p. 75). Ecotourism is being developed in Jamaica as well. Pattullo (1996, p. 120) amends that it is a form of ecotourism that is linked with sustainable environmental projects while trying to maintain traditional tourism. Ecotourism purists may criticize this approach. But in the face of Jamaican tourism reality, it is not as unreasonable as it may seem. After all, it is impossible to transform tourist accommodation for hundreds and thousands of tourists in just one go into an ecotourism venture. A good example of ecotourist developments is Jamaica's first national park, the Blue Mountain/John Crow Mountain National Park, which was opened in 1989 to stop deforestation and soil erosion. The concept of the park is to promote sustainable land use. In 1992, the park received a US$100,000 grant from the Puerto Rican Conservation Trust. A special conservation area is managed by local people to promote ecotourism and sustainable agriculture in the Blue Mountains. The park offers various sporting activities and tourists can spend time with local farmers and residents. At Maya Lodge, the headquarters of the Jamaica Alternative Tourism, Camping and Hiking Association, there is also a demonstration site for a community forestation program and it provides support, research, and training for other ecotourism operations. The park welcomes both foreign and local tourists (Pattullo, 1996, p. 119).

Government and NGOs have not yet fully developed their attitude towards ecotourism. Tourism development, economic development, and environmental issues lead to controversies and an ongoing struggle between government, developers, associations of hoteliers, NGOs, foreign aid organizations, and local people (Cater, 1995, pp. 25–28). Water and sea pollution, reef destruction, lack of sewage disposal systems, and lack of drinking water pose serious problems that have triggered initiatives to develop a "green" hospitality sector. While the parks are established to stop erosion, farmers are induced to go and live elsewhere or give up farming (Barker & Miller, 1995, p. 290; D. C. Smith, 1995, p. 256). Alternative employment is created for farmers and spear fishermen who are offered jobs as guides, rangers, or "board operators." The local population supports these initiatives, and environmental awareness is rising and will most probably gain importance.

Government and local people often have different opinions and interests. However, as far as tourism is concerned, Jamaicans understand the importance of this sector for their economy. Research by Stone (1991) has shown that out of a poll of 662 Jamaican citizens living in tourist areas, 75% of the respondents felt they benefited from tourism. With benefits, people referred mainly to economic benefits, while negative aspects were related to the social impacts of tourism. Among the negative impacts were rated drug problems and prostitution, which were seen as tourist-related issues (Stone, 1991, p. 8). Prostitution in Jamaica is characterized by local young men who prostitute themselves to foreign females, dubbed as "Foreign Service" and "Rent a Rasta" (Pattullo, 1996, p. 88). AIDS is increasing rapidly in Jamaica. In the mid-1990s, the Ministry of Health estimated that 0.1% of the population in Negril was HIV positive (Pattullo, 1996, p. 90). Drug-related organized crime, political violence, and gang shoot-outs may affect tourism (Pattullo, 1996, p. 98). A separate police task force was installed to combat drug dealers and illegal vendors after the shooting of tourists in the early 1990s.

Cuba

Prior to 1959, tourism in Cuba was characterized by gambling, liquor, prostitution, and as dominated by the Mafia. Cuba's turning to socialism turned out to be the end of tourism, at least for a few decades. Castro's idea of tourism and whorism being the same marked the death of tourism activities. Once banned, tourist arrivals dropped from 272,000 to 2000 between 1957 and 1971 (Van Iperen, 1996, p. 86). About 30 years later tourism was invited back in when Cuba ran out of funds due to bad sugar harvests, the decline of nickel prices on the world market, and the breakdown of the Soviet Union, Cuba's most important supporter (D. R. Hall, 1995, p. 102). Without forsaking socialism, Castro opened Cuba for tourism: "An appropriately structured tourism development program can help achieve such socialist objectives as spatial equalization of opportunities and imbuing visitors with a sense of the superiority of the socialist system" (D. R. Hall, 1995, p. 107). This led to a rapid growth of "international visitors" (Cuba does not have a registration of foreign "tourists"), from 745,495 in 1995 to 1,602,781 in 1999 (WTO, 2001, p. 181).

In the early 1990s Cuba enhanced its efforts to find investors in joint ventures to develop tourist destinations. Capitalist investors came to Cuba from all over the world, but especially, and ironically, from Spain, a country with which the (colonial) strings were cut about 100 years ago. "We learn from mistakes made elsewhere. Tourists don't want skyscrapers and tourism in Cuba will never affect the environment. Hotels can be built and pulled down, but once the environment is destroyed, it can't be reconstructed" (Castro, quoted in Van Iperen, 1996, p. 88). The tourism challenge was aimed at with zeal. Key resorts like Varadero and Cayo Largo received a $395 million injection (Figure 3.2). With a capacity of 14,600 rooms (in 1993) (Dubesset, 1995, p. 50) these resorts received package tourists, about 25% of whom came from Eastern European countries (D. R. Hall, 1995, p. 114). As far as resort development is concerned, the tourism product of Cuba does not differ from the trend toward "all-inclusives" as elsewhere in the Caribbean. Only gambling—not allowed on the island—takes place on ships as soon as they come into open sea.

Resorts are constructed in a way that foreign tourists remain separated from the local population, who are not supposed to be exposed to foreigners. For the time being, the management of most of the large hotels is in the hands of foreigners, as the Cubans lack experience with tourism. But training is now being provided in Varadero and Havana (Van Iperen, 1996, p. 87). Hundreds of students enrolled in the program of the Polytechnic Institute of Hotel and Tourism Services in the 1990s (D. R. Hall, 1995, p. 115). The segregation policy of the Cuban government does not prevent local people from trying to benefit from the presence of tourists. Many Cubans offer services (like transportation) to tourists, although the authorities may punish those who get caught doing so (Van Iperen, 1996, pp. 43-44). Eventually, local people will get involved on a large scale in petty tourist services,

Figure 3.2. Western tourists offer US dollars for a drink on the beach of Varadero (Cuba).

as has occurred in tourism destinations worldwide and in disregard of impediments by the government. In this respect, it is interesting to note that in particular people in the informal sector earn the much-desired dollars (hard currency) from tourism. Cubans employed by any of the 146 international joint ventures do earn a salary in dollars, but their employer pays their salary to a government-operated firm that exchanges this payment into pesos after extracting health and security benefits. Therefore, only those who obtain their money directly from foreigners (i.e., painters and writers who can sell their work directly to foreigners as well as unofficial drivers, tourist guides, and prostitutes) can buy products in dollar shops. These dollar shops tend to be better provided than the local, state-run shops. Dollars can also be earned through private enterprises that have been permitted to operate since 1994. Private enterprises are tolerated only for as long as they make a moderate profit. If they become too successful they are "nationalized" (Landau & Starratt, 1994, p. 8). This rule applies to private guesthouses and restaurants, which are required to comply with many rules. Many people run a small restaurant in their own home where tourists can taste the *auténtico ambiente cubano*. But the restaurants are forced to remain small and obey the *Ley de la última Cena* (Law of the Last Supper), dictating that no more than 12 guests at any one time will sit at the tables.

A special feature of Cuban tourism is the emergence of so-called health tourism, which attracted 2000 foreigners as early as 1990 (Hall, 1995, p. 113). This is not the kind of fitness tourism similar to what other Caribbean islands offer, with mud-wraps, beauty parlors, and gyms (Goodrich, 1994, p. 232). Cuban health tourism aims at medical care. It is organized by Servimed, part of Cubanacán, an enterprise especially aiming at the creation of joint ventures in the tourism industry (Espino, 1993, p. 50). Servimed advertises specialized treatment for vitiligo, heart and kidney problems, and, perhaps most importantly, eye surgery to prevent or repair blindness. Pacemakers are being implanted at US$5000 and open-heart surgery is performed at US$10,000. These operations are offered in an all-inclusive arrangement; only medicine and telephone calls are to be paid separately (Van Iperen, 1996, pp. 91–92). Thousands of radiation victims and other patients from the former Soviet Union are received as a way of paying off Cuban debt to the Soviet Union (Van Iperen, 1996, p. 190). The local population, however, hospitalized in worn-out rooms and worrying about lack of soap and other basics, is faced with a health care system that has increasingly less to offer (Van Iperen, 1996, pp. 193–194). Pharmacies lack simple things like aspirin and condoms, but keep hoping to be supplied "next week."

Cuban architecture has gained worldwide interest over the last few years. Habana Vieja, the old town center, dates from 1514. Since 1982 it has been on the UNESCO list of World Heritage Sites. In the same year, the Centro Nacional de Conservación, Restauración y Museologia (Cencrem) was created that works on the restoration of the whole of Habana Vieja. The Cencrem made a priority list for restoration on which museums came first and housing came last. The museums also serve as classrooms for the overcrowded schools. An interesting feature in Habana is its own Capitol (Carley, 1998, pp. 214–215). Other tourist attractions are beaches and mountains and, of course, the Che Guevara gravesite as a modern pilgrimage destination. As early as 1963, the Academy of Sciences set aside land for six national parks (4% of the national area) like Zapata, a swampy peninsula, and the Sierra de los Organos, a limestone stack area. Hunting and cutting trees are prohibited in this area. The management is in the hands of the National Center for Protection, and Conservation of National Treasures is the overseer (D. R. Hall, 1995, pp. 112–113). Mountain resort holidays are gaining popularity among the local population, while the government travel agency Havanatur organizes for foreigners mainly short trips to established tourist centers, such as old museum-like Trinidad on the south coast, Cancún (Mexico), and Nassau (Bahamas) (Van Iperen, 1996, p. 90).

It will be interesting to see how the Cubans will deal with environmental deterioration. Despite Castro's words about nature not being restorable, the coral reef around Cuba is damaged by the many cruise ships that anchor here. There is also sand loss on the beaches and the coastal waters are contaminated. The contamination is caused not only by sewage and garbage but also by industrial waste and fertilizer residues (D. R. Hall, 1995, p. 117). Research has been done in the Varadero area—one of the most important all-inclusive tourist areas—but hardly any information has been provided about the results (D. R. Hall, 1995, p. 117). Other than in Jamaica, the local population in Cuba is not likely to get involved in environmental protection, the organization of NGOs, or pressure groups. Private entrepreneurship is of very recent date (Landau & Sparratt, 1994, p. 8), and organized action is rare. Cuba, however, is a member of AEC—the Association of Caribbean States—and as such participates in the regional development of tourism and of environmental awareness. Though measures agreed on in an international organization need not necessarily be applied directly in every country, it is nevertheless a hopeful sign that Cuba participates in the development of ecologically sound tourism in the Caribbean and in Latin America.

Costa Rica

Tourism in Costa Rica is the second economic sector after agriculture (coffee and bananas) and the most important earner of foreign currency. Direct employment is estimated at 60,000 jobs and the number of jobs indirectly involved in tourism is estimated to be the same. In 1999, 1,031,585 tourists visited the country, almost 50% of whom came from North America (WTO, 1995, p. 42). Tourism employment is the foremost alternative for farmers who cannot compete with imports or sell their land to large enterprises, and for gold miners whose former mining areas have been turned into national parks. Tourists come mainly because of nature conservation and visit the official conservation areas. Those areas that are not explicitly labeled "national park," "refuge," or "reserve" are seriously threatened by ongoing deforestation for agriculture and industrial use. Costa Rica started with nature conservation by way of national parks in the 1960s, when government discovered the country's natural beauty as its strong point worth developing. It was then that interest rose for nature and nature conservation, which made all ministries and organizations in Costa Rica want to develop their own special department or subdivision focusing on these subjects. This is one of the reasons why nature protection in Costa Rica evolved in a haphazard and uncoordinated way. This lack of long-term planning is also rooted in the political system, which limits the president's term to 4 years. This implies that after each new election a new president takes over with a completely new set of ministers, introducing new projects and new policies (Carrière, 1991, pp. 193–194). Since 1990, the government has aimed at overall sustainable development, for which Costa Rica has been widely praised. What does this government-supported sustainable development entail?

The nature conservation movement of the 1960s was preceded and strengthened by an influx of foreigners who fell in love with Costa Rica's natural beauty, bought bits of land, and turned them into private parks. Cabo Blanco (Pacific coast) and Rara Avis (northeast) are examples of foreign involvement. Government followed suit by appointing some 12% of the country's surface as national parks, reserves, or refuges covering rainforest areas, dry savanna, beaches, mountains, and volcanoes, in which an abundance of birds, plants, and mammals is thriving. But not all parks were located conveniently close to Juan Santa Maria Aeropuerto Nacional as well as to one another. For many Americans and Canadians who flew to Costa Rica for a 1- or 2-week stay, distances between the various parks were hard to overcome. Tourists are used to going to the same places. This is why Manuel Antonio National Park, on the Pacific coast, received and still receives an enormous amount of visitors. As a consequence, prices in nearby Quepos are much higher compared with the rest of the country. Beautiful as beach and park are, overcrowding is a serious problem. In the season 1997–1998, the park had to set a limit to the number of visitors to the park: 100 at any one time. In the meantime, pollution from the hotels' primitive sewage systems is threatening the beach (Rachowiecki, 1997, p. 491).

So far, the government has no fixed rules for sewage treatment or for the treatment of other waste. Waste processing is the responsibility of the Ministry of Health. However, the regulations and technologies applied are not very sophisticated. There is no differentiation in materials to be recycled, burned, or dumped. Most solid waste is transported to large dumps. The only attempt at recycling consists of people picking reusable materials from the dump. In practice, waste disposal is left to private and community initiatives. The construction of a waste-processing plant near Paquera on the Peninsula de Nicoya—where many local people earn money from tourism—was opposed by the local population and cancelled. In Tamarindo on the Pacific coast, a community organization has taken over the waste disposal that, officially, was the responsibility of the municipality. Due to lack of funds, waste remained lying about. The members of the organization pay an annual fee for waste collection and disposal, and they also clean the village once a year. They have requested more help on environmental matters from the Dutch government within the framework of the Dutch–Costarican Treaty on Sustainable Development (DOV). The community organization is set up by a number of hotels and restaurant owners who are worried about the sustainability of tourism in Tamarindo and the adjoining park Las Baulas. Some 70% of all Tamarindo tourism entrepreneurs are of foreign descent.

Small dumps can be found behind ranger stations in the national parks. In La Sirena, as well as behind other stations in the beautiful, remote, and sparsely visited Parque Nacional Corcovado, one finds piles of tourist waste: empty beer cans, cola cans, plastic wrappings, and other waste dumped in large holes that will later be covered up. There is a long way to go from the first step towards "nature conservation" and the creation of national parks to achieving the ecologically sound and sustainable exploitation of these parks. There is—as yet—no coordinated policy and approach towards conservation; the training of people and their employment in the parks leaves much to be desired. However interesting the tropical forest may be to many visitors, the park rangers have different interests in life besides receiving guests and providing information. Many of the *guardaparques* are police officers who are posted in the parks for a number of years. They count people entering the park, collect entrance fees, and keep an (armed) eye on poachers. Being a park guard is not a respected profession yet, the more so because professional training has only very recently been established.

The concept of ecotourism has gained considerable attention in Costa Rica. The first to realize the potential were foreign tour operators. They started to offer ecoholidays with accommodation in ecolodges and nature-based activities like canoeing, hiking, crossing rivers, and rafting, advertised as "adventure tourism." Prices are high, when taking into account that tourists are required to be self-sufficient; spending US$100 a day is no exception. But there are also local initiatives to organize ecotourism. A good example is the CoopeSilencio near Quepos, a farmers' cooperation where the women run a small "soda" (shop) and a chicken farm and the men till the land and grow trees. Tourism is their new activity. The farmers have built tourist accommodation (*cabinas*) and established trails. They promote their product by putting brochures in the expensive Quepos hotels (Scheepmaker, 1998, p. 27). At first sight this may be a strange strategy directed at the wrong category of people. But considering that most tourists who go to a luxurious Quepos hotel (with three-course meals, swimming pool, and a well-provided bar) will want something special to experience in such a silent and remote place, a visit to CoopeSilencio may provide them with that experience. The problem with this initiative, like with the other 15 to 20 small-scale and locally owned ecoprojects in Costa Rica, is that the people managing these projects lack training and experience with running an enterprise. In this respect, local eco-projects differ from foreign-managed initiatives. Foreigners often have the professional background and knowledge needed to cope with tourists.

Costa Rica has a tradition of foreign involvement. While Costa Rica is not welcoming just any migrant and generally gives out visas for only a short stay, those foreigners who invest more than US$50,000 may stay permanently. In this way, Costa Rica, a country with a relatively stable government and economy, has attracted a large number of foreigners, most of whom have arrived at some point in their midlife when they are looking for a break from their former life. Many of these immigrants have invested in tourism. While in the capital city San José hotels are generally Costa Rican run, outside the city many hotels and guesthouses are owned and managed by (white) foreigners. The vast majority of accommodation, however, is small scale (with less than 50 rooms) and locally owned (Rachowiecki, 1997, p. 25). Foreign hotel owners often have strong bonds with the owner's native country and do business with tour operators from this country (Groen, 1996, pp. 41– 42). The attitude of the local population towards foreigners is basically a friendly one. Not hampered by recollection of slavery, as are the inhabitants of most Caribbean islands, white people do not cause resentment in

Costa Rica. Whereas the tourists' preferences, especially regarding food, caused sheer amazement in the early days of tourism, Costa Ricans gradually added pizzas and pancakes and other Western foods to their restaurant menus, though still preferring rice and beans themselves. Nowadays, public transport reaches far-off villages, bringing in backpackers who stay in locally provided accommodation. Regular domestic services are maintained by Sansa and Travelair with very small airplanes to various airstrips, several of them close to tourist destinations, like Tamarindo, Quepos, Tortuguero, and Puerto Jiménez.

After 1993, the growth of the number of tourist arrivals slowed down and the fear of decline was spreading among the Costa Ricans (Rachowicki, 1997, p. 31; Instituto Costarricense de Turismo). This development was due to rising prices and competition from other destinations that promote ecotourism. With tourism entering the phase of stagnation or even decline, Costa Rican economy would be in serious trouble. Therefore, voices called for government intervention to enhance nature conservation and the improvement of ecotourist facilities in order to live up at Costa Rica's green image. Between 1996 and 1999 the total number of tourists entering the country rose from 781,127 to 1,031,585 (WTO, 2001, p. 168).

The Future of Ecotourism in Jamaica, Cuba, and Costa Rica: Some Concluding Remarks

In the preceding section the role of government and local people in tourism development in Jamaica, Cuba, and Costa Rica has been described. It has been shown that in Costa Rica, where government adheres more or less to a laissez-faire policy, more ecotourism projects have come into existence than in Jamaica, where government has been actively participating in the development of the sector for decades. In Cuba, where government encouragement of tourism in relatively new, it remains to be seen whether ecotourism will be developed. It is only in Costa Rica that ecotourism can be found as explicit policy objectives. This does not alter the fact that ecotourism projects are not facilitated by the government, but are largely left to market demand and entrepreneurial activity. The general lack of ecotourism planning in the Caribbean and even in Costa Rica, a country with a "green" image, raises questions regarding the future of ecotourism in the region. This question will be dealt with by way of concluding this chapter.

However marginal, ecotourism is being developed in Jamaica, Cuba, and Costa Rica. At least, if the ecotourism projects are taken at face value (i.e., if they are labeled "eco"), this qualification is accepted as such. In the three countries, government has little involvement in the development of eco-projects. In Costa Rica ecotourist projects are usually initiatives that are privately developed, privately run, and modestly successful from a commercial perspective. The latter applies in particular to foreign-owned projects. Then again, one should to keep in mind that, in "eco" terms, profit should be outweighed by the positive impact on nature and environment. Jamaica, with a far more intensive government involvement, can hardly boast of any successful ecotourism projects. A few projects seem to be in the process of being developed. And it seems that the local population is the main driving force behind these initiatives. Cuba, where government dominates tourist development and controls private entrepreneurship, has only recently turned to tourism in order to revitalize its economy. Ecotourism lags far behind. The local population has to wait to receive permission to get on with private initiatives. It remains to be seen whether ecotourist projects will be among these private initiatives in Cuba.

It has become obvious that existing eco-projects generally range among small-scale tourism developments. These projects appeal to independent travelers or small groups interested in nature-based activities. This clearly distinguishes ecotourism from packaged beach tourism, which is mass tourism. In the case of Jamaica, it is found that tourism entrepreneurs who cater to ecotourists have more difficulties complying with environmental measures imposed by the government than do resorts. The large-scale all-inclusives backed by foreign investors can more easily raise the money that is needed for appropriate environmentally friendly infrastructure and technology. At the same time, ecotourists—being independent travelers—are more difficult to control and their patterns of touring and spending are difficult to forecast. In Costa Rica there are many foreign-owned, small-scale holiday resorts that call themselves "ecolodges" or "biological reserves," which provide their guests with ecologically sound lodging, biologically grown food, traditional hammocks, fans (instead of air-conditioning), and candlelight (instead of electric light). Small-scale accommodation, however, is not always ecologically sound and can have negative impacts on the environment. Locally owned hotels and lodges often let the sewage flow directly into the sea or the ground (Rachowiecki, 1997, p. 25). Even if the garbage from these small-scale lodges is collected by a government-controlled organization, appropriate waste disposal is not guaranteed, as waste processing is virtually unknown in this country.

The World Wildlife Fund estimates in the 1990s that 15% of all tourists "go green" with backpacks and hiking boots (Pattullo, 1996, p. 118). Ecotourism projects thrive on jungle trails, wild rivers, observing wild animals, the experience of nature, and the natural qualities of the lodges concerned. However, involvement of "local people" performing "traditional" crafts and performances are also an integral part of the ecotourist experience. While the label "eco" attracts attention to the nature-based and environmentally friendly aspects of related tourist activities, the social and cultural consequences of foreigners prying into the lives of local people also require consideration.

Moreover, the question should be raised whether nature-based activities, like watching turtles laying their eggs on beaches at night, are less threatening to nature than traveling through swamps by speedboat. Ecotourist activities in no way secure the ecological future of the project area and of the people living there. Issues as to how energy is provided, how waste and sewage are being disposed of, what materials are used for buildings and means of transport, how nature is being conserved (and which parts of it), and how sustainable the project is, are generally not raised by tourists and project managers. If an ecotourism project is sustainable, what will happen if the local population increases in numbers? And, if the project is to be successful, in what terms is success to be measured?

It has become a politically correct statement to advocate small-scale, low-density tourism, also referred to as "green," "alternative," "nature based," or ecotourism, mostly located in developing countries. However, considering that between 600 and 700 million people travel for purposes of leisure each year, it may be obvious that ecotourism will never be an alternative for mass-scale package tourism. It is therefore necessary to focus on ways to adjust mass tourism to make this type of tourism more "green" or ecologically sound, instead of denouncing the principle of mass tourism altogether. There are many ways in which mass tourism can be adjusted; for instance, using locally produced nature-based building materials and paint, equipping accommodation with fans instead of air-conditioning, selling drinks from casks or bottles instead of cans and food in paper bags instead of plastic wrappings, reducing the amount of garbage by using materials that can be recycled, installing a double water pipe system to prevent the waste of drinking water for flushing toilets, to mention only a few measures.

The weakness of any form of tourism that pretends to be "eco" and requires traveling of considerable numbers of people to other places is energy waste and pollution. The type and amount of energy used and spilled by airplanes cannot be compensated by a "green" vacation. This applies to all transportation: trains, buses, cars, or taxis. The dilemma is that tourism cannot be stopped anymore; even attempts to diminish the numbers would meet with furious reactions worldwide of entrepreneurs and governments depending on tourism. The question is: What can be done to solve this dilemma? International conventions are continuously held and agreements ratified in order to protect nature, lower the emission of pollution, fix the amount of fish to harvest from the sea, conserve wetlands and areas of historical and natural interest. It is here in the international arena where the quest for ecotourism has to start.

So far, countries have been responsible themselves for the ways in which they developed and exploited tourism. As has been shown in this chapter, private interests or bureaucratic barriers often impede the efficient management of natural and tourist resources. Governments do not succeed on their own to develop ecotourism. As the world is turning into a smaller place where more and more people are living ever closer together, responsibility cannot be with individual countries and their national governments. It is vital to have international rules and laws that are enforced through control mechanisms emanating from the international community. But it is not reasonable to expect developing countries—whether they are situated in Latin America, the Caribbean islands, or Africa and Asia—to abstain from tourism altogether when it is one of their main sources of income. If small-scale ecotourism projects took the place of large-scale, all-inclusive resorts, airline companies would no longer offer cheap flights to many tourist destinations. The impacts on the economies of these destinations need no elaboration. The impact of ecotourism would be disastrous. Instead of replacing mass tourism by ecotourism, stricter international guidelines should be advocated, organizations should be established and equipped with power and funds to implement international agreements, and the enforcement of measures should be controlled. In this way tourism may contribute to more sustainable development worldwide.

Acknowledgments—For information relevant for this chapter I am indebted to A. Hoes (Dutch geographer, who worked for the UNDP during eight years in Costa Rica) and A. Sizoo (Dutch Law student who studied waste distribution and processing laws within the framework of the Treaty on Sustainable Development Netherlands–Costa Rica).

Chapter 4

How Eco Is Costa Rica's Ecotourism?

René van der Duim and Jan Philipsen

Introduction

In 1993 the Minister of Tourism of Costa Rica was awarded the "Green Devil" prize at the International Tourism Fair in Berlin (ITB) for the hypocritical ecotourism policy of the Costa Rican government. Despite his appeal for ecotourism, a luxury hotel had been built in Nicoya at the West Coast of Costa Rica, even though there had been legal infringements and a long list of ecological objections (Van Berkel, 1994). This is one of the many examples that fuel the question: How eco is ecotourism in Costa Rica? In answering this question, many issues are at stake (Buckley, 1994). For example: Who are the ecotourists that visit Costa Rica? In which way and to what extent does "nature" make Costa Rica attractive for tourists? In what ways are attempts being made to control the impacts of tourism on nature and the environment? To what extent does tourism contribute financially to nature conservation in Costa Rica? To what extent does the local population benefit from tourism and to what extent does tourism offer an acceptable alternative to employment in sectors that, from the point of view of nature conservation, are perhaps less desirable (e.g., forestry and animal husbandry)?

Although all these issues are relevant for ecotourism developments in Costa Rica and will briefly be addressed in this chapter, the focus will be on the way tourism contributes to nature conservation, in a material as well as in a symbolic sense (Van der Duim, 1993). In order to illustrate the relationship between tourism and nature conservation, examples from Monteverde, a private reserve, and Manuel Antonio, a national park, will be presented (Figure 4.1).

Ecotourism in Costa Rica

In order to get a picture of tourism in Costa Rica, it is important to present a brief overview of the way in which tourism has developed in the country. The emergence of international tourism in Costa Rica can, to an important extent, be

Figure 4.1. Map of Costa Rica. Source: Adapted from "CIA: The World Factbook 2000" (www.odci.gov/cia/publications/factbook/).

attributed to the interest displayed by biologists, geologists, soil scientists, geographers, and other scientists in the natural resources of Costa Rica. This interest has increased steadily since the 1970s and has led to initiatives in the field of nature conservation. Over the past two decades, more than a quarter of the surface area of Costa Rica has been designated as protected either as a national park or as a (private) nature reserve. In this way, a large number of tourist attractions have been created. In addition, the results of scientific research spread, for example, through stories, newspaper articles, television, and magazines such as *National Geographic*. This circulation of information has generated considerable interest among the general public. Each year, Costa Rica receives about 250 researchers who make use of the facilities provided by the Tropical Research Studies Institute (OTS). More than 2000 articles and doctoral theses and dissertations have been produced as a result. The research carried out by the Costa Rican National Institute for Biodiversity (INBIO) is also well known throughout the world. These are among the main reasons why Costa Rica has assumed a market position as one of the ecotourist destinations (Inman, 1998; Laarman & Perdue, 1989; Rovinski, 1991).

However, ecotourism in Costa Rica is at a crossroads (Lumsdon & Swift, 1998). At first, the growth of tourism in Costa Rica was explosive. The number of international arrivals tripled in the period 1985–1995 from 260,000 to 748,000. After stagnation in the period 1996–1998, more than 1 million visitors came to Costa Rica in 1999. In recent years, tourists have been coming from increasingly diverse countries. Before 1989, most tourists came from Central America, but, from 1989 onward, North America (particularly the US) and Europe have become particularly important.

The strong growth of tourism has been coupled with a shift in the nature of tourism. The first ecotourists in Costa Rica were scientific researchers and those who were not very different from the scientists themselves in terms of their interests. However, as Costa Rica became increasingly well known as a holiday destination, more and more tourists with rather a different profile began to arrive. While 60% of the tourists who came to Costa Rica stated that they wanted to visit one or more of the national parks (Boo, 1990), those among them who wanted their visit to contribute to a sustainable society were the exception rather than the rule. As Lumsdon and Swift (1998) observe: "Market expectations have shifted form a scenario where the visitor feels that he or she is making an eco-pilgrimage, to one where the destination is perceived as a center for activity and adventure in a tropical paradise" (p. 164). Research projects among visitors to the Manuel Antonio National Park and the Monteverde private reserve (Cramer & Van Lierop, 1995), for example, have identified the type of tourist who alternates a pleasant (beach) holiday in an unusual environment with visits to the national parks.

Heykers and Verkooijen (1997) and Van der Heyden and Vierboom (1997) also show that most of the tourists are in search of a combination of beach, nature, and (sports) activities. Primarily, the fact that many of the tourists to Costa Rica who were interviewed stated that they were looking for more information about nature (and culture) opens up an important avenue for achieving ecotourism goals. However, conclusions from these research projects show that the increase of charter flights from Europe also attracts another type of tourist, one that is far less concerned with the future of Costa Rica. This development seems to be diametrically opposite to Costa Rica's official tourist strategy as expressed by former Minister Castro Salazar, who envisioned: "Tourism for the few who are prepared to pay more." Apart from the fact that this strategy has been adopted by a large number of mainly developing countries, it also gives rise to practical problems and questions of principal. The issue is whether keeping ecotourism small and expensive is socially and politically compatible with the fact that an ever-increasing number of people want to experience nature in another part of the world and particularly in a region that researchers have lavished with so much praise. It is questionable how long a society will support international nature conservation if it is only the new middle class who are able to enjoy it (Urry, 1990, 1992; Van der Duim & Philipsen, 1995).

In practical terms, it is difficult to guide developments in supply and demand in the field of ecotourism. An important obstacle to developing effective guidance in ecotourism is that the market itself is developing in an unpredictable way. The growing popularity of Costa Rica among ecotourists is the result of such stable factors as the enormous biodiversity present in the country, its political stability, and the establishment of reserves and national parks. However, other more coincidental issues also play a role, such as the Nobel Prize awarded to President Arias for his prominent role in the peace process in El Salvador and Nicaragua and the sudden interest of the media in the activities of the Organization of Tropical Studies or of INBIO. The preference of ecotourists for certain destinations offering nature-based activities is only influenced by ideas of nature conservation to a very small extent. Equally important is the introduction and development of recreational facilities and services such as four-wheel-drive terrain vehicles and terrain bikes and advanced equipment for sea fishers, climbers, and deep-scuba divers. In addition, advertisers and other media focus attention on outdoor sports and this has influenced the way preferences have developed. Many ecotourists are searching for a "camel trophy type" of experience.

Nature as a Tourist Attraction: The Cases of Monteverde and Manuel Antonio

Generally speaking, Costa Rica's competitive advantage is its high biodiversity located within small distances from the beaches, which makes the attractions easily accessible to tourists. The most visited parks in Costa Rica are Vulcan Poas and Manuel Antonio (both about 200,000 visitors a year). The private reserve Monteverde is the most visited private reserve in Costa Rica (around 50,000 visitors a year) and may therefore be an excellent illustration of the history of Costa Rica as an ecotourism destination.

The genesis of Monteverde can be traced to the 1950s when Quaker settlers from North America acquired 1200 hectares for agricultural purposes and allocated 554 of these for watershed protection (Honey, 1999). In 1972, a Costa Rican NGO—the Tropical Science Center (TSC)—acquired the first 328 hectares of forest for a reserve. In 1974, TSC reached an agreement with the Quakers to manage their 554 hectares and the two properties became the original Monteverde Private Cloud Forest Reserve (MPCFR). Following several very successful fund-raising campaigns, the MPCFR now protects over 10,500 hectares of forest (Baez, 1996; Honey, 1999).

The Monteverde reserve has very good facilities compared with the public national parks (Rovinski, 1991). For US$8 foreign tourists get access to well-kept trails. Information brochures are available and for US$15–20 well-educated guides show tourists around. In the souvenir shop equipment can be rented. In Monteverde, only 2% of the reserve is open for the public. Around 90% is not even open for research purposes. The maximum number of tourist allowed to visit the reserve at one time is 120 (Honey, 1999). The idea behind the limited access is that not only the ecological value, but also the experience value, of the reserve would be in danger if a larger number of tourists used the limited facilities. There is no way to prove without causing ecological damage that these measures are effective than to support this precautionary principle.

When tourists visit Monteverde their expectations are often very high. The reserve is well known from television documentaries and magazines. In general, tourists have far too high an expectation of the experience that the reserve can offer. Often the visit is a disappointment because the golden toad that figured in the *National Geographic* documentary has now been declared extinct and a meeting with the quetzal (one of the most colorful birds in Costa Rica) is very much a matter of chance. Because the reserve is small in size and its paths have been thoroughly surfaced, human intervention and management is clearly visible (Figure 4.2). Tourists who want to experience a wilderness will probably get more out of the 35-kilometer-long route that leads to the park, which is particularly difficult to negotiate in the rainy season. This route, in fact, gives the reserve an air of remoteness and inhospitality.

Figure 4.2. In the Monteverde reserve, Costa Rica.

Whereas the Monteverde reserve has souvenir shops and well-posted walking paths, the Manuel Antonio national park has very few facilities for visitors. Two routes have been laid out for walkers and a few information boards have been provided. For guidance, however, visitors have to rely on local guides from Quepos if they want to enjoy all the riches that nature has to offer. The visitor center offers minimal facilities because of lack of money and the park rangers provide little information themselves. Despite all this, Manuel Antonio Park exerts a strong attraction. On the one hand, it has a number of very beautiful beaches and, as Luft and Wegter (1990) note, "The water is blue, clear and cool. If a top-ten was to be drawn up of the most beautiful beaches in the world then those of Manuel Antonio would certainly be among them" (p. 276). There is also a great variety of flora and fauna for visitors to enjoy in those areas of the park open to the public (10% of the total surface area). During a 1-day working visit, rare species of monkey, iguanas, a boa constrictor, and a leopard were spotted.

Outside the parks and the reserves, attractions and facilities have sprung up as a result of private initiatives that try to meet the wishes of as broad a group of tourists as possible. Land is being bought around the national parks and reserves by (mainly foreign) tourist entrepreneurs who are trying to promote and exploit ecolodges (relatively small-scale but luxurious accommodation situated either in or near the tropical forests). These are often substantial sites and many additional attractions have been installed varying from short nature trails to technical equipment that makes it possible to travel through the roof of the rain forest.

Holiday spots such as Manuel Antonio/Quepos have been compared to very popular and overcrowded tourist destinations in Europe (like a number of Mediterranean shores). Since the mid-1990s, the number of hotel rooms in the Manuel Antonio area has doubled to 1200, and the number of visitors to the national park has increased fivefold to nearly 200,000. About 50% of these hotels and boarding houses are in the hands of foreigners. This development has been described by one of the local people as a third cultural revolution: first there were the Spanish, then the owners of the large banana plantations, and today it is the turn of foreign investors, some of whom use Quepos to whitewash their black money. Referring to this phenomenon, Inman (1998) draws attention to "green-washing" whereby tourist operators, and foreign operators in particular, tend to promote their holiday packages in a green wrapping, taking advantage of Costa Rica's ecotourism image. Critics are concerned that these organizations are appropriating the returns on investments made by ecotourist pioneers.

Rapid tourism development has not been well planned. In many respects, supply lags behind demand. This is evident in the transport sector but it is also reflected in the low standard of education of personnel. The former National Parks Service (SPN), now known as SINAC (National System of Conservation Areas), for example, does not appear able to sufficiently train guides or to provide tourist facilities such as visitor centers and information panels. The influx of tourists has increased as travel agencies situated in the large-scale coastal resorts around Golfo de Papagayo (see below) offer excursions to the parks and reserves in this area. In this way close linkages have been established between sun-sea-sand tourism and the nature-based tourism that centers on parks and reserves.

Mitigating the Negative Effects of Tourism on Nature and the Environment

The rapid and poorly controlled tourism development and the absence of physical planning and legislation gave rise to serious environmental problems not only in Quepos and Manuel Antonio, but also in other places in Costa Rica (Caalders, Van der Duim, Van der Boon, & Quesada Rivel, 1999; Van Berkel, 1994; Whelan, 1991). Amidst an atmosphere of growing concern, attempts have been initiated to reduce the effects of tourism on nature and the environment. A certification program, for example, is being developed for environmentally friendly hotels. The Instituto Costarricense de Turismo or ICT (Costa Rican Tourist Board) is currently implementing a certificate for sustainable tourism. On the basis of sustainability criteria derived from the physical, social, and economic characteristics of the environment as well as the quality, service, and client friendliness, hotels can earn from one to five stars. CANAMET (The National Chamber of Tourist Micro-entrepreneurs) is also working on a trademark in which sustainability criteria play an important role. In addition, there is an increasing number of training schemes in the field of environmental education and ecotourism. Studies in environmental impact assessment are being carried out, especially in coastal areas where hotels are being built (for a critical review of these studies see Van Wijk, 2000), and management plans for national parks are being compiled. In the meantime, management plans for a number of protected areas in Costa Rica have been established.

The implementation of these plans, however, is difficult because of deficient financial resources, lack of knowledge on environmental policies, the large number of public and private organizations involved, and the unclear competencies between them and the (rapid) changes of legal provisions and policies after elections (Inman, 1998; Van Wijk, 2000).

The development and implementation of these plans has been further complicated by a lack of continuity in government services such as the ICT and SINAC, the department charged with national parks within the Ministry for National Resources. In Costa Rica, it is the practice that after the four-yearly election results have been made known, there is a change not only of elected representatives, but also of civil servants. In addition, the government is constantly being confronted with the need to economize and there are very few effective control mechanisms to ensure the implementation of laws and regulations. Finally, ICT and SINAC fall under different ministries, although there is regular contact and discussion between SINAC, ICT, and the tourist industry (CANATUR). One result of these regular consultations is that legislation to deal with tourism is being prepared including measures in the field of environmental protection. Characteristic of this tourist policy, however, is the intrinsic tension between economy and environment.

The debate that surrounds the so-called Papagayo project in Guanacaste is a good illustration of this tension. The project involves an investment of US$2300 million (mainly expatriate) and would alone double the nation's accommodation by adding 25,000 hotel rooms to the inventory (Weaver, 1998). Although the plans are about 15 years old and the building of the first hotel began in 1992, there has been a lively discussion between opponents and proponents of the project on the subject of the size and the way in which the project fit into its physical location. Under pressure from the environmental movement, many changes have been made to the original plans; hotels must not be more than three stories high, for example. However, the opening of the national airport in Liberia, the establishment of other infrastructure, and the continuous role played by powerful (foreign) investors and project developers will undoubtedly work in the advantage of the realization of this plan. As a consequence, Costa Rica will suffer from the "Banana Republic Syndrome" in which wealthy multinationals dictate tourism development (Van Wijk, 2000).

The Financial Contribution of Tourism to Nature Conservation

Ecotourism policy should not only focus on minimizing the effects of tourism on nature and the environment. Ideally, ecotourism should also contribute financially to the economic development of the country in general and the conservation of nature in particular. In Costa Rica the development of tourism is motivated by the prospects of (supposed) economic benefits. These are, in fact, very significant. Tourists spent US$940 million in 1999. Total employment in tourism is estimated at 140,000 jobs, half of which consist of indirect job opportunities (Pashby, 2000; Van Leiden, 1995). In Monteverde the explosive growth of tourism has had an important effect on employment. It has been estimated that more than 400 full-time and 140 part-time jobs in the tourism sector have been directly generated, not to mention those created indirectly. In 1993, the Monteverde Cloud Forest Reserve employed 53 people, with a total annual salary of US$400,000 (Baez, 1996). Commerce has been stimulated and women had the opportunity to set up cooperatives to produce craft products. According to Baez (1996), the tourism industry in Monteverde has resulted in the creation of some 80 different businesses, of which a significant number are locally owned.

However, there has been no policy focused on ecotourism development. Although official policy focuses on its development, in practice there is a tendency in government and business to focus on traditional forms of tourism with an eye to short-term economic returns (Rovinski, 1991). The government argues that developing ecotourism alone is not enough to generate the returns needed to work away the enormous shortfall in the balance of payments. There is thus almost no question of a transfer of economic benefits from ICT to SINAC, for example. Between 1991 and 1995, ICT allocated some 4% of its budget to environmental projects (Inman, 1998). SINAC had to secure its own income and, in fact, does this to an increasingly significant extent. In order to generate funding for nature management, the training of guides, and the provision of tourist facilities (such as visitor centers and information panels), the former SPN decided to increase the admittance fees from US$5 to US$15 for foreign tourists wishing to visit the national parks. This price increase was introduced despite strong protest from ICT and the local population and was motivated by the argument that it was reasonable that foreign tourists, in exchange for experiencing the pleasures of the Costa Rica's national parks, should contribute to their maintenance (Salazar, 1995). This increase in entry fee resulted in a decline in the number of visitors, but a substantial increase in income from about US$1 million in 1993 to about US$1.5 in 1994 and US$2.6 in 1995 (Bermudez, 1995; Inman, 1998). Under pressure from tourism organizations such as ICT and CANATUR, however, entry prices were lowered in 1996 to US$6.

The role of tourism in the private reserves is equally important for the future of nature conservation in Costa Rica. There are about 100–150 private reserves, ranging in size from 5000 to 10,000 hectares (Honey, 1999), covering an estimated 5% of the total area of Costa Rica. The owners of the private reserves finance their management to a large extent by running ecolodges. Ecolodges can generate an annual income of as much as US$300 per hectare (Bien, 1995). In contrast to this, cattle husbandry generates no more than US$10–20 per hectare per year.

In the Monteverde area, income from tourism plays a very important role as well. At least 70% of the income in the area comes from tourism, leaving agriculture far behind. Maintenance of the reserve is paid from tourism revenues for almost 100%. In 1992, tourists spent some US$37 million in the Monteverde area. Thirteen percent was spent on the development of the reserve and the remaining 87% went to the local community, that is to say, the residents of Monteverde including foreign businessmen. In 1995, tourists spent about US$50 million of which 90% went to the local community. In this way the average income from tourism in Monteverde is three times as high as from other sources, such as agriculture. Echeverría, Hanrahan, and Solórzano (1995) shows that, when the contingent valuation method is used, the per hectare economic value of the Monteverde reserve appears to be significantly higher than it would be if it had other user functions such as agriculture or cattle husbandry. Monteverde's overall contribution to the economy was calculated at approximately 18% of Costa Rica's total tourism revenues (Baez, 1996). Using the travel cost valuation technique, Tobias and Mendelsohn (cited in Inman, 1998), using a 4% real interest rate and assuming that the real value of the site remains constant over time, calculated the present value of the Monteverde Cloud Forest Biological preserve between US$2.4 and $2.9 million. In another study, Menkhaus and Lober (1996), using a sample-derived travel-cost model, calculated that the average US tourist placed a value of $1150 on a trip to Monteverde, when all expenses involved in the trip were taken into consideration. Extrapolated to all US visitors to Monteverde, this means that the Reserve accounted for $4.5 million of the total tourist expenditures in Costa Rica.

In 1988, an attempt was made to determine the total economic value of ecotourism in Costa Rica. According to Inman (1998), an ecotourist from an industrialized country pays an average of US$288 a day. This amount of money is spent on the following items:

- US$95: airline
- US$65: foreign wholesalers, tour operators and travel agencies
- US$18: Costa Rica land operator
- US$110: local Costa Rican entrepreneurs

The US$110 spent locally is distributed as follows:

- US$23: ground transport
- US$28: hotel accommodation
- US$20: catering
- US$11: entrance fees to protected areas
- US$12: guiding service
- US$16: overhead of the country operator.

The Distribution of Tourism Benefits

The question is, however, how the benefits of tourism are distributed. According to Valentine (1992), the successful development of ecotourism depends largely on whether or not the local population benefits from nature conservation and related tourism developments, not the least because this income should offer an alternative to current economic practices, such as agriculture, the timber industry, and hunting, which are very dependent on natural resources. The income and the number of jobs that tourism generates in Costa Rica have been specified above. From the figures it would appear that 56% of the money spent by the ecotourists who travel to Costa Rica is spent outside the country. Taking leakage into consideration, Inman (1998) estimates that ultimately 37% of expenditure remains in Costa Rica itself. Therefore, it is very important that tourism development is more firmly coupled to the local economy than it is at present. In the Bilateral Agreement on Sustainable Development drawn up between the Netherlands and Costa Rica, tourism is defined as a spearhead (Caalders et al., 1999; Van der Duim, 1997). From 1999, within this context projects will be carried out that combine tourism and agriculture, and fishing and ecotourism. These projects make use of local labor and local materials and encourage the development of local handicrafts and local souvenir production (Lindbergh & Hawkins, 1993).

Despite the accomplishments at, for example, Monteverde, many recent studies show that foreigners often own tourist facilities in Costa Rica. For various reasons, there is little local control on tourism developments. First, the influence of foreign capital is clearly visible in Costa Rica. Despite the fact that tourism is relatively small scale, a high proportion of the hotels and ecolodges is in the hands of foreigners. The high interest rates (more than 30%) on bank loans have created a barrier to local investment. According to Place (1991), the rapid growth in the number of visitors of the Tortuguero National Park has led to a decrease in the opportunities available to local businessmen who want to take part in tourism as employers. The speed with which foreign investors took up investment opportunities did not give villagers enough time to generate their own capital to invest in tourist facilities and services. While the Costa Rican government has been successful in protecting endangered species and locations in the parks, it has done little for local people to make the transition from an economy based on the exploitation of natural resources to a new economy based on the conservation of these resources. In this respect, as Hagenaars (1995) notes, the Costa Rican economy is equivocal. Sustainable development is promoted in national and strategic plans. In practice, as a consequence of the dominance of neoliberal policy, tourism emphasizes economic growth with the assistance of foreign capital and investment instead of developing a policy that aims at strengthening the microentrepreneurial sector.

Schemes promoting the small firms should be geared to the network of actors engaged in the production, dissemination, and consumption of tourism goods and services. As Verschoor (1997) demonstrates, the feasibility of small-scale entrepreneurial projects depends on three interrelated factors: first, the ability of a project to maintain a global network that is intended to contribute resources (i.e., tourists) to the project; second, the capacity of the project to assemble a local network of actors, with the ultimate goal of offering a tourist product; and third, the degree to which an entrepreneurial project succeeds in imposing itself as an obligatory point of passage between the global network and the local network. "This means that if successful, the project should first have the ability to shape and mobilize the local network and second, that the project is able to exercise control over all exchanges between the local and the global network" (Verschoor, 1997, p. 29). Organizations such as CANAMET could facilitate network building locally as well as globally, but above all in the transactions between the local and the global (Van der Duim, 1997). However, from the point of view of sustainable development, it is vital that different kinds of local and nonlocal actors (both formal and informal) cooperate (i.e., tourism entrepreneurs, as well as environmental or cultural organizations). The more links and exchanges (of ideas) between the different types of actors in these networks, the higher the innovative capacity of a region. Actors who can act as a "bridge" or gatekeeper, trying to link global and local networks, can play a central role in the creation of time- and place-specific innovations that are so welcome in contemporary tourist product development (Caalders, 1997; Caalders & Philipsen, 1998).

An important condition for the participation of the local population in tourism is that they have experience with and knowledge of tourism and that the local and regional government has this as well. There is a particular lack of insight into the consequences of tourism for the local population and for nature and the environment (Boo, 1990). For example, in Monteverde people have the feeling that they no longer have any control over developments. Monteverde has not escaped one of the most common problems associated with tourism development: the increase in land value and cost of living. According to Baez (1997), one square meter of land sells for US$10–20, which is comparable to the price of land on the outskirts of San José, the capital city of Costa Rica. The same holds true for the cost of living. According to Vargas Leiton (1995), Monteverde has always been a close and democratic community in which the local population was closely involved in decision making. In order to realize projects in nature conservation, health, food production, road building, and education, people often work together in cooperatives. There used to be general agreement about the speed at which change should take place in the local community. The explosive growth of tourism (between 1985 and 1995 the number of tourists increased from 6000 to 60,000 per year) gave the local population the feeling that they no longer had developments in their own hands. The growth of tourism was coupled with a local growth in population from 3000 to 6500 in the period 1985 and 1995. It appeared that more and more cooperatives were necessary to organize everyday life in Monteverde. Tensions emerged between various organizations. Towards the end of the 1980s, an umbrella organization was called into being with the objective of formulating a common vision on the future: Monteverde 2020. It was a failure. It no longer seemed possible to reach an agreement about the pace of development. Part of the community benefited if tourism continued to developed at the same rate, while other sections put up resistance because of the negative effect the tempo had on life in the area (long lines of banks, traffic congestion, rising prices, the disappearance of local solidarity). According to Chamberlain (1995), the social capacity of Monteverde has been reached with the arrival of 50,000 visitors. At the moment, an attempt is being made to stabilize the stream of tourists at that level. Maintaining the poor condition of the access road to Monteverde plays a key role here. If no management measures are taken, the number of tourists in Monteverde can be expected to rise to 200,000 a year in the near future.

Finally, the degree to which local people can identify with a national parks policy is important. If this identification is strong there will be less inclination to use natural resources for economic objectives in the short term. By suddenly raising the entrance fee to the parks in the 1990s the SPN seriously disturbed relationships with the local population. In Cahuita the local people barred personnel from SPN from the park and tourists were allowed to enter free. Elsewhere, local inhabitants were driven from their land when national parks were set up and the promised financial compensation never materialized (Blanco & Lipperts, 1995; Whelan, 1991). In fact, of the 1.3 million hectares earmarked for conservation in various categories, 44% set aside is still under private ownership, putting the government's outstanding debt at $655 million (Dulude, 2000).

Conclusion

Ecotourism in Costa Rica is at a crossroads. Costa Rica has reached what is classically described as the early mass tourism stage where the volume of tourists and the development in tourism supply can no longer be categorized as niche, eco, or nature-orientated tourism (see also Lumsdon & Swift, 1998). As a consequence, the contributions of tourism to nature conservation are contradictory. On the one hand, it cannot be denied that tourism provides a very significant financial contribution to maintaining both national parks and private nature reserves. Ecotourism has motivated the private sector to conserve or even restore natural environments. In this sense, ecotourism has, to a very important extent, contributed to halting the large-scale deforestation that has lead to the disappearance of two thirds of Costa Rica's tropical forests since the 1950s.

On the other hand, tourism development in the immediate vicinity of these nature reserves has led to negative impacts on nature and the environment and has given rise to serious concern. These impacts cannot be adequately countered because of a lack of (implementation of) effective physical planning and legislation. The Costa Rican government does not seem to have made a clear and strategic choice for ecotourism. In order to ensure economic benefits in the short term, traditional forms of (sea-sun-sand) tourism have been and will be developed. In addition, the income derived from ecotourism does not benefit local people sufficiently and the tourism sector is still to a very large extent in the hands of foreign business. Local people have not been drawn into or involved in tourism development or in decision making as far as the national parks are concerned. Because of this, the emotional and economic basis, which could support their involvement in an effort to maintain the national parks and reserves, is still lacking.

Chapter 5

Locals and Foreigners: Tourism Development, Ethnicity, and Small-Scale Entrepreneurship in Cahuita, Costa Rica

Anne Marie van Schaardenburgh

Introduction

As is shown in the previous chapter, the rapid growth of tourism in Costa Rica over the past two decades has partly been generated by the country's image as an eco-destination. Many tourists are attracted to Costa Rica for its natural beauty and unique ecosystem with a great diversity in flora and fauna. But there are other assets that make the country an interesting destination for international tourists, one of these being Costa Rican culture and, in particular, the ethnic diversity of its population. In general, the population of Costa Rica can be distinguished into five ethnic categories:

1. The Hispanics, 80% of the population, descendants from the Spanish explorers of the 16th century, constitute the majority of the population (Van Berkel, 1994). They call themselves Ticos and Ticas (from *hermaniticos*, which means little brother/sister).
2. The indigenous people, less than 1% of the population, descendants from several tribes that originally lived in Costa Rica before the arrival of the Spanish explorers, establish another ethnic group.
3. The mestizos, 14% of the Costa Ricans, are a result of mixed marriages between Hispanics and indigenous people (Van Berkel, 1994).
4. The descendants of former slaves from Afro-Jamaican origin form 5% of the total population.
5. Foreigners of two "generations" live in Costa Rica. The first generation came as hippies in the 1970s. More recently younger ("second-generation") foreigners, looking for adventure and attracted by a relaxed way of life, come to stay and start (tourism) businesses in Costa Rica.

While these five categories may enhance the attractiveness of Costa Rica for cultural tourism, their access to and actual participation in tourism development is rather unequal.

In order to explore this aspect of ethnically defined inequality in tourism participation, this chapter will focus on the ethnically diverse village of Cahuita, which is located in Talamanca, a coastal region in the province of Limón, the southeastern part of Costa Rica. The Costa Rican national government ignores the region of Talamanca in their developmental programs, which contributes to its backward position compared with other provinces in the country (Van Berkel, 1994). Talamanca is the region with the lowest population density but a high diversity in ethnic groups. There are three reserves for indigenous peoples in the Talamanca highlands. These reserves accommodate the Talamanca-Bribri, the Talamanca-Cabécar, and the Kéköldi. These indigenous tribes try to maintain their traditional lives through their customs and ancient beliefs. At the coast, the majority of the population is of Jamaican origin. The ethnic diversity in the small villages along the coast provides a major cultural attraction for tourists.

In the southeastern part of Costa Rica small-scale tourism organizations are predominant. In this respect the region contrasts with the Pacific coast, where large-scale tourist projects, especially luxurious resorts, are developed. Resort development is strongly promoted by the government, as resorts cater to the demands of the international tourists, most of whom come from North America. Not surprisingly, the flow of international tourists is concentrated on the central highland around the capital city of San José and the provinces of Puntarenas and Guanacaste at the Pacific coast in the western part of Costa Rica.

The small village of Cahuita is located on the Caribbean coast of Limón, 44 kilometers south of Puerto Limón (Figure 5.1). Adjacent to it lies the Parque Nacional de Cahuita. Because of the small-scale organization of its tourism and its ethnic diversity, this village provided the perfect location for the research on which this chapter is based. The research, which focused on the strategies of local participation in tourism, was conducted in 1995, using methods of anthropological fieldwork (cf. Van Schaardenburgh, 1996). In this chapter, local participation is defined as the ability of local people to influence the outcome of development (Whelan, 1991). The concept has a dynamic character, moving from passive participation to self-determination. Referring to tourism development, local participation implies that people benefit from and are given opportunities to participate actively not only in decision-making processes but also in the initiation and implementation of tourist projects. This includes empowering people to mobilize their own capacities, be social actors rather than passive subjects, manage the resources, make decisions, and control the activities that affect their lives (Cernea, 1991). The structures of influence and the mechanisms of control and dependence are crucial factors in the empowerment of people and will be discussed in this case study of local participation in tourism development in Cahuita.

In this chapter the question will be raised to what extent and in which ways the local community of Cahuita benefits from the opportunities offered by tourism development. In order to answer this question, the role of two actors will be highlighted in particular. The first is the role of the government as facilitator or impediment of local participation in tourism. The second is the role of small-scale

Figure 5.1. Map of Costa Rica with research location. Source: Adapted from "CIA: The World Factbook 2000" (www.odci.gov/cia/publications/factbook/).

entrepreneurs, and in particular the factors that determine their success or failure in local tourism development. Before turning to Cahuita, the relationship between government intervention and local entrepreneurship in tourism will be briefly discussed based on a literature review.

Government Intervention and Local Entrepreneurship

Whereas national governments in many developing countries promote tourism as a passport to development, the role that these governments attribute to the participation of small-scale entrepreneurs in the developments is highly limited. In developing countries, government policies towards community development in general and the local tourism sector in particular vary widely. In terms of Midgley (1986), state involvement in community development can range from an overtly antiparticipatory to a participatory mode. Where state bureaucracies expect tourism to contribute significantly to national development, tourism policy is directed towards large-scale investments in cooperation with foreign investors and project developers. Small-scale businesses surviving under these circumstances are regarded as an obstacle rather than an asset in tourism development. If this is the case, then government usually exerts an overtly antiparticipatory attitude: local participation in general and business initiatives of small-scale entrepreneurs in particular are not supported by government policies. Instead, governments often counter deregulatory measures at the top with more regulation and control below (cf. Dahles, 1998; Dahles & Bras, 1999). Critics point to large resort developments, particularly resort enclaves, as being major contributors to the negative impacts of tourism (D. Harrison, 1992; Wood, 1993). Not only are they often out of scale with the indigenous landscape and ways of life, it is argued, but they consume large quantities of capital that could be more usefully applied in other ways. The involvement of foreign investors is necessary because of large capital requirements, which are far beyond the resources of local people. The result is that tourism development is insulated and communities miss out on the opportunities brought about by tourism. Management positions often go to outsiders, as few local people have the appropriate skills. Local residents are often denied access to resources, such as beaches, that they previously used, and reap few benefits from the developments.

A participatory approach, on the other hand, is characteristic of situations where the potential of tourism is exploited for sustainable developments. In that case, tourism consists of smaller-scale, dispersed, and low-density tourism developments located in and organized by communities where it is hoped they will foster more meaningful interaction between tourists and local residents (Brohman, 1996). These forms of tourism depend on ownership patterns, which are in favor of local, often family-owned, relatively small-scale businesses rather than foreign-owned, large-scale companies and other outside capital. Small-scale developments are less disruptive, have modest capital requirements that permit local participation, are associated with higher multipliers and smaller leakage, leave control in local hands, are more likely to fit in with indigenous activities and land uses, and generate greater local benefits (Dahles & Van Meijl, 2001; Wall & Long, 1996). It is assumed that small-scale tourism development and active resident involvement are "much less likely to produce negative sociocultural effects associated with foreign ownership, are much more likely to enhance local tolerance to tourism activities, and can respond more effectively to changes in the market place and fill niches overlooked by larger, more bureaucratic organizations" (Echtner, 1995, p. 123). In addition to the concern for small-scale tourism as a strategy in sustainable developments, much of the recent literature is dealing with the question whether small-scale entrepreneurship in tourism provides feasible employment opportunities (Cukier, 1996).

In Costa Rica, the promotion of ecotourism by the government has not yet resulted in a participatory approach to local entrepreneurship. Tourism entrepreneurship at a local level is dependent on government policies and planning processes at the regional and national levels. The main national institutions that are responsible for tourism development in Costa Rica are the Servicio de Parques Nacionales (SPN; the National Park Service; recently changed into SINAC—National System of Conservation Areas), the Instituto Costarricense de Turismo (ICT; the Costarican Tourism Institute), and Coalición de Iniciativas para Desarrollo (CINDE; the Costa Rican Coalition for Development Initiatives). Both ICT and CINDE support the improvement of infrastructure in some regions of the country to enhance their potential for tourism growth. They have directed their efforts especially at the Central Valley, North Pacific coast, and the Middle Pacific coast as the country's main tourist regions. National policy makers are particularly interested in the provinces of Guanacaste and Puntarenas. Infrastructure is rapidly improved in these areas. In tourism terms, these areas are more productive because they enjoy a longer dry season and therefore a longer tourism season as well. Investors are also interested especially in these parts of Costa Rica and, as a result, large-scale resort developments are concentrated here. The Caribbean coast, however, is not a target for tourism development in the national policy. Despite its agricultural productivity and its tourism potentials, the coastal province of Limón is not regarded as an economically important area and remains an underdeveloped part of the country. In disregard of government failing to generate appropriate policy measures to support local entrepreneurship, there is small-scale tourism development, which occurs in an unplanned and uncontrolled way. Participation in the tourism sector is initiated by and benefits different categories of "local" people, as will be shown in the case study of Cahuita, one of the tourist villages at the Caribbean coast of Limón.

Tourism Attractions in Cahuita

Tourism entered the village of Cahuita in the early 1970s. For many tourists, Cahuita is an interesting destination because of a combination of attractions. The success of tourism in Cahuita basically depends on four complexes of tourist attractions: the National Park Cahuita, the beaches, local culture, and easily available drugs. These four attraction complexes will be discussed in detail below.

The main reason for tourists visiting Cahuita is the National Park, which covers 1667 hectares of land with mangroves, swamps, and rainforest and 600 hectares of sea consisting of a coral reef with 34 species of coral, over 100 species of seaweed, and 500 species of fish (Pariser, 1992, p. 309). The number of visitors to the park increased significantly during the 1980s and the first half of the 1990s (Table 5.1). Before that time, the flow was relatively stable. Traditionally, the park was visited predominantly by national tourists. Only since 1991 has the number of international tourists exceeded the number of national tourists.

The beaches of Cahuita—another important reason for tourists to visit the village—are situated within the park boundaries. This implies that to visit the white beaches of Cahuita one has to enter the park first. The National Park Cahuita is one of the four most visited parks in Costa Rica and the beaches contribute largely to its popularity among tourists. Less popular but quite unique are the "black beaches" on the other side of the village. These beaches consist of black sand of volcanic origin, which is sediment from a small river from the Talamanca mountains discharging into Kelly Creek.

Besides for the natural beauty of the National Park and the beaches, tourists visit Cahuita because of its Afro-Caribbean culture and atmosphere. This culture expresses itself through reggae music, reggae gadgets as souvenirs, and, of course, through the life style of the local people, especially those who present themselves as Rastafaris. In particular, female tourists from foreign countries feel attracted to the rastamen as they offer romance and excitement. The women offer some material rewards (food, drinks, presents, and even money) in return for sex (cf. Dahles, 1997; Pruitt & LaFont, 1995). This "romance tourism" occurs on a small scale, and those who indulge in it usually legitimize it in terms of an "open and sharing culture," a concept that is derived from the Rastafarian movement.

Table 5.1. Number of National and International Visitors of National Park Cahuita, 1982–1995

Year	National Visitors	International Visitors	Total
1982	26,779	4,369	31,168
1983	12,712	3,559	16,271
1984	18,490	5,270	23,760
1985[a]	16,585	5,628	22,213
1986	25,278	8,383	33,661
1987[a]	24,999	9,917	34,916
1988	52,239	22,773	75,012
1989	67,478	34,683	102,161
1990	45,065	31,471	76,536
1991[a]	48,444	53,154	101,598
1992[b]	—	—	—
1993	51,967	15,388	67,355
1994	22,330	18,270	40,600
1995[c]	6,008	781	6,789

Source: ICT (1995).
[a]The years 1985, 1987, and 1991 are projected for lack of data.
[b]In 1992 the park was closed due to an earthquake.
[c]Number until March.

Drugs, particularly marihuana, are seen as a part of the local culture, by both residents and tourists. Many locals use marihuana regularly (daily or weekly) and some use cocaine (less frequently, as it is more expensive). The drug culture has a strong appeal for particular tourists but is rarely an attraction by itself. The old and new hippies from North America and Europe are attracted by this use of drugs, which they see as a "relaxed way of life." Many local inhabitants are afraid the drugs will damage the image of the village and will have a negative impact on tourism. This effect already occurs when Ticos spread rumors about the region and advise tourists not to go to the province of Limón because of drug-related criminality. One incident in which a Canadian tourist was killed during a hold-up by armed men near Cahuita caused a series of protests throughout Costa Rica. Many Ticos saw their prejudices regarding the Blacks in Limón confirmed and they warned the tourists of the criminality in that province. There was even a big billboard placed at the international airport in San José warning arriving tourists not to visit Limón. The residents of Limón perceived this government measure as another expression of the ongoing discrimination and stigmatization by the Ticos and an attempt to keep the area in its backward position.

Tourism Development in Cahuita

The early tourists exploring the coast of Talamanca in the late 1960s and 1970s were hippies from the US and Europe. Some of them stayed and integrated easily in the local community. They first rented rooms on the locally owned *fincas* (farms). The local people were basically farmers who grew cash crops such as cocoa and coconuts. As more foreigners and Ticos came to enjoy the natural beauties of the Talamanca coast, local people started to build more rooms and facilities for tourism. When the agricultural production of cocoa diminished through a crop disease, tourism was embraced as a new source of income and the local community of Cahuita started to see the commercial value of tourists. Many locals sold their land to foreigners or some rich landowners (most Ticos), gave up farming, and tried to make a living from tourism. Tourism development expanded quickly in a short period of time, and the village became largely dependent on tourism.

Infrastructure played a crucial role in the development of Cahuita in general and as a tourist destination in particular. The Talamanca region was geographically and socially isolated from the rest of the country for a long time. The first road to connect the communities in the Talamanca area was constructed in 1967. When the bridge across the Estrella River at Penshurst was finished in 1976, Cahuita and the rest of Talamanca were finally accessible by road from Limón. This road reduced traveling time to and from the city of Limón considerably. Even San José, the capital city and political center, came within reach. As a result, Talamanca was integrated more and more into the national society. Cahuita became more interesting to visit for Ticos, as well as foreign tourists. The improved infrastructure accelerated the flow of tourists, but soon turned out to be inadequate because of booming visitor numbers. As government measures took too long to materialize, Cahuita people started construction works themselves to respond to the needs of tourism.

Tourism brought economic prosperity to Cahuita as many local people started businesses in the tourism sector. None of the enterprises enjoyed sound financial backing or large investments in the beginning. All economic activities in the tourism sector were small scale and expanded eventually due to the increasing numbers of (international) tourists. The most common way of participating in the tourism sector in Cahuita is by offering accommodation, particularly *cabinas* (cabins/rooms). These are often family businesses, but most of the work is done by women, who provide tourism services such as checking in, preparing food, and cleaning the rooms. The men are more concerned with the maintenance of the rooms. Sometimes, the children help their parents when they are free from school, by cleaning rooms and preparing food. Most of the owners of *cabinas* make a living exclusively from tourism. Others have kept their *fincas* and continue to produce fruits and vegetables. Still others make additional income by selling goods, such as handicrafts or ice cream. Still more *cabinas* are being built. The average number of rooms per accommodation business is two, but some local businesses comprise up to 15 rooms. Besides the *cabinas*, there are five small hotels in Cahuita with about 30 rooms. It is forbidden by law to construct buildings within 50 meters of the coastline. Moreover, the law restricts the number of floors per building to three. Hence, only small-scale and low-story accommodations can be found in Cahuita. Other small-scale enterprises are the travel agencies providing tours and renting equipment for snorkeling, surfing, etc. Also, many restaurants and bars can be found in the center of Cahuita. Most of these restaurants are locally owned and serve Caribbean dishes; others, such as pizzerias, provide tourist food. All these businesses were specifically created to satisfy tourist demand.

Entrepreneurship is one way in which local residents participate in tourism. Another way is through direct or indirect employment in the tourist industry.

Some Cahuitans work as rangers in the National Park, others are employed as receptionists in hotels or as guides on boat tours. Many Cahuitans are self-employed as street vendors selling fruit or handicrafts. Finally, some individuals participate in what has come to be known as the "sunset" industry, such as self-employed local guides, drug dealers, "gigolos," and rastamen. Although these categories are often seen as "marginals," their role in the tourism industry should not be underestimated. For many tourists, they act as "cultural brokers" as they smooth the way into the local tourist scene. Due to their direct contacts with tourists, they have great influence on the tourist perception of Afro-Caribbean local culture and their "don't worry be happy" life style constitutes a major tourist attraction.

Local participation in Cahuita's tourism development is particularly initiated by foreigners and significantly dependent on the younger generation of local and foreign origin. The older members of the Afro-Caribbean families do not agree with this rapid development. They try to maintain their traditional life style rooted in agriculture and want the community to return to its relatively isolated way of life. They especially oppose the prominent role that the foreign entrepreneurs play in the village's tourism development. Some young foreign entrepreneurs are progressive in their policy to develop tourism in Cahuita and the region. For example, they themselves want to construct a paved road from the main road to a park with *cabinas*. In their opinion, the government fails to improve the infrastructure in the area. These foreigners want tourism to grow more rapidly in Cahuita as they expect that it will bring prosperity to the whole community. For this reason, they participate in projects of the Camara de Turismo. Some old residents resist this policy and prefer tourism to develop more slowly or even to remain at the current level. They feel a loss of control over their lives and their culture.

The younger Cahuitans think differently, as they are more outside oriented. After all, the younger generation has enjoyed a better education. Nowadays, children visit schools in other communities in the province of Limón, such as Puerto Limón and Bribri. Some Cahuitans have studied and worked in San José or even abroad. This experience has an impact on how the younger generation participates in tourism. They are more aware of the requirements of hospitality and the needs of tourists. They are more assertive than the older generation and behave as innovating and risk-taking entrepreneurs. They are more active in their marketing strategies towards tourists. For example, they approach the tourists that arrive by bus in the village to bring them to their *cabinas*. They also use their contacts outside the region in order to promote their tourism enterprise. These well-educated youngsters constitute the engine of tourism development in the community. But not all young people who leave Cahuita for education or work return to their home villages. Many seek their future outside the area.

Ethnic Diversity and Tourism Participation in Cahuita

Compared with the ethnic landscape of the country as a whole, Cahuita has an exceptional position in Costa Rica. The Afro-Jamaicans, who are one of the minority groups in Costa Rica, actually form the majority in Cahuita. The Afro-Jamaicans' first language is Pidgin English, an English dialect that integrates some Spanish expressions. Their second language is English and their third language is Spanish, although nowadays the basic education is Spanish oriented. The area has a strong cultural identity because of these Black immigrants and the long isolation of Talamanca from the rest of the country. In Costa Rica, the region and the Afro-Caribbeans living there are stigmatized for their way of life and the alleged drug abuse that is strongly associated with their culture. They feel discriminated by the Ticos in particular.

Who is to be considered "local" in Cahuita? The first inhabitants of the region were the indigenous people, such as the Bribri, Kéköldi, and Cabécar. These indigenous groups lived in the Talamanca highlands, while the first immigrants from Jamaica settled on the coast in the beginning of the 20th century. Before roads connected the Talamanca region to the rest of the country, only a few Ticos settled in the region. The area could then only be reached over water. When the area became accessible by road in the 1970s, the first foreigners came into the Talamanca region. Those who stayed and started a life in Cahuita are looked upon as locals nowadays. Other foreigners followed. The "second-generation foreigners" settled in Cahuita in the 1980s and 1990s. These foreigners came to Cahuita either to live a life in retirement or to start a business in tourism. These foreigners came mainly from Canada, the US, and England. They are not perceived as locals.

Segregation along ethnic distinctions has not yet appeared in Cahuita. In everyday life, the different ethnic groups share the same facilities, participate in the same social activities, and share the same interests. But ethnicity emerges as an issue when tourism participation is at stake. The ethnic affiliation of the village residents plays an important role in the tourism sector in the first place because the Afro-Caribbeans constitute an attraction for the tourists and, in the second place, because tensions arise among the different ethnic groups when tourism development is discussed.

The indigenous people hardly participate in tourism and, if they do, it is only through occasional jobs, such as guiding tours in the high season. They still live predominantly on agriculture outside the village center. As they benefit only moderately from tourism, they are quite reluctant to get more involved in its development. Basically, they regard tourism as a threat to their traditional way of life.

The local Ticos are more involved in tourism, but seldom as entrepreneurs. They often find jobs as employees in tourism businesses. An exception to this rule is a travel agency owned by two local Ticos. They have many contacts outside the area and are very active in tourism development in Cahuita. They also collaborate with foreign tour operators in the international tourism market. These two play a central role in the community and hold important positions in the local tourism sector. This may be illustrated by the fact that, in this village that has only two telephone lines, they own the only fax machine and offer the only public phone to tourists.

The majority of actors in Cahuita's tourism industry are of Afro-Caribbean origin. About 75% of the small-scale *cabinas* are run by members of this ethnic group. They participate in the tourist sector in all kinds of ways, either being self-employed or as an employee in the accommodation or restaurant sector. They benefit from an increased tourism market and play a crucial role in creating the "tourist site" and the image of Cahuita.

A minority of local residents is involved in tourism through "romance tourism" and/or drug dealing. These activities become increasingly significant in the tourism development. While attracting female love seekers or young drug users, they can have a detrimental impact on the attractiveness of the area for other visitors. Romance and drug tourism particularly benefit those males who assume the Rastafarian identity, also known as "Rent-a-Rasta."

Local people who prosper through tourism—mainly foreigners and the younger Cahuitans—acknowledge the economic opportunities and advantages brought about by tourism development. Others—the older Cahuitans and the indigenous people—feel left out and envy the second-generation foreigners who are successful in the tourism sector. The first-generation foreigners live either a retired life and do not participate in the daily life of the community or they run a small tourism business successfully. They complain less about the current situation than the original residents of Cahuita. The group of second-generation foreigners is very successful as entrepreneurs and is therefore becoming more influential in the development of tourism. Local people prefer to be employed by these foreigners instead of working for a local business owner, because they receive better payments and agree more, in general, with the attitude of these foreigners regarding the development of tourism as an economic opportunity.

Local entrepreneurs have mixed feelings regarding the dominance of foreigners in Cahuita's tourism development. Particularly the older residents are concerned about the impact of foreigners on the attitude of the young locals. They state that the Afro-Caribbean residents lose control over the development of Cahuita when the land is sold, particularly to foreigners. All residents want to benefit from tourism, but some locals point out that they should maintain their land and some of their agricultural activities. They do not object to the development of tourism in general, but criticize foreigners occupying the better positions. The Afro-Caribbean residents increasingly look at themselves as being disorganized compared with foreigners. They feel a loss of control when they realize that they leave their agricultural way of life but cannot compete with the foreigners in the development of tourism. As the second-generation foreigners possess more financial means, more knowledge about tourism and business management, and have contacts outside the area, they benefit more from tourism.

Most of the second-generation foreigners are involved in the international tourism market. They came to Cahuita when tourism development had taken off and offered economic opportunities. This group rejects the criticism by the older generation Cahuitans and points out that the locals also benefit from the tourism sector and the activities undertaken by foreign people like themselves. Some second-generation foreigners return the criticism by pointing out that locals could benefit more if only they were "not so lazy." Moreover, the foreigners blame the Black residents for the bad image of Cahuita caused by their drug abuse and their involvement in prostitution and crime. The foreigners have a great deal of control over tourism development in the community. They are very active in organizing activities to improve the tourism sector, such as infrastructure and trash collection. Because they are more active compared with the other actors, they put pressure on tourism development and gain even more control. Some of the foreigners are disappointed in the tourism development, which does not meet their expectations. Crime—many local people claim the crime rate has increased over the years—has caused the first foreigners to sell their business and move to other areas, such as Puntarenas on the Pacific coast. The success of tourism fuels the contradictions between locals and foreigners. One of the first-generation foreigners, who lived in Cahuita for over 20 years, was well integrated, and never experienced any problems with the other villagers, was increasingly being approached as an outsider when tourism started to boom and his handicraft/souvenir shop was doing well. The same happened to another foreigner who built a successful business over a period of 15 years. When he owned only two *cabinas* nobody made any problems for him, but when he constructed two extra rooms every year and finally called himself owner of a 30-room accommodation complex, he was said to be "one of those foreigners who comes to Cahuita to take over the business."

Tourism Policy and Planning

In 1994, the community of Cahuita was among those that protested against the decision of the SPN to increase the entrance fee of all national parks (cf. Chapter 3). The community claimed that this policy would discourage tourists from visiting Cahuita, which would result in a reduction of vital income. At this point, the local population realized the extent of their economic dependency on tourism. The conflict between the community and the SPN resulted in the Cahuitan people deciding to disregard the national policy measures and to take the park management into their own hands. They started to run the park themselves, admitted visitors for free, and took care of the maintenance of the park. Eventually, a commission was established consisting of representatives of the SPN and the community to solve the conflict. However, the local representatives argued that this intervention came too late because the important decisions had already been made by the national policy makers. For example, the entrance fees were increased at a national level. This incident illustrates the community's lack of influence on national tourism policy making. Nevertheless, the local community was still in charge of the National Park Cahuita at the time this research had come to an end. At that time, they reopened the entrance post and provided information for tourists and requested visitors pay a voluntary contribution, which they used to finance the maintenance of the park.

The weak confidence of Cahuitan people in the national government is further diminished, as there is lack of financial support for the province of Limón. Some residents believe the government is leaving the region structurally underdeveloped because of racial considerations. After all, it is accommodating one of the country's ethnic minorities. At regional and local levels, several NGOs are actively attempting to improve tourism development in a sustainable way. The Asociación de Desarollo Integral de Cahuita (ASODEINCA; Association of Integrated Development in Cahuita) is a political organization that aims at the empowerment of the local inhabitants through tourism development. The Junta de Administración Portuaria y de Desarollo Económica de Vertiente Atlantica (JAPDEVA; the Board of Marine Administration and Economic Development of the Atlantic) operates at a regional level and is concerned with the economic development of the port of Limón. They had intended to send experts to Cahuita to train entrepreneurs and employees in tourism marketing. So far, these plans only exist on paper and have never been implemented. In practice, JAPDEVA is only concerned with the port of Limón, which has economic priority because of the export of fruit from the plantations. Another nonprofit organization is the Asociación Talamanquena de Eco-Turismo y Conservación (ATEC; the Talamanca Association for Ecotourism and Conservation), which promotes tourism in a sustainable way through small-scale and locally owned businesses. Practically, they are involved in solving problems of water supply and waste disposal, which are basic needs that are under pressure due to the increasing numbers of tourists. These organizations have set goals to achieve sustainable tourism development but experience great problems motivating and activating the local population. Due to the top-down decision making, the local people have no trust in the national policy makers and, therefore, react apathetically to a change of organization. Although their opportunities to participate in the process of decision making have increased at a regional level, they lost their interest after disappointments when initiatives were never implemented.

The province of Limón being left out of tourism development plans is symptomatic for the political relations in the country, which are characterized by a structural discrimination of the people of Limón. Although local people can participate in tourism, they have little influence on national policy making, including tourism development. The structure of national institutions does not facilitate small-scale tourism businesses or enhance the participation of the local community in decision-making processes. The empowerment of locals through NGOs is not very successful, as they are not capable of activating the local community, because these NGOs go without the support of more powerful organizations operating at the national level.

The national government policy towards tourism is ambivalent. On the one hand, the government strongly promotes the increase of international arrivals to Costa Rica; on the other hand, it intends to reduce the number of visitors to the national parks by raising the entrance fees. The latter is motivated by the need to control the impact of tourism on the natural resources. The government is also engaged in large-scale tourism projects in other provinces on the Pacific coast. While government agencies issue permits for the construction of large hotels in Puntarenas, they neglect the development of tourism in Limón at the same time. They also discourage tourists from visiting the province of Limón because of the alleged increase of crime in this region. The Afro-Caribbeans structurally run into problems if they require facilities for their tourism businesses. Many are refused a bank loan, the more so as they have sold their land (which could be their security) to foreigners, while these very foreigners get easy access to loans. The locals in Cahuita feel discriminated against by these measures. In their opinion, they are marginalized because they constitute a minority in the country.

Discussion

The case study of Cahuita has shown that national tourism policy in Costa Rica does not apply a participatory approach. The government does not stimulate small-scale tourism businesses, but focuses its resources and efforts on large-scale developments that promise large returns. The Costa Rican government neglects tourism on the Caribbean coast in favor of the popular resorts on the Pacific coast. Finally, it fails to increase the participation of ethnic minorities and, instead, supports campaigns that discourage tourism in areas such as Cahuita because of alleged increase of deviance.

Tourism has become the main economic activity in Cahuita, where most inhabitants participate in tourism as a small entrepreneur, employee, or self-employed person. While tourism development in Cahuita offers economic opportunities for all members of the community, it does not do so to all equally. Not everybody participating in tourism has the same opportunities and access to the necessary facilities. Tourism businesses may be generally small scale and family owned, but contrary to Brohman's (1996) optimistic diagnosis of small-scale tourism developments, it is not necessarily "local" hands in which control is invested. Instead, as tourism development in Cahuita shows, people from outside the region, foreigners and Ticos alike, generally have better access to information, because they possess more elaborate networks, and to financial facilities, because they possess more securities. Outsiders are more flexible in catering to the changing demands of tourism and, as a consequence, operate more successfully in the tourism sector. The indigenous and the local Afro-Caribbean are not trained and prepared to operate in the tourism sector. Often they feel like tourism "happened" to them and they try to do their best to benefit economically, but generally they do so not as independent entrepreneurs but as employees or self-employed persons in the "informal" tourism economy. As has been pointed out in the literature (Dahles, 1999; Echtner, 1995), employment in tourism does not generate empowerment of local people, only lasting dependency on a volatile tourism sector.

Foreign participation in tourism is not confined to large-scale resort development, as is often suggested in the literature. In Cahuita, where all tourism development is small scale, most tourism businesses are owned by "outsiders" (i.e., foreigners and Ticos). This imbalance in local power relations brings about covert frictions. Some locals complain they get the worst jobs. Although this may seem to be motivated by envy, there is some truth in these complaints, as the Afro-Caribbean minorities face more problems in participating in the tourism development than the Ticos and foreigners. Behind these complaints is the fear of foreigners and Ticos taking over the tourism sector of Cahuita. All in all, ethnicity plays a central role in tourism development in Cahuita. It influences directly or indirectly the way in which the inhabitants participate in tourism (as entrepreneur, employee, or self-employed) and relate to others in the community. Cahuitan people feel that the significance of ethnicity is reflected in national tourism policy, which seems to marginalize the province of Limón because of its large Afro-Caribbean population.

Although tourism has brought prosperity to Cahuita, it does not mean that local people have control over tourism development in their community. The local residents are not empowered, but have become more dependent on tourism. Decreasing numbers of visitors not only put the local economy under pressure, but also jeopardize the social relations between ethnic groups and generations. Therefore, small-scale tourism development without proper government support does not enhance sociocultural stability, but can be quite disruptive in terms of increased deviant behavior on the part of the underprivileged among the local population.

Success in tourism participation is volatile and dependent on factors beyond local control. In the province of Limón, basic facilities for local entrepreneurs to operate successfully are lacking, such as tourism education, access to financial means and information, access to business networks, and training in professional skills. Besides the ability to persevere, small entrepreneurs need to understand the market and new developments in that market. Those people who have not enjoyed a special training in tourism—as is the case with the older inhabitants of Cahuita of Afro-Caribbean descent—find themselves overtaken by people often younger and/ or from the outside with a higher level of education and more experience in the tourism industry. In Cahuita, successful competitors are second-generation foreigners who are generally well educated and more experienced in tourism.

For Costa Rica to use tourism as a strategy for sustainable development, the government needs to develop a participatory approach by putting more effort into small-scale entrepreneurial opportunities and access to education and financial means for people of different ethnic backgrounds and in different regions of the country. Small-scale tourism development needs to be prioritized on the national political agenda. Only if more equal opportunities for local people are realized will tourism contribute to sustainable development in Costa Rica.

Chapter 6

The Feasibility of Sustainable Tourism Development: A Case Study in El Salvador

Maryse Brouwer

Introduction

El Salvador is not a well-known tourist destination. This is partly due to the country's recent history. The war in El Salvador officially ended on January 16, 1992, with the signing of the peace treaty in Mexico. The practical effect of the 12-year hiatus between 1980 and 1992, when there was a general perception overseas that it was unsafe for tourists to travel to El Salvador, was that no coherent policies for the tourism sector—and all other economic activities for that matter—could be developed. El Salvador, therefore, has a significant amount of catching up to do in developing its tourism industry because its neighboring countries in Central America, particularly Costa Rica and Guatemala, have moved aggressively to position themselves in specific market niches. Lately, El Salvador has been putting a lot of interest in promoting international tourism, a concept that was inherited from the Strategy for Tourism Development in El Salvador, which was established in 1994. Some NGOs and small private enterprises have taken up the challenge to develop small tourism projects and to build new hotels, looking for new development alternatives and a new source of income and employment.

The CORDES foundation (Fundación Para La Cooperación Y El Desarrollo Comunal De El Salvador) was founded on June 20, 1988, during the armed conflict. Its creation was motivated by the urgent need of projects of self-development by the then many displaced people looking for resettlement, and already resettled groups. CORDES is a nonprofit humanitarian institution. Although its basic function lies in the agricultural field, it is also involved in the construction of basic infrastructure such as roads, drinking water, and housing as well as in services like health, education, and public security.

In the area of San Carlos Lempa, located in the southern part of the country (Figure 6.1), CORDES has promoted the creation of the Sistema Economico Social

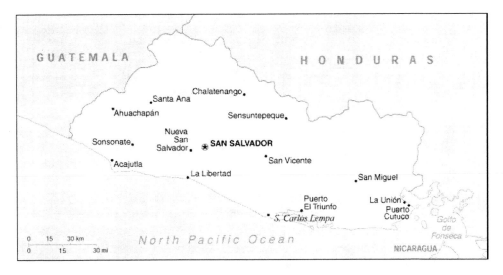

Figure 6.1. Map of El Salvador with research location. Source: Adapted from "CIA: The World Factbook 2000" (www.odci.gov/cia/publications/factbook/).

(SES), which is a form of organizing the economic and social activity in this area. The objective is to put the economic and social decision making in the hands of the people that live in the area to achieve a real and sustainable self-management. In search of new development alternatives the idea was created to develop an ecotourism project—as the NGOs would call it. CORDES and SES try to spread in this area a vision that is different from the rest of the tourist activities that are developed in the region by introducing alternative (eco)tourism activities.

Based on the above considerations, the central question to be dealt with in this chapter is: What conditions need to be satisfied to develop a tourist attraction system that contributes to the sustainable development of the area of San Carlos Lempa?

This question is composed of different elements:

- natural, cultural, and human attractions that are the basis of tourism (Hummel, 1992; Leiper, 1990);
- sustainable development: the ultimate goal of CORDES/SES;
- conditions: economic, social, cultural, ecological, and infrastructure;
- area San Carlos Lempa: a rural area in a developing country. In particular the people in the receiving areas will need to have a bigger say in the planning and decision making and a bigger share in the profit making of tourism development.

Sustainable Tourism and the Role of NGOs

Over the years, sustainable development has come up as one of the new paradigms of development. A wide range of nongovernmental and governmental organizations embrace it. Removal of poverty, ecological conservation, economic sustainability, and participation are the real fundamental objectives of the sustainable development paradigm (Hummel, 1992). The use of tourism as a development instrument for local communities is applicable everywhere but is especially important in developing countries that do not have the economic resources to meet both conservation and socioeconomic objectives (Inskeep, 1991).

The general dimensions of sustainable tourism can easily be related with the principles of a sustainable development. Sustainable development can be defined as

> a process which allows development to take place without degrading or depleting the resources which make the development possible. This is generally achieved either by managing the resources so that they are able to renew themselves at the same rate as which they are used, or switching from the use of a slowly regenerating resource to one which regenerates more rapidly. In this way, resources remain able to support future as well as current generations. (McIntyre, 1993, p. 10)

According to McIntyre (1993), "tourism can be one of the answers if it is environmentally sound and based on sustaining the natural and cultural base rather than eroding this resource capital" (p. 4). Thus, sustainable tourism means balancing ecological, economic, and sociocultural objectives within an ethical structure. A project of sustainable tourism in the area of San Carlos Lempa needs to fit into the philosophy and aims of CORDES, which also in its other projects strives for sustainable development. Under this focus, sustainable tourism can be integrated in the context of human and overall development of the region. Therefore, the central question is not whether it is possible to develop tourism in whatever way, but rather whether there are tourist attractions that comply, and continue to comply, with certain conditions, such as ecological sustainability and participation of the local population. Is such a project able to activate the social/economic life of this traditionally extremely poor area?

But a critical note is in order here. Despite the growth in tourism worldwide and the appearance of new forms of tourism such as ecotourism, green tourism, or responsible tourism, reservations about the phenomenon, impacts, and consequences of tourism have multiplied. As tourism develops as a major economic sector internationally, debates about sustainability, authenticity, social impacts, and cultural commodification take place. El Salvador is a small developing country. Is it justifiable and sensible to import the product "tourism"?

To facilitate an active participation of the local people in the host communities, an important role can be played by nongovernmental development organizations (NGDOs). They see themselves in many cases as representatives of the poorer segments of the local population. As actors in development, they will need to take up positions and become partners in the planning and implementation of tourism development (Engelenburg & Van Duijvenbode, 1995).

In the past, tourism has been looked upon by most NGDOs and foreign donor agencies alike as a sector not to get involved in as it was considered to have too many unwelcome effects in economic, social, and environmental terms. Recently, this attitude has changed and a lot of interest has been shown by NGDOs to play a more active role in the development of sustainable tourism. The reason for this is in fact twofold. First, it has been generally recognized that the trend within the tourism sector of fast expanding its economic importance is ongoing and can no longer be ignored. Second, an active stand not only enables them to counter the negative effects of tourism development, but it also provides them with the opportunities to reap the benefits, namely tapping the income-generating potential. Thus, NGDOs have the potential to play an important role in the development of sustainable tourism. A more active attitude of these organizations allows to adapt better to potentially negative aspects and to change them into a source of important revenues, also necessary to continue their own programs. NGDOs generally work at the grass-root level, intensively with and on behalf of the local communities. They strive to improve the quality of life of the poorer segments of society through a multitude of programs and activities. These include income-generating activities, business development, empowerment, social organization, education, and resource management. In fact, the challenges for sustainable tourism match nicely with the mandate, objectives, and programs of NGDOs.

The positive role that can be played by NGDOs is obvious. However, it is by no means the case that involvement of NGDOs will automatically lead to successful sustainable tourism development. A number of preconditions have to be met: institutionalized participation of local people in planning and decision making, integration of the tourism program in the overall development program, links with the government and with tour operators, cooperation with other NGDOs, and consensus about the balance between conservation and profit making.

An interesting point in this discussion is the changing attitude of Dutch development organizations and donor agencies. Recently, a careful start has been made to translate the possible contribution of tourism into policy. The first initiatives in the support of small-scale (eco)tourism development in Tanzania, Namibia, and Ecuador (SNV, Novib) have taken place. But as a consequence of these initiatives, discussions have arisen about the role and function of development organizations. Does tourism—as an economic sector—fit into the objectives of these organizations?

El Salvador

El Salvador is bordered by Guatemala to the west, Honduras to the north and east, and 320 kilometers of Pacific coastline to the south. It has the smallest and most densely populated area of the Central American countries. Volcanoes dominate the landscape, providing incredibly fertile soils. Cities have been built on the foothills of the largest volcanoes, a seemingly foolhardy place to position settlements, but these precarious locations support the most abundant agriculture.

El Salvador is not a nature-lover's paradise and is not noted for its abundant wildlife. Most of the country's natural rainforest has disappeared, and topsoil erosion and pesticide poisoning are unfortunate side effects of intensive cultivation.

Tourism currently contributes very little to the gross national product of El Salvador. The amount of international tourism receipts of US$75 million in 1997 (WTO, 1999, p. 56) is one of the lowest that is experienced by all Central American countries. Visitor arrivals to El Salvador amounted to 541,052 in 1998 (WTO, 2000, p. 209), many of these for business motives.

The growing interest for rural tourism, farm tourism, and special interest tourism as well as active or adventure vacations is a tendency that is expected to accelerate in the following decade. An innovative tourism product for El Salvador will be a mixture of the history of the country with certain forms of natural attractiveness (Vasquez, 1992).

San Carlos Lempa

History

The process of economic and social reconstruction of the San Carlos Lempa area started with the signing of the Peace Agreements between the FMLN and the Salvadorian government in 1992. The repopulation had already started in 1991, after the area had been a scene of combat and had been abandoned by the civil population for almost 12 years. The reconstruction process was initiated by a variety of NGOs. During this development process they felt the need to achieve a better coordination between the population and the supporting agencies and in this context the SES was founded.

Social Aspects

The area of San Carlos Lempa is formed by 14 communities with a total of 4000 inhabitants: persons demobilized form the guerilla and the army, former refugees returned back from Nicaragua or Honduras, internally displaced persons and former residents. The extension of the area is about 56 hectares and the population density was 74 inhabitants per square kilometer in 1998. As for the age distribution, the population is very young, with a great percentage of children under the age of 15. In the medium term, this implicates a great need of work opportunities. The implementation of nontraditional activities such as tourism may create these opportunities for the (adolescent) inhabitants and potentially assure their permanency in the area.

Economic Aspects

The most important economic activity is the production of basic grains, sesame seed, melons, and cattle raising, primarily at the family level. A major problem is the lack of work and income. Thanks to the PTT (Programa de Transferencia de Tierras, program for the transfer of the lands), major achievements have been obtained concerning access to land and the organization of the different communities to better administrate their territories. The structure of UdPs (Unidades de Producción, production units) facilitates the administration of funds and credits for the realization of projects, provided by organizations of financial or technical support such as CORDES and SES. The high level of people's organization has allowed the population to carry out diverse nontraditional activities (organic cashew farming, agriculture under irrigation) and apply for services that, until then, had been denied to them (electricity, drinking water).

The development goals of the SES are diversified. SES is looking for diversification of the local economy by exploiting the natural potential of the area to make it more competitive as well as to strengthen the organizational process of the communities. Next to the other agricultural objectives of the SES—organic farming, nontraditional cash crops under irrigation, traditional agriculture, and cattle raising—ecotourism could become an important strategy for the SES and its productive organizations.

Institutional Aspects

The presence of national and international NGDOs has been one of the biggest resources in the formulation and implementation of viable solutions to the problems with which they where confronted. The CORDES foundation has been the one that has taken the leadership in the reconstruction process of the area of San Carlos Lempa, working together with several other NGDOs. The local women's organization ASMUR focuses its attention on gender issues in the area. At the national level, CORDES has built relationships with diverse governmental and nongovernmental agencies, universities, and the parliament. At the international level there are contacts with various governmental and nongovernmental agencies.

Infrastructure

The main road of the area has been improved, but the current state of the other roads is characterized by their continuous deterioration, especially during the rainy season. The transportation system has improved. A couple of collective buses and a pick-up service cover a great part of the area, although many communities still lack any form of transportation, especially during the wet season. In several communities, electric power has been installed (since March 1996). Some families make use of solar energy for light, radio, and television. At the beginning of 1998, a drinking water system was introduced in the whole area, except for the island of Montecristo; previously, the people had to make use of drilled wells or river water.

A main problem that affects the area is the inadequate (organic and inorganic) waste treatment. Actually, two types of contamination can be identified: contamination by solid waste such as cans, papers, bottles, etc., that are not recyclable; and excretion in the open fields and contamination by organic garbage, which eventually breaks down. Health workers, trained by PROVIDA and endowed with a first-aid kit, cover most of the communities. There is a general clinic in San Carlos Lempa and a women's clinic in San Nicolas. For more specialized medical attention one has to travel to the hospital in Zacatecoluca or to San Salvador. In most of the communities, an educational infrastructure exists. The level of education, however, is still low and a high level of illiteracy is observed among the women in the area.

The soccer fields in most of the communities are the principal recreation facilities. La Sabana and Taura have built a play area for children. The cultural center in San Carlos Lempa offers some entertainment especially for the youth, and the community buildings in the other communities are sometimes used for gatherings or parties.

Ecosystem

The pressures that are exercised on the natural resources nowadays have an historical antecedent. Cotton cultivation during much of the 20th century led to an ecological disaster (caused by cutting of trees, pesticides) and also the extensive cattle exploitation resulted in big environmental impacts. Furthermore, population growth has had its influence, because it was necessary to increase the exploitation of the natural resources. Besides promoting a political consciousness, it becomes indispensable to assure the conservation of the natural resources by classifying and monitoring them to ascertain their correct use. Each community has designated an area as an ecological reserve, preventing in that way any commercial exploitation or intensive use in that section. These areas are only used to capture some mammals and reptiles. As for the forests, neither management systems nor regulations concerning their rational use or protection are set up. A latent threat is the constant and limitless cutting of trees used for cooking or making charcoal. The Río Lempa, which forms the eastern border of the area and which is the biggest and most important river of the country, is highly contaminated, which could affect the feasibility of an ecotourism project.

Tourism in San Carlos Lempa

Beaches continue to be popular tourism destinations. Most of the beaches in El Salvador present some level of ecological deterioration and a high degree of division into private landholdings. The CORDES foundation, together with the inhabitants of the area, has already started a small tourism project on the island of Montecristo and in the hamlet of La Pita. The local people show a growing interest in exploiting their rich natural resources through the introduction of a low-impact type of tourism.

The Potential Attractions

Analysis of the tourism potential is one of the main steps within the development of sustainable tourism. The potential attractions as seen by the inhabitants and CORDES are mainly based on the natural resources of the area, such as the sea, the beaches, and the mangrove forests. But in comparison with other tourism destinations, these attractions are not unique. The biggest attraction might be the fact that the region is still not developed for tourism, which gives it a rustic and quiet element.

From a more cultural point of view, a strong characteristic is the history of the area and its development process of the last years as represented in various (agricultural) projects. The recent history of the area is exhibited in a small war museum in one of the communities. It can better be characterized as an exposition of arms than as a real museum, but it certainly contains some elements to develop it into a real attraction.

Attractions can literally be created or invented, in the sense of integrating an existing aspect with tourism in such a way that this aspect gets a different meaning. "It is necessary to create attractions, apart from the natural ones that we possess now" says an employee of CORDES. A first possibility is to develop "special interest tourism," based on the recent history of the area. Another possibility will be the elaboration of the educational aspect. Starting from a clear development perspective, there are two ways to carry this out. First, the tourist can be made aware of the historical and current situation and can be offered the possibility to help personally in improving this situation: "project tourism"—in the construction of facilities, working in a social project, or the protection of turtles, etc. Education by the people themselves is a key aspect of this idea. The second way is to initiate an environmental education program with the objective of true improvement in local circumstances: "self-development" of the area. CORDES has a strong background to elaborate this educational aspect.

Infrastructural Needs

Apart from the primary attractions a tourist also expects certain facilities and complementary amenities, such as transport, lodging, services. The infrastructural necessities are divided into three groups:

- Basic infrastructure such as drinking water, electricity, sanitary services, waste treatment, telecommunications, stores and trade, health services.
- A system of terrestrial and aquatic transport.
- Tourism infrastructure: lodging, restaurants, information centers.

The area of San Carlos Lempa is lacking many of these facilities and services, especially in the transport and tourist infrastructure. For the improvement of basic infrastructure they have to cooperate closely with government authorities, which will be a slow process because of the extent of bureaucracy. Besides the tourism infrastructure in La Pita and the island of Montecristo, there is a lack of lodging facilities, eating facilities, and other services in the form of excursions, souvenirs, etc.

Target Groups

For the San Carlos Lempa area, the most feasible target group is a more "primitive" type of tourist, whose demands for infrastructure are considerably smaller than those of the conventional beach tourist. This group is willing to accept more easily the local conditions (regarding food and lodging, for example), because it considers this a part of the attractiveness of the trip. A new tendency in tourism is the experience of normal daily activities. MacCannell (1976) points out that a piece of work or an item is defined as authentic after the first copy is produced. CORDES can find a market niche in providing excursions and visits to the cashew plantation and the cashew processing plant, organic farming projects, housing projects, etc. The market of workers from NGOs and other national and international organizations forms a new and specific target group. Because CORDES has a wide net of contacts and alliances, it can use that network to offer a package for trips or meetings of these organizations.

Aspects of Sustainability and the Role of CORDES/SES

Ecological Approach

Tourism in the area not only arose as an economic alternative, but also as an alternative to create a rational balance between nature and the communities of the area. This could be attained not only by means of providing direct revenues, but also by a growing environmental conscience and recognition of the importance to conserve the natural resources. Therefore, the expected positive effects are articulated more strongly than the possible negative impacts. Such impacts are not expected because a selective and regulated tourism is envisioned, with responsible people who do not damage the places that they visit. But one cannot trust the behavior of the tourists; the natural ecosystems will require being regulated, monitored, and subjected to conservation actions. When tourism is developed without any form of control the danger is high that the infrastructure will be subjected to high external pressures that can cause environmental costs. Also, to transform a culture toward more environmental conscience is a long-term and slow process. CORDES attributes a big role of tourism in the promotion of an environmental conscience. But if the natural attractions are not very strong, how will the relation be established? The fact that in the other projects more and more attention is paid to environmental issues means that there is space to apply this knowledge in a new field like tourism. Moreover, tourism can even provide a new point of view by introducing novel concepts and showing relations between conservation (of turtles) and income (visits to turtle farm).

Social and Cultural Approach

On the part of the population the current attitude toward tourism can be marked as rational, sometimes indifferent. It is observed that although certain interest exists, the opportunities for exploitation and the possible contributions of tourism are not yet very clear. This is understandable, however, because these are completely innovative ideas for a semirural community.

In terms of hospitality, the matter is more complicated: people are willing to adapt to the interests of the tourists, although in general there does not exist a lot of knowledge about tourists or their behavior. There are groups that favor tourism development, providing it represents tangible benefits. The CORDES foundation recognizes that the development of tourism implies a process of transition and that it is necessary to promote another way of thinking by showing the benefits of tourism.

Within the SES, management directs the administrative assistance for the projects. The planning phase is delegated to a group of technicians, who elaborate a work plan that details the resources that are required, the costs and expected income, programming of the machinery and the transport, etc. This work plan is passed to the hands of management of the SES, which, after its study and approval, proceeds to the search for financing. The CORDES foundation accepts the role of receiver of the funds, being responsible for its administration and evaluation. At this time, there is no structure for tourism and this complicates the process of formulating and developing tourism projects in the area.

The CORDES foundation and the SES are specialized in the agricultural field, not in tourism. They are looking for assistance from outside, and also in the organizations themselves, in the incorporation of new ideas and visions, which is a slow process. Tourism is a very specialized sector that requires specific knowledge and for which space and mechanisms have to be found to participate effectively in a global market. It has been observed that some communities in different countries are successful in the use of tourism in preserving and diffusing their cultural traditions and using their natural resources in a sustainable way. Sustainable tourism represents, in this sense, an opportunity for the incorporation of community institutions by establishing innovative ways for development.

The development of tourism in the area as seen from a sociocultural perspective seems feasible because of the open attitude towards tourists (micro-level). The rational attitude can be changed into an active contribution when the possibilities to execute a project become more concrete. At this time it is difficult to offer perspectives for the communities or the groups who are interested, because of the lack of knowledge in the organization as well as the lack of project proposals and funding. However, these are necessary conditions if communities are to maintain a certain degree of interest. The administrative and organizational part continues being a point of discussion. Who will be responsible? How can the participation from those who are really interested be guaranteed?

Tourism is a more abstract sector than agriculture, where the results can be easily related with the inputs. At this time no tourism tradition exists in the area, nor are the perspectives on a national level very promising. Tourism is a very marginal sector for the country and there is little support from the government. The cooperation between NGDOs and government institutions is complicated by the fact that El Salvador is a very politicized society.

Economic Aspects

The first stage of the ecotourism project in the area can be seen as an experiment, a pilot plan. The project has been developed in an ad hoc form, with little long-term planning. This is partly due to the lack of structural funds. The financial resources are limited: the SES depends on external funding for the execution of its projects. The contributions of the SES and the UdPs consist of the land they own, existing constructions, and human resources (manpower). International cooperation is more and more scarce and demanding; that is to say, the donating organizations are worried about efficiency and effectiveness. Economic viability is an important indicator, and project proposals will be tested thoroughly on this aspect. In the same sense, the government has also put its attention to the NGDOs to exercise control on the destination of the resources coming from the external cooperation without considering the purely political aspect of this instrument.

From the economic point of view, it does not seem very feasible to develop a tourist project in the area. First, there are no approved funds; there is no money for investments in basic facilities. It is necessary to develop proposals and specific budgets with states of expenses and projected earnings. The question arises whether NGDOs will be the appropriate parties to contribute to the development of tourism. Working on the basis of projects and outside funding, there is little room for ongoing investment.

When implementing a tourist project one needs to place attention on the potential profitability. Real prices should be calculated, based on the costs and expenses for the several elements of transport, lodging, activities, etc. It is not a tradition to calculate manpower in the prices of food or services (e.g., the work of women), but they have to give a price to their work. Unavoidably, there is a flow of money away from the area, because of the purchase of goods and services from outside (leakages), which should be reduced to the minimum. One can affirm that for the desired type of tourism (small scale, not very demanding, ecotourism) and for the materials to be used (traditional, local), the investments will be relatively smaller than in the rest of the market. Nevertheless, longer terms for profitability and the return on capital have to be applied. The hope of NGDOs that involvement in the tourism industry can mean an interesting new source of income, highly needed to continue their programs because they are confronted with a drying up of financial support for development programs from industrialized countries, could be a faint one. It is justified to expect direct (revenues and employment) and indirect benefits (diversification in economic activities, improved infrastructure), but not from the very first moment. Finally, a multiplier effect is assumed for the rest of the area in the sale of products, sale of crafts and souvenirs, and benefit of services.

The Future

Tourist scenarios can now be defined, which consist of different products, elaborated together with all the involved parties. Five scenarios are formulated for the area.

Scenario 0: *Somos Campesinos* (We Are Farmers)

(Eco)Tourism development seems difficult. The attractions are not unique and perhaps it is too early to introduce this new sector. Maybe it will be better to consolidate the projects that are already in operation. Also, if the idea is abandoned, one does not have to worry about the impacts and problems associated with tourism development.
Scenario: Leave the new development axis aside and place attention on organic farming and the fair trade market.

Scenario 1: *Estar en Contacto con la Naturaleza* (Being in Touch With Nature)

This scenario is based on the nature of the area and of the island of Montecristo. In a later stage, the rest of the area can be integrated under this scenario.
The elements are:

- Attractions: mangroves, beaches and sea, the Río Lempa, turtles, crocodiles, iguanas, fish.
- Activities: rest and recreation, journeys by boat, walks, eating, swimming.
- Conservation of nature, increase of the biodiversity, environmental education, reforestation, promotion of rational use of the natural resources.
- Fair perspectives for funding.

Tourist type: all target groups.
Arguments against:

- Mangroves are a vulnerable ecosystem and not very accessible.
- Little diversity of flora and fauna, which limits repetition of visits.
- Contamination of the Río Lempa.

Scenario:

- Expansion of lodging facilities and restaurants. Development of (aquatic) activities, purchase of boats and kayaks.
- Determination of limits of tourism development.
- Think about garbage treatment, sewage system, etc. Establish rules for accessing and using the natural areas.

- Pay attention to participation of the actors involved.

Scenario 2: *El raíz muy Fuerte* (Strong Roots)

This scenario is based on the history of the area and of the larger region.
Arguments in favor:

- Attractions: ruins in the municipality of Tecoluca, war museum, the recent history, FMLN influence.
- Activities: visits to the museum or ruins, chats with local organizations, accompanied by local guides.
- Part of a larger whole: integration with Tecoluca, packages.
- Possibilities for the restoration of cultural-historical patrimony.
- Retaining the sociocultural history, and remembrance of the conflict.

Tourist type: national visitors, special interest tourism, schools.
Arguments against:

- For museum project, specific knowledge is required, implying dependence on the municipality of Tecoluca.
- Little spreading into the area; contacts of short duration between tourists and the population.
- High investments: profitability low, few direct effects.

Scenario:

- Restoration of the war museum; investigation and reconstruction of the ruins.
- Creation of lodging facilities and of an information center in San Carlos Lempa.
- Put attention on contamination or destruction of the ruins; include the communities in the development.

Scenario 3: *Educación Integral!* (Integrated Education)

This scenario seeks to carry out an integral educational focus towards the tourists as well towards the local population. It is based on the whole area, but first to be elaborated at the island of Montecristo and in La Pita. The scenario embraces three aspects:

1. nature/ecology,
2. politics and development,
3. economy/production.

Arguments in favor:

- Attractions:
  —River, flora and fauna, forest areas, mangroves, turtles.
  —Museum, San Carlos Lempa, the communities.
  —Organic agriculture, traditional fishing.
- Activities: walks with guide, chats, visits to projects (cashew cultivation, cashew plant, farm school), volunteer work, organization of conferences and courses.

- Ecotourism in a perspective of integral development. Integration with the working method of the SES, possible to enlarge interest in the area.
- It is related to the two development possibilities mentioned earlier; CORDES possesses a strong position to elaborate the political and educational aspects.
  —Protection of nature, scientific investigation, volunteer work.
  —The maintenance of the memory of the armed conflict.
  —The exploitation of local production for tourism purposes.
- In the future the foundation of a Spanish language school and (eco)tourism school can be integrated with these ideas.

Tourist types: small groups, special interest, schools, NGDOs.
Arguments against:

- Very long-term vision required and very complicated concept.
- It requires a lot of organization with the other NGDOs.
- Dispersed initiatives in the area, difficult to integrate them, decentralization.
- Small market, look for promotion channels.
- Less interest on the part of the population.

Scenario:

- Construction of an information center, basic (tourism) services, lodging, transport to and in the area, formulation of packages.
- The encouragement of the different groups to cooperate, integrate the daily life; training local guides because explanation by local people forms an important element.
- Pay attention to: idealism is not enough, it also has to offer revenues. Danger of only consultation and information instead of real participation by the population.

Scenario 4: *Vamos a la Playa* (Let's go to the Beach)

This scenario is based on the sea, the river, and the island.
Arguments in favor:

- Attractions: beach, sea, river, forests, mangroves, flora, and fauna.
- Activities: horseback riding, boat trips, bicycle rides, camping, fishing, swimming.
- Possibilities for small entrepreneurship, employment.

Tourist types: consumers, sportsmen, national visitors.
Arguments against:

- Dispersed, difficult coordination.
- Relationship with the sustainability aspects (mainly ecological) more difficult to elaborate; contamination.
- Danger of the emergence of conventional tourism that does not match the objectives of ecotourism development.
- High investments.

Scenario:

- Construction of facilities, paths, signs, tourist infrastructure, purchase of kayaks, horses, bicycles, etc.
- Determination of the prices for the activities.
- Pay attention to regulations and control.

Maybe in the end, CORDES/SES and the area will need all these types of tourism to assure a mix of experiences for the visitors. At this moment, however, at the starting point of tourism development, it seems more useful to define a phased scenario to pursue diversity in the attractions in the long term:

- Stage I: Definition of the role of ecotourism within the development strategy of the area and the integral development plan.
- Stage II: Concrete elaboration of the basic product, construction of the basic tourism infrastructure (with the help of the brigades or voluntary work).
- Stage III: Organization of pilot tours for small groups (a maximum of 15 people) of interested tourists and the NGDO market.
- Stage IV: Expansion of the tourism infrastructure, expansion of the tourism activities, and the integration with economic activities. Definition of the limits of tourism development in the area.
- Stage V: Elaboration of the project to the "consumerist" tourist, work on profitability.

Conclusion

Tourism is a growing economic sector worldwide and new forms of tourism are growing rapidly. Can developing countries benefit from this tendency and in what way can they guarantee that tourism is developed in a cautious way? CORDES is a NGDO in a developing country searching for new economic alternatives in the process of sustainable development of the area of San Carlos Lempa. The question is if its experience, its specific position close to the local people, and its method of participation can contribute to the development of a more sustainable form of tourism.

The population of the area is directly involved in many of the decisions to be made. They are beneficiaries of the program for the transfer of the land and therefore the owners of the land. The organizational level is in an advanced stage. Therefore, the contact with the communities through their leaders and representatives facilitates a better interaction and an opportunity for empowerment of the poorer segments of the society. In this sense the answer may be yes.

On the other hand, the development of tourism requires another way of thinking and specific knowledge of the tourism market. CORDES has to develop these skills—together with interested community members—when promoting tourism as a new economic alternative and opportunity for environmental conservation. In an advanced stage it will be necessary to establish a structure separate from CORDES/SES because of the specific knowledge required. Tour operators already possess these skills and in this sense they might be the right agencies to initiate these types of projects. In the current trend of a greater awareness of the possible negative effects of mass tourism, tourists are also moving to a more sustainable form of tourism because of marketing and promotion issues.

To reinforce the attractiveness of the area, the integration of diverse educational–scientific activities has to be sought. To make this work it is necessary to give priority to the education of people and their organizations so that they can play the role of true actors. CORDES, with its experience in providing educational programs, can incorporate these aspects, thereby supporting the introduction of tourism and related concepts. But, at the same time, one should consider whether this is idealism and at what length it will be feasible.

Another point of concern is the precondition of establishing contacts and relationships with the government and tour operators. El Salvador is a very politicized country and, therefore, it is difficult to meet this requirement. The government has a very limited proactive attitude towards small-scale tourism development, and possibilities for subsidies and credits are almost zero. Finding funding is also a difficult challenge, because the theme of tourism and development is still a young one. Most donor agencies are skeptical towards the commercial sector tourism being a new alternative in the sustainable overall development of an area. It will take a lot of effort from the NGDO to convince them of the possibilities.

Although the interest is growing to spread (theoretical) information and knowledge gained in the last couple of years, concrete initiatives are very dispersed and there is little exchange of information, mainly due to the level of development, which is mostly at the community level. More research into concrete tourism development projects is needed to answer the question whether sustainability of tourism development is more likely to be articulated in projects led by NGDOs than by private enterprises. The conclusion of this case study is that at some point NGDO involvement seems desirable in that it can build a bridge between the supply (the region) and the demand (tourists). Also, the NGDO can more easily open ways for participation, and can relate tourism development to overall community development.

Finally, what will be the future of the sustainable tourism project? When the expansion of tourism reaches its critical limits, external tour operators often exert pressure to extend these limits. The NGDOs and the local population constitute forces counteracting these pressures. The question, however, remains whether CORDES and SES can and will observe the formulated limitations and principles. After all, they are also actors involved in the broader development process.

Chapter 7

Fighting Over Tourists: A Case Study of Competing Entrepreneurs in a Small Town in Belize

Suzette Volker and Jorinde Sorée

Introduction

The odd man out. A small country with a remarkable colonial past, enclosed by the superpowers of Central America. A country where tourism is responsible for most of the nation's income. A country of entrepreneurs who use their personal backgrounds and knowledge to survive in a small economy. This is Belize in a nutshell.

In 1984, the government of Belize established the first policy plans for developing the tourism industry. According to these plans, the entire Belizean population had to be able to participate in and enjoy the economic benefits of the tourism sector. Active implementation of these objectives, however, failed to occur. When in the 1990s new forms of tourism emerged, Belize was among the Central American destinations for cultural and nature-based tourism. In 1997, against the background of sustainable tourism development, the Belizean government finally took measures to actually intervene in the activities of entrepreneurs at a local level. By then, Belizeans as well as foreigners had invested money, knowledge, and experience in tourism without any governmental assistance, interference, or control. As a consequence, local tourism businesses in Belize show a remarkable diversity. As has been discussed for the case of Costa Rica in one of the previous chapters, ethnic relations in general and (Western) foreigners in particular play a crucial role in the local tourism sector of Belize, as well. The penetration of the local tourism sector by government intervention, though intended to enhance local participation in tourism, was not received well by all entrepreneurs. After all, government measures disturbed the established relationships characterized by rivalry and solidarity, and benefited some while impeding others.

In order to understand the changing relationship between the actors in a local tourism sector on the one hand, and between this local sector and government interventions on the other hand, this chapter will focus on the everyday dealings of small-scale tourism entrepreneurs in a local Belizean community. San Ignacio, a small town located in the Cayo district, has been one of Belize's most important commercial centers since the end of the 18th century (Figure 7.1). This region has been renowned for its mahogany lumber and chicle industry, which attracted many entrepreneurs of different social and cultural backgrounds. Conveniently situated along the trade route to neighboring Guatemala in the Belizean inland, San Ignacio is long familiar with (commercial) travelers in need of a meal and a place to sleep. When, in the 1980s, tourists from the US and Europe started to pass by, local entrepreneurs welcomed them as a new source of income. This applied in particular to those entrepreneurs who originated from Western countries and settled in San Ignacio in the early 1970s. It is this kind of expatriate entrepreneur who developed the local tourism sector, followed by Belizeans who were attracted to this promising new business. By the early 1990s, tourism in San Ignacio had become one of the most important sources of income for the local population. In this situation, the implementation of new government policies in favor of sustainable tourism had far-reaching consequences for the relationships within the heterogeneous business community of San Ignacio.

This chapter is based on anthropological fieldwork conducted in San Ignacio in 1997 (cf. Soree & Volker, 1998). It presents a case study focusing on the process of change that occurred in the local tourism sector against the background of intensified government intervention. The central question that will be raised focuses on the ways in which power relations between small, interdependent entrepre-

Figure 7.1. Map of Belize. Source: Adapted from "CIA: The World Factbook 2000" (www.odci.gov/cia/publications/factbook).

neurs changed due to the implementation of sustainable tourism by the Belizean government. In order to address this question, this chapter starts with a theoretical discussion of cooperation and networking in small-scale businesses. The chapter proceeds with an analysis of Belizean tourism policy since the 1970s. Against this background, the case study of San Ignacio is presented, focusing in particular on the shifting relationship between two interdependent actors in the local tourism sector: a foreigner and a local-born entrepreneur. New business opportunities created by government intervention brought about shifts in local power relations, which triggered a conflict between the two. In the conclusion, this local conflict is interpreted against the background of the theoretical literature on small-scale entrepreneurship.

Social Networks and Small-Scale Entrepreneurship

Studies of small-scale entrepreneurship define social networks to be central to their functioning. According to Bourdieu (1977), the accumulation of capital constitutes the main structuring principle of society. In addition to economic capital, actors in the social arena strategically use social, cultural, and symbolic capital to position themselves. The concept of social capital (mobilized through networks of social relations) seems to be particularly useful when analyzing economic and political relations among entrepreneurs on the one hand and between (small-scale) entrepreneurs and the state on the other hand. The presence of large numbers of small-scale businesses leads to the formation of dense social networks. Such relations reduce the dependence of small firms on larger ones and increase their possibilities for independent access to markets and supplies of raw materials. Moreover, large groups of small entrepreneurs have a voice in local politics. However, as small entrepreneurs do not constitute a homogeneous group with similar economic positions, social backgrounds, and political orientation, the accumulation of social capital implies social struggle. As a heterogeneous category, they continuously compete for enhancing their access to different forms of capital.

The creation of complex networking relations among entrepreneurs appears to be the central strategy in the development and operation of small enterprises. Networks are used not only to develop business contacts but also to raise social standing and enhance political influence, which in turn contribute to economic success. Networks are a crucial resource for small-scale entrepreneurs not only for successful business dealings and the enhancement of prestige, but also as insurance against an uncertain future. As has been elaborated by Dahles (1999), based on Boissevain (1974), a distinction has to be made between two types of resources that are available through network relations and used strategically in the competition between entrepreneurs: first-order and second-order resources. The first-order resources include land, equipment, jobs, funds, and specialized knowledge, which entrepreneurs control directly. The second-order resources consist of strategic contacts with other people who control first-order resources directly or who have access to people who do. Entrepreneurs who primarily control first-order resources are denoted as *patrons*; those who control predominantly second-order resources are known as *brokers*. Patrons manipulate the private ownership of means of production for economic profit. Brokers act as intermediaries, they put people in touch with each other directly or indirectly for profit, they bridge gaps in communication between people. Entrepreneurs can become brokers if they occupy a central position, which offers them strategic advantages in information management. The capital of brokers consists of personal networks of relations with people, communication channels, and role relations, which are governed by notions of reciprocity and transaction.

As has been observed, small entrepreneurs are reluctant to organize themselves in formal associations. Independent patrons seem to fear the loss of their autonomy if they get involved in any organization, including private local initiatives. Among small owners of accommodations, restaurants, and travel agencies informal self-help organizations do emerge, but generally they do not represent a vigorous force. Instead, elaborate networks of cooperation are strategically used for solving problems and reducing risks (Dahles & Bras, 1999). Risk is the probability for small businessmen to achieve a sustainable level of income (i.e., emerging as successful entrepreneurs, making profits on a permanent basis, and eventually formalizing their enterprise). If this works out well, sustainability comes within reach not only for entrepreneurs but also for their communities. Hence, the claim is made by many scholars that local ownership of tourism enterprises would result in benefits for the local community as a whole.

Although economic considerations are the basis for much of the cooperative efforts of small entrepreneurs, personal networks, family obligations, and friendship are necessary for mutual support. This is where local brokers are integrated into the local tourism industry. At first sight, these locals who get involved in tourism by means of second-order resources seem to have a weak position. As one of their main resources, the tourist, is accessible only for a limited span of time, many brokers are pressed to benefit as much and as quickly as possible from the tourists. In the local tourism sector, the role of brokers can become rather prominent. Local patrons suffer from the same fluctuating customer–provider relationships as brokers do, as tourism flows are irregular and unpredictable. While most patrons have only limited opportunities to control these flows, brokers often have direct access to and knowledge of this resource (Dahles, 1998). Moreover, they are familiar with the local market and the opportunities to match demand with supply in a way that enables them to make a profit. That is why local businesses often rely on brokers to provide them with tourists. Small entrepreneurs—patrons and brokers—form an integral part of the tourism sector in developed as well as developing countries. Their role is acknowledged by more and more governments in search for new forms of tourism with unexpected consequences for power balances between local actors, as will be illustrated below by the case of a small town in Belize.

Tourism and Government Policy in Belize

Like its neighboring countries, Belize has a colonial past, first under Spanish and then under British rule. The Spanish, who initially were not interested in the inaccessible coral reef coastline and swampy inland of what is presently known as Belize, did assume authority over the region in 1521. The native Maya population, who suffered from slave raids, diseases, and warfare, was severely decimated under Spanish rule (Roessingh, 1998).The Spanish conquerors left the area for what it was after British pirates and adventure seekers, who during the 17th century sought refuge in the area, defeated the Spanish in the battle of St. George's Caye in 1798. Eventually, the area developed into a self-governed colony, which prospered through its logwood and mahogany trade. In 1862, the colony officially became part of the British Empire under the name of British Honduras. In 1981, Belize became independent (Key, 1993; Moberg, 1993; Roessingh, 1998).

Upon independence, Belize's economy entered a recession, which was fueled by the worldwide oil crisis. The Belizean government had to resolve deficits in their balance of payments. Under World Bank and IMF pressure, plans for the economic recovery were established that were strongly in favor of the diversification of Belize's economy and recommended the development of the tourism sector as a potential sector for economic growth. With a financial injection from the World Bank and the American development organization USAID, Belize's infrastructure (such as roads and the national airport) was modernized and prepared for tourism (Wilkinson, 1992). These preparations paid off as tourism development had a promising start with a tripling of revenues between 1984 and 1989 and a doubling between 1989 and 1997 (see Table 7.1).

In the new plans that were developed for the period between 1994 and 1998, the Ministry of Tourism and the Environment distinguished a number of Key Result Areas (KRAs), which were supposed to organize tourism and attribute an overall professional appearance to this sector (Soree & Volker, 1998). Emphasis was placed on the development of planning and management, the formulation of appropriate policies, the tightening of relationships with the private sector, the realization of a convincing public education plan, the establishment of strong international ties, and the development of capacities in efficient project management to be evaluated on a yearly basis. A crucial role was defined for the Belize Tourism Industry Association (BTIA), which was founded in 1985 by private sector tourism entrepreneurs, but recognized as a lawful and official organization only in 1989. From

Table 7.1. Tourist Arrivals in Belize in the 1990s

Year	Number of Tourist Arrivals
1988	134,318[a]
1989	156,120[a]
1990	189,775[a]
1991	77,542[b]
1992	99,308[b]
1993	103,609[b]
1994	120,069[b]
1995	133,097[b]
1996	—
1997	146,000[c]

[a]Source: Statistical Office (1995).
[b]Source: Belize Tourism Board (1995).
[c]Source: WTO (1999).

that moment on, the BTIA started to lobby and negotiate with the national government in the interest of its members and the tourism sector as a whole.

One of the tasks of the BTIA is to establish and maintain standards for tourism professionals, among whom are the tour guides. With increasing numbers of tourists visiting Belize in the 1990s, tour guiding became a popular sector for unskilled and unemployed Belizeans to seek an income from tourism. Although many of these people had expertise on Belize's natural environment, the uncontrolled proliferation of guiding as an area of informal employment threatened efforts of professionalization of the tourism sector. In 1997 tour guides were forced by law to obtain a guiding license. These licenses are issued only if an applicant successfully attends a training course for Belizean tour guides and can produce a letter of recommendation from the tour guide association (which is part of the BTIA). Guiding courses have to be attended also by those guides who need to extend their licenses. Only those guides who have been working as a professional guide for at least 10 years are exempt from this obligation. In addition, a special tourist police has been established, which enforces the law on tour guiding and controls tour guides' licenses.

According to its Mission Statement of 1997, the BTIA aims at the development of "sustainable eco-cultural" tourism. This terminology is used without further explanation. The combination of sustainable tourism, ecotourism, and cultural tourism in one conceptual reference is striking. The lack of elaboration raises the question what kind of tourism the BTIA intends to establish under this label. As for the eco part, the BTIA maintains firm ties with environmental organizations and nongovernmental organizations (NGOs), such as the World Wildlife Fund. The BTIA is also actively involved in the Belize Center for Environmental Studies and the Belize Audubon Society, responsible for the initiation of many wildlife reserves. De Belize Eco-Tourism Association was set up in 1993 as part of the BTA. Against this background, the focus on ecotourism is clear. The concern for culture-based tourism, however, lacks a clear basis. One may guess that "culture," like "eco," is a strategically chosen concept in order to distinguish Belize from other Central American countries advertising themselves as ecotourist destinations.

The government of Belize expects that responsibility for new investments in the tourism industry will be taken by the private sector. Nevertheless, the government is prepared to contribute its share by assisting in the process through the creation of a suitable investment climate including special incentives for certain types of investment in tourism development in order to encourage maximum participation by Belizeans in the industry (Soree & Volker, 1998). The fact that the government is only modestly involved in the tourism sector makes Belize attractive for entrepreneurs who intend to start a business in tourism. Not surprisingly, initiatives in the Belizean tourism sector come from private entrepreneurs.

Pioneers in the San Ignacio Tourism Sector

In the Cayo district where San Ignacio is situated, the population is as heterogeneous as in the rest of Belize (Shoman, 1994, p. 257). The majority of the population in Cayo consists of Spanish-speaking mestizos, the descendants of the Maya or Hispanic-Amerindian immigrants from Yucatan. Their number is still increasing with refugees from El Salvador and Guatemala. The second largest group is the English-speaking Creoles who are the descendants of African slaves (imported to work in the colonial mahogany industry) and the first European settlers. Smaller groups of migrants are the Arabs, Turks, Lebanese, and Syrians who came to Belize and Cayo in the late 19th century and figured prominently as middlemen in the chicle trade. A few Chinese came to Belize in the 19th century as contract workers, later joined by others who opened Chinese restaurants or became involved in the lottery business. Old-German-speaking Mennonite farmers came from Mexico and Canada in the 1950s. They turned out to be fabulous carpenters and farmers. Nowadays they are the main producers of poultry and dairy products in Belize. Rich Hong Kong and Taiwanese entrepreneurs entered the country in the 1980s. Most of them use their Belizean residence as a springboard to the US. People from Western Europe and North America came to Belize in search of adventure or a new life. They were "either wanted or unwanted," as a Belizean informant described their motivation jokingly. One of these Westerners is John (a pseudonym), who was among the first to start a tourism business in San Ignacio and who offered his services to international tourists in particular. In the following section his career will be described in detail. Special emphasis will be placed on the networking strategies he developed to establish himself as a local entrepreneur.

John, the Englishman

Born in 1947 in England, John grew up as an orphan and subscribed in the British army at the age of 19. For 18 years he served in the British army, part of this time stationed in Belize. Upon leaving the service, he married Rhonda, a local woman from San Ignacio, where the couple took up residence. During the first months of their marriage, John earned some money by selling snacks and sweets.

> I sold empanades in the streets. My wife cooked them at home. Because we lived nearby a school, we also sold candy. I bought a big bag and sold them by piece for 5 cents. That's the way I went into business. Not many people know this.

By the end of 1984, Rhonda was offered to take over Ella's, a local restaurant in the center of the town, frequented primarily by local and English military men, and infamous for brawls and fighting. John and Rhonda entered into a very favorable lease contract for a period of 20 years, setting their first serious steps into business life. These first years, the couple made friends in the local business community. The Lebanese greengrocer Habib was one of them. He supplied the restaurant with vegetables, often on credit. John still buys his greengroceries from Habib, even though other local suppliers are less expensive. Once the reputation of Ella's changed, John made a deal with the local police who have their daily lunch in Ella's at a special rate. John and Rhonda worked long days, but with the support of Rhonda's family they managed.

In the mid-1980s the first Western tourists found their way to San Ignacio. Often they were just passing through on their way to Guatemala or Mexico. More and more, these tourists stopped at Ella's for refreshments and a meal after a tiring journey. While they were enjoying their meal they asked questions about hotel prices and tourist activities, questions that John would answer patiently. Out of this grew a kind of tourist information office. John, being an Englishman and, to a certain degree, sharing the cultural background of his Western customers, adds to the attraction of Ella's. The Western travelers feel that John understands their needs and will give them appropriate and trustworthy information. With tourism being developed in the area and tourist arrivals increasing, the need for a tourism information and communication center is becoming more prominent. John succeeds in turning this need into an opportunity for his business. His intention to diversify his business meets with the cooperation of local hotels, a number of tour guides, and the Cayo branch of the BTIA. His restaurant is widely recommended to tourists in the Cayo district. In exchange, John offers other local tourism entrepreneurs the opportunity to promote their business for free by placing flyers and advertisements in Ella's. In this way, John ensures himself of a continuous flow of customers and establishes the reputation of being as a reliable tourist information center. Eventually Ella's expanded, while other local people benefited from this development. Local artists were allowed to exhibit their works in front of Ella's. Some family members of Rhonda started a gift shop in one corner of the restaurant. Another corner of Ella's is set apart as a cybercafé, where tourists can send and receive e-mail messages. A befriended computer expert helps John run this section. Encouraged by John, Rhonda's four brothers also attempt to make a living from entertaining tourists. Rhonda's father owns an old self-made canoe and the brothers had it prepared to take tourists on trips on the Macal River. This idea was soon copied by other local young men.

Together with his wife, John built up a successful business. Upon leaving the army, he had his savings and his pension to purchase the restaurant, which he never would have been offered if it was not for his wife. His marriage to Rhonda opened many opportunities to expand his social capital locally with Rhonda's network of relatives and friends. Rhonda was experienced in the hotel and catering sector, which smoothed her way into running a restaurant. Rhonda's brothers were familiar with San Ignacio's natural surroundings and were eager to become tour guides. Apart from John's strategic use of the social and cultural capital of Rhonda's family, his own Western background benefited him as well. As a Westerner, John could imagine what Western tourists wanted when they came to Cayo. He was able to judge what kind of accommodation, food, and entertainment these tourists expected to find. Although John does not have any specific knowledge of the tourism industry himself, he knows how to use the knowledge and expertise of others to benefit his enterprise. John has built a network in which many other local entrepreneurs participate. Business relations assume the characteristics of friendship and comradeship in order to strengthen ties of mutual dependence. There is one exception to this rule: Michael, a local tourism entrepreneur with whom John maintains a long-standing conflict.

Michael, the Man From the Jungle

This 37-year-old Belizean is from a poor Creole family. He grew up in the jungle with his nine brothers and sisters. From the age of six, he often stayed with relatives in San Ignacio, where he attended school. After having completed secondary school, he went to a teacher's training college and became a primary school teacher. After 7 years of teaching, he gave up his job and started working for San Ignacio's Star Campsite.

When I quit teaching, I knew this was my plan in life—to deal with tourists. At the time, it wasn't an easy trade to get into. You could work for a foreigner who had already set up a business in the tourism industry—that was your only opportunity. For me, it was easier. I was involved in the Star Campsite. I lived there for a while, and the Turkish owner noticed that I was knowledgeable. I know everything about my country, and I am a teacher.

Apart from organizing guided river tours for the tourists staying at the Star Campsite, Michael developed his former home in the jungle as a campsite for tourists. He hired a couple from Texas to run the place, while he himself stayed at the Star Campsite. Apart from these activities, Michael organized guided river tours. He advertised these tours primarily at Hakim's hotel and restaurant, across the street from Ella's.

Hakim gave me the opportunity. When I started as a tour guide, it was not possible for me to advertise in Ella's. If I had, I would be competing with the family. Ella's has more or less a monopoly position. The family controls the river, Mountain Pine Ridge and Caracol. It's a family business. That's why it was easier for me to advertise at Hakim's.

Michael relates that he and John did not get along so well from the beginning. John discredits Michael in front of other local business people and tourists. He never fails to elaborate on Michael's violent behavior, his criminal record, his drug abuse and harassment of female tourists. Michael, on the other hand, calls John a thief. He is convinced that John sent people to the Star Campsite to steal tourist property.

John only did that because he did not want me to go into the tourism industry. He knew that I could pose a serious threat to him and his business because of my background and my education. From the very beginning, there have been conflicts, in the sense that John ordered thieves from Santa Elena [a small village near San Ignacio] to go to the Star Campsite to steal from the tourists. Because I lived near the campsite, I was the first suspect. It took me two months to catch the thief. The thief told me who had sent him and why. The reason was to give me a bad reputation, so that people would no longer want to go to the Star Campsite for reasons of safety. The thief told me who had sent and paid him. They never caught John, and he kept making things difficult for me. One day he was not in Ella's, but his wife was, and some British soldiers. That evening the incident came up, and then Rhonda did not want to serve us beers anymore. We exchanged some words, and when we decided to leave, the soldiers started to fight with Jimmy and myself. I just wasn't satisfied, and I knew that the police have been bribed by John. So we demolished Ella's. After we had done that, everybody applauded. I went to the river and came back with loads of stones, . . . and started to throw them at everybody, including the soldiers. From that moment, John and Rhonda realized that maybe it is alright to mess with people, but not with people who fight back.

Since this incident, John and Michael have not been on speaking terms. In the meantime, Michael's business prospered. In 1992, Michael and a Belizean archeologist discovered a cave in Barton Creek that had been used for offerings by the Mayas. With government permission, Michael included a visit to the cave in his river and jungle tours. By the end of 1994, Glenda, a Belizean hotel and restaurant owner, offered Michael the opportunity to advertise "Michael's Adventure Tours" in her restaurant. Michael's "Adventure Tours" soon became a success. He employed Jimmy, a former pupil, as his assistant and offered other tour guides the opportunity to take over tours from him, provided they hired his boats.

Due to his childhood in the jungle, Michael knows a lot about nature, and, as he was a teacher for years, he has the skills and the experience to transfer this knowledge to others. In his career in the tourism sector, Michael found support from other local entrepreneurs. With the help of the Turkish owner of the Star Campsite, Michael was able to enter the tourism business and to buy his first canoes. Both Hakim and Glenda, and later Leon, the chairman of the Cayo Tourguide Association, offered Michael the opportunity to promote his business through their enterprises. In return, Michael recommends their business to the tourists who stay on his campsites.

The Bone of Contention

In the spring of 1997, the government took steps to implement one of the most important parts of its policy plan: the professionalization of the tourism sector. This affected primarily the tour guides. In San Ignacio's tourism sector, most of the tour guides were unlicensed freelancers. Licenses were issued only to those who were recommended either by the Cayo Tourguide Association or a "respectable" person in the tourism sector. However, the new and stricter government policy obliged guides to become a member of an official tour guide association and to enroll in special training courses. These courses are accessible only for members of such organizations. Apart from the tour guides, most tourism enterprises, such as resorts, hotels, and restaurants, were also affected by the new regulations, as they used to hire unlicensed tour guides to show around and entertain their guests. Under the new government regulations, these enterprises could be fined for doing so. They had to check whether the guides they hired had a license.

Michael and John differ strongly in their opinion and attitude towards this professionalization policy. Michael intends to adhere strictly to the new regulations and is prepared to report negligent colleagues to the tourism police. Tour guides who work for him have to have a license. John, on the other hand, feels that the tour guides who have been working for him for years are professionals due to their long experience on the job. Therefore, John advises them against submitting themselves to the new rules and does business as usual. In his present position as one of the leading entrepreneurs in the local tourism sector, he protects them against government intervention and in the process boycotts the new policy.

Michael's law-abiding attitude has to be understood against the background of his position in the Cayo Tourguide Association, which organizes 120 tour guides in the Cayo district. In 1994, with his business prospering, Michael tried to become a member of the Cayo Tourguide Association. However, because of his criminal record, he was refused membership. Two years later, he was admitted upon recommendation of one of his friends in the Belizean Tourism Association. Shortly after his becoming a member, he was even elected secretary to the board of this association. Michael took his new position seriously. He checked whether members paid their contribution, attended the monthly meetings, and enrolled in the required courses. Apart from the tasks deriving from his function, Michael tried to teach other tour guides the code of conduct and responsibilities.

> Sometimes tourists want to mess with you. Sometimes you meet a nice female tourist. . . . People come here for different reasons. I want the tour guides to be able to deal with that. We want to set limits for them. What would you think if you saw me walking with different female tourists all the time? As a tour guide, you have to have some sort of discipline. If a tourist has a bad experience, the whole world knows.

His position as a board member of the Cayo Tourguide Association bestows power upon Michael. He can exert influence on the recommendation that tour guides need to obtain a license. He is well informed about the whereabouts of the guides in the district. He knows who has and who does not have the required licenses, and who needs to obtain an extension and has to enroll in the course. He is aware of the fact that a number of tour guides working for John are up for renewal, and that they, if they do not abide by the rules, will break the law. His position provides him with the power to undermine the activities of his rival John. After all, the newly created tourism police cooperate closely with the board of the Cayo Tourguide Association, and thus with Michael.

However, Michael must be careful not to make enemies among the tour guides when applying the letter of the law too strictly. The tour guides in San Ignacio vary in their attitude towards the professionalization policy from passive to active resistance. Those who overtly object to the new rules feel that the Cayo Tourguide Association is not critical of the government. Instead of standing up for its members, the association acts as executor of government orders. Some think that the regulations apply only to those guides who cannot bribe the authorities. As one of the tour guides says:

> I am sure that people who earn a lot of money, and thus can pay a lot of money, can just buy a license. The freelance tour guides here do not earn so much money and therefore do not have that opportunity.

Another factor that arouses criticism, directed at both the government and the Cayo Tourguide Association, is that Westerners, resident in Belize, are granted easy access to the tourism sector. Belizeans feel that these Westerners are already ahead of Belizean entrepreneurs because they have been exposed to Western culture and therefore possess intimate knowledge of tourist demand. Upon entering the training courses, these Westerners in fact enjoy additional opportunities to improve their knowledge. As a consequence, they will easily promote to leading positions. As one of the tour guides remarks:

> A Belizean saying goes as follows: "The big fish eats the small fish." When we get to the point that we become poorer, it is the white man who will die first. I will personally see to it that my son doesn't die from hunger because they [the white foreigners] take the bread from my mouth. We were born here, and they came later.

Shifting Power Relations in San Ignacio

The implementation of the policy of professionalization heralded a new era for the development of the tourism sector. With increasing government intervention, the context in which tourism entrepreneurs in San Ignacio operated underwent changes that impacted on local relations of power and dependency. New government regulations introduced the difference between the formal and the informal tourism sector, which labeled the unlicensed and unregistered activities as illegal. As a consequence, the strategies employed by various entrepreneurs either gained or lost strength effect.

There was an asymmetric relationship between the tour guides and other entrepreneurs in the tourism industry that dates back to the early years of tourism development. Tour guides always depended on hotel owners, restaurant owners, and travel agents for their work. They required the recommendation of a "respectable" person in the tourism sector to become officially registered. With the new government policy, this dependency diminished, as tour guides had to meet the demands of the Cayo Tourguide Association, an organization that took over the role of the "respectable" person in terms of recommendation and licensing. By organizing themselves in a local tour guide association, tour guides created another instrument to protect themselves against exploitation by other actors in the tourism sector. They gained respectability by means of formalization.

In the past, John succeeded very well in accumulating power. He derived his central role in the tourism sector, on which his status and power in San Ignacio were based, from his networking skills in the "informal" circuit—"informal" as there was no formalization then. He has been able to create and maintain this position mainly because of the support of his wife's family network. He preferably employed in-laws in his diverse ventures, and when he did business with non-kin, he demanded direct reciprocity. His business innovations (introducing information technology) gave him a clear advantage above other tourism businesses in San Ignacio. However, the implementation of the professionalization policy undermined John's position. His resistance to the new regulations regarding tour guides led to a breach with formal tourism organizations (such as the BTIA and BTB), with which he once maintained good relationships. More and more he is thrown back on his private network, which is now defined as informal. This clearly entails an infringement on his power position.

His competitor and personal enemy Michael, on the other hand, succeeded in riding the waves of the professionalization process of the tourism sector. Not only did he abide by the rules, he himself came to enforce these rules when he accepted the board membership of the local tourism association. Michael learned to operate successfully in the formal circuit. As a consequence, power relations in the local tourism sector were changing to his advantage. Due to government-initiated regulations, the functionaries of the institutions that enforce these regulations are bestowed with the power to control access to the tourism sector. They can make or break people. In the case of Michael, his official position enables him to exert control on John's network, while, at the same time, he can further his own commercial interests. Compared with the early years of John's and Michael's participation in the local tourism sector, a complete turn-about of their position has taken place as a consequence of government intervention. John, the respectable business man, has lost his monopoly in the San Ignacio tourism business community, while Michael, the unlicensed tour guide with a criminal record, has become a representative of state authority and a major actor in the tourism sector.

Conclusion

The case study of the tourism sector of San Ignacio provides an example of how government intervention can impact on local power relations among local entrepreneurs. In San Ignacio, the tourism sector was built by innovative and competitive entrepreneurs who initiated small-scale hotels, restaurants, souvenir shops, and tour guide services. This process started at a time when the Belizean government refrained from interventions in the tourism sector and entrepreneurs operated uninhibited by regulations. Entrepreneurial success was dependent on personal networks and reciprocal relationships. There was no clear difference between formal and informal activities.

In terms of Boissevain's distinction between patrons and brokers, the Belizean case shows that ownership of first- and second-order resources cannot be separated. A business, to be successful, requires both, as is illustrated in the case study of John, owner of a centrally situated restaurant (first-order resource) and main actor in an elaborate personal network (second-order resource). With state control lacking, John acted as patron as well as broker. The combination of both resources is a powerful one, as it enables the owner to exert power over those lacking either one of them. John certainly used his network to develop not only his business contacts but also to raise his social standing and to secure future success. Power is not derived from either being a patron or a broker, but from accumulating a wide variety of capital, such as economic (money, a business), social (network), cultural (knowledge), and symbolic (social standing, good reputation) capital.

Private entrepreneurs are reluctant to organize themselves in associations, as these may impose rules that may impede their strategic dealings. The significance of organizations as sources of power becomes clear once the government tightens its grip on the local tourism sector. In the case study, Michael who at first, as a tour guide, lacked first-order resources, managed to acquire a thriving business and respectable position in the local community by strategically using an organization as an instrument to obtain power. John's reluctance and Michael's eagerness to use this resource may be related to the difference between an established patron who feels threatened and hindered by these organizations and a broker who realizes the potential of organization as a source of power. Local tour guides followed in his step once they understood that shifting power relations in the local arena diminished their dependence on individual entrepreneurs. As a consequence, a tour guide association is more effective to deal with impersonal forces like government agencies, which replaced personal ties.

The claim that local ownership of tourism enterprises may result in benefits for the local community as a whole requires some adjustment. The Belizean case study illustrates that small entrepreneurs establish a vigorous force in local tourism development, which benefits the local economy and creates employment for local people. However, for tourism to contribute to sustainable developments in a local community, private local entrepreneurship requires the support as well as regulation by the government. It is the responsibility of the government to facilitate local entrepreneurship, which requires the education of and control of local people working in this sector. In the Belizean case, the government measures introduced in 1997 have undoubtedly left their mark on a local community like San Ignacio. However, it remains unclear to what extent these measures will contribute to *eco-cultural* tourism.

Chapter 8

Indigenous People and Local Participation in Tourism: Two Case Studies From Ecuador

Carin de Bont and Wendy Janssen

Introduction

The tourism sector is still growing worldwide and so is the impact of tourism on host communities, especially in developing countries. Researchers such as V. L. Smith and Eadington (1992), Pearce and Butler (1993), and many others foresee severe problems unless tourism is planned and organized in different ways. Most theories take the tourists' needs and expectations as a starting point when looking for ways to minimize sociocultural and economic threats generated or accelerated by tourism. Usually they emphasize the necessity for developing a sustainable form of tourism. However, as can also be argued, tourism development should fit in a broader context of sustainable development, contributing to the improvement of the sociocultural and economic situation of the community as a whole. This implies that tourism should not be isolated from other sectors. As Inskeep (1991) argues, tourism can be viewed as a socioeconomic activity or sector with social, cultural, environmental, and economic dimensions. Local participation, instead of the tourist, deserves to be the focus of attention, as it constitutes one of the main preconditions for sustainable tourism development. The local people are very well capable of initiating and monitoring tourism development that meets their needs and wishes. If the local community is not involved in tourism, tourism projects will have little chance of continuation once outside initiators and investors back off. Forms of so-called "alternative" tourism (e.g., indigenous tourism) acknowledge the importance of local participation. However, whether this form of tourism is really sustainable (i.e., fitting the concept of sustainability and the sustainable context of the local community) depends on how tourism is planned, implemented, developed, and controlled (Hunter & Green, 1995).

Ecuador has been chosen as a case study because, unlike in many other developing countries, tourism in Ecuador is usually initiated at a local level, although few initiatives are actually taken. The Ecuadorian government gives little or no support to local tourism initiatives. On the other hand, the government does not thwart plans for establishing tourism projects. There are no properly defined policy guidelines for state intervention in tourism projects, although the government does have priority lists concerning tourism destinations. Once the state recognizes a place as a tourism resort (such as the Galapagos Islands), it usually will promote this place. When a place is not considered to be economically profitable and important as a tourism destination, it is ignored by the government, as will be shown for the case of Misahuallí, a village in the Amazon rainforest. However, when tourism is developing well and the local population benefits, the government does not actively promote, stimulate, or support the place either. Nevertheless, some places do extremely well in terms of tourism development, as will be illustrated by the case of Otavalo, a market town north of the capital city of Quito (Figure 8.1). In this chapter, both places, Misahuallí and Otavalo, will be compared in terms of a central hypothesis that is derived from the work of Midgley (1986) and Paul (1987). This hypothesis proposes that if the local population takes initiatives for tourism development and the state supports these initiatives, the best opportunities for sustainable development are provided. The two case studies will examine to which extent this hypothesis applies to the indigenous people of both places: the Otavaleños and the Amazon Indians of Misahuallí. The question that will be raised is: In what ways do local indigenous peoples partici-

Figure 8.1. Map of Ecuador with research locations. Source: Adapted from "CIA: The World Factbook 2000" (www.odci.gov/cia/publications/factbook/).

pate in the tourism sector of Otavalo and Misahuallí and to what extent does this participation contribute to the improvement of the sociocultural and the economic situation of the local indigenous population?

Sustainable Tourism

The impact of tourism is predominantly measured in terms of economic growth. However, tourism development generates impacts that reach beyond the economic sector and into the social, cultural, environmental, and even political areas. The sector still grows, and this trend is expected to continue into the future. This means that tourism impacts will continue to expand. Although these impacts can be positive as well as negative for a tourist area and its population, the question remains to what extent tourism can grow without damaging the cultural and natural environment of the host population. Most developing countries have little or no experience with tourism. Those countries that venture into this area have great expectations in terms of economic profit, but lack the tools to ensure that tourism development benefits or at least is in harmony with the sociocultural, ecological, and heritage values, goals, and aspirations of the host communities. The relationship between tourism and development through local participation has emerged as a reaction to mass tourism. "Local participation" became a concept of increasing importance when it was defined as an indispensable ingredient of sustainable development, introduced by the Brundtland Report in 1987. The idea is that tourism with an emphasis on local participation can contribute to sustainable development, in particular to the improvement of the sociocultural and economical situation of local peoples.

According to Pearce (1992), the local population should become involved in all aspects of tourism planning, implementation, and monitoring in order to enhance their own well-being (economical and sociocultural) and establish a more satisfying experience for both the visitor and the visited. Assistance from the "outside" (the state government, international organizations and investors) should be welcomed to complement local financial, political, and institutional inputs and thus promote new developments such as "alternative" tourism (V. L. Smith, 1989). Many researchers claim that forms of alternative tourism are small scale, frequently developed by local people, and comply with characteristics of sustainable tourism, such as conservation of natural resources, respect for limit of growth, and respect for local cultures and local community involvement. But the scale of tourism alone does not determine the extent of sustainability. Therefore, it is premature to automatically equate alternative tourism with sustainable tourism. But alternative tourism might be viewed as an opportunity to develop sustainable tourism, for it shows the importance and necessity of local participation within tourism. A precondition is that local people must be willing and able to participate in tourism. One form of alternative tourism in which social contact with the local people is prerogative is indigenous tourism. Indigenous tourism is based on the territory and cultural identity of an ethnic group and is controlled by this group from within. The indigenous people are directly involved in tourism, either through local control and/or by having their culture serve as the essence of the attraction. A balance has to be found to what extent tourism should be admitted to prevent tourism from becoming a threat to the well-being of the indigenous people and their social and natural environments.

The Setting: The National and Local Level

Ecuador

The República del Ecuador, the smallest of the Andean countries with a total area of 283,560 square kilometers including the Galapagos Islands, is situated in South America. The capital of Ecuador, Quito, is located at 13 kilometers below the equator (after which the country is named), at a height of 2850 meters. It is the second highest capital in the world (second to La Paz, Bolivia). Ecuador has a population of approximately 12 million people and the official language is Spanish. The indigenous people also speak their own languages, mainly Quichua. Besides oil, Ecuador's major export products include bananas, shrimp, coffee, and cacao. Tourism is becoming more and more important for the Ecuadorian economy, holding a fourth position of importance in the economy. Since 1990, the number of visitors to Ecuador has increased considerably from 362,072 foreign visitors in 1990 to 439,523 in 1995, a 21.39% growth. The two most important institutions concerned with tourism in Ecuador are the Ministry of Tourism and the Cooperación Ecuatoriana de Turismo (CETUR). The country is an attractive destination for tourists to visit because of its large variety of landscapes (coastal region, Andean highlands, and Amazon region), cultures (the Otavaleños, Shuar, Huaorani, and Quichua-Indians of the Amazon region are just a few of the many different indigenous groups living in Ecuador), and unique flora and fauna (Figures 8.2 and 8.3). The most popular tourist attractions are the Galapagos Islands (where Darwin formulated his evolution theory), which are situated about 600 miles from the continent. Among other tourist attractions, two places on the mainland will be of pivotal interest in this chapter: Otavalo, famous for its Indian market, and Misahuallí, starting point for treks into the Amazon jungle.

Otavalo

Otavalo is situated in the province of Imbabura, at 95 kilometers north of Quito. It has about 60,000 inhabitants living in the town itself and in 75 small surrounding communities (Meisch, 1995). The largest part of the local population is of indigenous origin, the so-called Otavaleños. Most tourists visit Otavalo because of its famous Indian market, where on Saturdays the Otavaleños sell their handicrafts, particularly woven tapestries and ponchos. The Otavaleños are well known for their weaving art, traditional costume, and hairdo. Their long experience and success as traders and market vendors has enabled many Otavaleños to travel to Europe and North America, where they play their folk music in the streets and sell their handicrafts. Due to the flourishing tourism industry in Otavalo, a number of locals have built up a substantial capital and are, according to local standards, millionaires.

Textile production in Otavalo has gone through ups and downs. After World War II the indigenous weaving industry suffered a depression when the Ecuadorian textile industry mechanized. The Otavaleños could not compete with the cheap

Figure 8.2. Three Indian women in the Andes mountains, Ecuador.

Figure 8.3. An Indian woman crossing a river by canoe in the Amazon rain forest, Ecuador.

mass production of cloths and fabrics. However, tourism changed this situation to the advantage of traditional hand-woven products. In the early 1960s, only a few tourists visited the Otavalo market on Saturdays when the textile sale was still held in the open air at Plaza Centenario. In 1973, the Dutch government sponsored a development project to pave the Plaza Centenario, which today is known as the Plaza de los Ponchos (Meisch, 1995). Tourism activities are concentrated in this square. The Otavalo market is one of the most famous Indian markets in South America and also one of Ecuador's most popular destinations for travelers. The market itself is very old and dates back to pre-Inca times, although much has changed over the years. The number of tourists is subject to seasonal fluctuations, but in general it is increasing. In 1987, the Saturday market received about 600 tourists per week in high season. In 1994, this number had risen to as many as 2000 Western visitors in high season, besides equally large numbers of Colombians and Ecuadorians from outside Otavalo (Meisch, 1995). The increase of tourism generated a growth in the export of textile products as well. Today, many Otavaleños merchants produce textiles to export to countries abroad or by order of foreign exporters, for they have a great talent to satisfy market demands and they have understood the lucrative business that export production entails. Nowadays, the Otavaleños are one of the richest indigenous groups of the Americas. They have the ability to use their knowledge of commerce in a way that stabilizes and even improves their position. They know how to influence and manipulate the tourist market because of their awareness of being indispensable in the tourism sector of Otavalo. The fact that they have managed to maintain their culture and identity is also used a means to attract tourists and functions as a marketing instrument at the same time. The Indians of Otavalo who sell their handicrafts at the market actually constitute the cultural attraction of this town. Whereas not only the Indians benefit from tourism, as it offers jobs to other people living in the area, the indigenous inhabitants of Otavalo are practically in control of the tourism sector. Their participation is a precondition for the existence of both tourism and employment in Otavalo. Hence, tourism offers economic, social, and cultural stability and development to the local population, provided that the indigenous part of this local population participates in the market and in the production of handicraft. Therefore, local indigenous participation plays an indispensable role within the tourism sector of Otavalo.

Misahuallí

Misahuallí is a small village situated in the Ecuadorian Amazon with only 1000 inhabitants, among which is a group of Quichua Indians. In contrast to the Otavaleños, the people of Misahuallí do not distinguish themselves by a special costume or hairdo and the village does not have any remarkable buildings or monuments. Tourists visit Misahuallí almost exclusively to go on a jungle tour to enjoy the flora and fauna of the Amazon rainforest. About 50% of all Ecuadorian jungle tours start from this place. Most inhabitants are involved in tourism, although only few of the Indians (about 10%) are involved as guides or canoe operators. Until now, they have not been able to really benefit from tourism.

In this area, tourism took off about 25 years ago, leading to the transformation of two towns into "jungle towns" (i.e., places from where tourists start their jungle tours): Misahuallí and later also Puerto Francisco de Orellana, better known as Coca. When the number of tourists to these towns increased in the 1980s, the mestizo inhabitants gained control as they began to cooperate in order to cope with the situation. At the time, there was a tourist information office in Misahuallí and 22 private agencies were offering tours. When mestizos from Quito and Ambato moved to Misahuallí and a few foreigners opened hotels, competitiveness grew and local entrepreneurs discontinued their cooperation. The tourist office disappeared and control of tourism businesses shifted away from the mestizos towards the small group of foreign hostel owners. The latter had the financial means to invest in their hostels in order to meet the needs of the Western tourists and therefore gained control of tourism development. When the competition between the cheaper mestizo hostels became stronger, the number of hostels, stores, and agencies decreased, as only a few could survive under these harsh conditions. Today, there are only four mestizo-owned hostels and about seven stores.

The Quichua Indians have never been much involved in tourism. There were some Indian guides, but, with the introduction of licenses for guides by CETUR, they had to stop because they did not have the required basic education or money to enter the courses. Until 1993, there were no licensed Indian guides in Misahuallí. However, during the early 1990s, their situation changed. When the number of visitors increased, so did the negative impact on the Indian communities. They felt exploited by tourists visiting their homes, disrespecting their privacy. This was shown to the extreme when the neighboring Huaorani tribe (known for their "shrunken head" rituals) protested against tourism with violent actions against everyone entering their territory in 1992. Unlike them, the Quichua Indians decided that, if they could not stop the tourism boom, they should join it and benefit from it. Today, about 10% of the Quichua Indians who live in the parish of Misahuallí have exchanged their agricultural jobs for jobs in tourism, mostly as guides. The Amazon Indians have an advantage over others to become guides because they generally have better knowledge (passed on from generation to generation) of the flora and fauna. The feeling of exploitation decreased due to the fact that more often groups of tourists were taken to visit Indian homes by Indian guides. Today, there are about 60 licensed Indian guides and some canoe operators working in tourism in Misahuallí. On the other hand, 90% of this Indian community is not involved in tourism, mostly because they are not familiar with industries other than agriculture and they do not speak languages other than Quichua. Those who try to start their own business in the town feel that the local mestizos, foreigners, and policy makers in the province make it difficult for them in particular and give them no support at all. In other parts of the tourism sector, such as the accommodation industry, the indigenous population does not play any role. For example, there were no Indian hostel owners or store owners in Misahuallí at the time of our research in 1996.

In general, the inhabitants of Misahuallí feel that they are not well represented in the local government. They think that the policy makers in Tena do not act in their best interest. Misahuallí is still not recognized as a major tourism destination and for years there have been almost no improvements of basic supplies, such as water, sewerage, waste processing, and electricity. Because there is no cooperation between the entrepreneurs, there are also no mutual funds to invest in these facilities. Although everyone agrees that there are several ways to improve their social, cultural, and economic situation, and that a change for the better is welcome, actually no one likes to put in the effort and take the initiative. A good example of this attitude is the issue of learning other languages. It is generally agreed that learning to speak English would generate more income, because most tourists speak English and always ask for English-speaking guides (of which there are very few in Misahuallí). However, no one wants to learn another language, partly because they do not like to put in the effort of studying and partly because they simply like to speak their own language best. The Indians speak Quichua, which is totally different from the Spanish language. Needless to say, this often leads to misunderstandings and communication problems when dealing with tourists.

Tourism in Otavalo and Misahuallí Compared

When comparing tourism development in Otavalo and Misahuallí, it becomes clear that tourism in the two places is very different, although in both cases the indigenous component is present. Tourism in both Otavalo and Misahuallí can be considered as indigenous tourism, not only because the indigenous population is part of the tourist attraction, but also because the indigenous population actively participates in the tourism sector. The extent to which an attraction is focused on indigenous culture is an indicator of indigenous tourism. Control is just as important for that matter, because whoever has control can generally determine factors as scale, speed, and nature of tourism development. Butler and Hinch (1996) have brought together these two key figures—the presence of the indigenous theme and the degree of control—in a classification scheme that distinguishes four types of indigenous tourism (Figure 8.4).

The extent of control that indigenous people have over a tourism activity is presented horizontally. This control can include ownership and management positions in the industry and decision-making power in tourism policies and politics. The vertical axis shows the degree to which a tourist attraction is based upon an indigenous theme. This implies some kind of involvement of local indigenous

		Indigenous control	
		Low degree	High degree
Indigenous theme	Present	*Culture dispossessed*	*Culture Controlled*
	Absent	*Non-indigenous tourism*	*Diversified Indigenous*

Figure 8.4. Indigenous tourism. Source: Butler and Hinch (1996, p. 10).

people, for example, by means of employment or voluntary participation of indigenous people. Of the four different types of indigenous tourism that emerge from this scheme, two (i.e., "culture dispossessed" and "diversified indigenous") may lead to mass tourism developments, because in the former type the local people exert too little control and in the latter local people are too little involved. The only type of tourism that represents a truly indigenous form is "culture controlled," because local people are deeply involved as well as in control of this kind of tourism development.

Turning to Otavalo and Misahuallí with this scheme in mind, one cannot fail to realize that the extent to which the indigenous people are in control of tourism development in their community differs in both places. Referring to this model, it can be stated that tourism in Otavalo can be considered as a true form of indigenous tourism, because the indigenous theme is clearly present. Tourists who visit Otavalo focus on cultural manifestations such as handicrafts (at the Saturday market), music, dance, and aspects of the traditional way of life. In Misahuallí the indigenous theme is present as well, but the natural surroundings, especially the flora and fauna, clearly dominate the tourists' motivation to visit the place.

When looking at the extent and the way in which the indigenous peoples participate in the tourism industry in both places, the differences become even more pronounced. In Otavalo, the Indians more or less create the tourist attraction by their presence at the market, where they sell their handicrafts. Without the participation of these indigenous people, the market would lose its significance for most (foreign) visitors. Therefore, the extent of control by these indigenous people is very high. In Misahuallí, on the contrary, the Amazon jungle constitutes the main tourist attraction. The Indians contribute to the attractiveness of the rainforest as they fit in with this/their natural surrounding. They make the jungle more authentic, so to speak; hence, the prominent role that the Indian people play in guiding jungle tours, operating canoes, and hosting tourists who visit their *cabañas*. However, the number of Indians who work in the tourism sector is very small and limited to the lesser-paid professions (such as guiding), while they are largely absent among the business owners (e.g., hotel owners or travel agents). Thus, the extent of control by Indians within the tourism sector in Misahuallí is much lower than in Otavalo. It may even be decreasing because of the harsher competition with nonindigenous people who participate in the tourism sector in areas that used to be controlled by Indians.

The level of prosperity of the Otavaleños has increased with the growth of tourism in this town, and some individuals have become very rich. The Amazon Indians, on the other hand, have become more exploited and suppressed, and their level of prosperity hardly improved when tourism in Misahuallí increased. Besides, the Otavaleños have managed well to maintain their own culture and identity, both as a cultural heritage and encouraged by tourism as a marketing strategy. The position of the Otavaleños within the tourism sector and the tourists' reactions towards their presence condition these indigenous people to carefully watch their authentic culture. There is little discrepancy between the tourist image of the Indians from Otavalo and their cultural identity. For example, most Otavaleños in their daily lives often wear the costume in which they are represented (especially by women and older men) and also perform activities and traditional celebrations in which they are depicted. The contradiction or difference between the tourist image and the sociopolitical situation is much greater for the Indians of the Amazon jungle than for the Otavaleños. The indigenous people of Misahuallí seem to have assimilated more to Western culture and therefore disregard the demands of the tourism industry. The Amazon Indians seem to prefer Western clothing to their traditional way of dressing. Tourist culture seems to provide the examples that are easily imitated. However, this does not mean that the Amazon Indians have lost all of their authentic culture and heritage. They still practice their nature-based ancient rites and rituals.

Understanding the differences between both Indian groups, the Otavaleños and the Amazon Indians, requires a closer analysis of their entrepreneurial skills in general and their tourism mindedness in particular against the background of their broader relationships with the outside world. To start with the latter, Otavalo has a long history of trade since pre-Inca times, which marked the beginning of a trade culture in the community. This trade culture and the Otavalo weaving art enabled the Indians to develop a handicraft industry that still flourishes. The handicraft industry has given a sense of pride and cultural identity to the Otavaleños and, at the same time, has enhanced the cultural competence of the Indians to deal with outsiders. Neither the state nor foreigners have been able to interfere with the strong sense of community in Otavalo. Misahuallí, on the other hand, does not have a history of trade. Since the Spanish domination foreigners have been able to develop an industry in the province of Napo based in particular on oil and tourism. The Amazon Indians have become used to a situation of dependence upon foreigners in their own community. This has had consequences for the entrepreneurial attitude and skills exerted by the indigenous people in both communities. Otavaleños are rather shrewd business people and experienced in commercial and marketing strategies. The following example may illustrate this: Otavaleños like to tell tourists that they are very poor and that they badly need the money they earn from selling their handicrafts at the market. During a conversation that the authors had with two of the indigenous market vendors, these vendors tried to get more money for their products by claiming that they needed it to "feed their donkey." Later the authors discovered that these vendors drove a big four-wheel drive pick-up truck. Many tourists fall for this act of the "poor Indians" and pay much more money than they initially intended or they fail to bargain, because they feel sorry for them. These explicit strategies to squeeze money from tourists were still absent in Misahuallí at the time of the research. Otavalo and Misahuallí also differ in terms of the indigenous attitude towards tourism and towards being an entrepreneur/participant in the tourism industry. In Misahuallí, most entrepreneurs are foreigners, while in Otavalo the local indigenous people participate as entrepreneurs at a large scale. This highly participatory role of the Otavaleños makes them benefit from tourism more than the Amazon Indians from Misahuallí.

In many developing countries, tourism initiatives emerge at the national level and find their way to the communities in a top-down manner. Plans to develop tourism are often implemented at the community level, lacking local support and participation. When tourist numbers in these communities increase and mass tourism starts, tourism development becomes a burden instead of a benefit for the local population. In contrast to this, tourism development started at the local level in both Misahuallí and Otavalo. However, this is true for the tourism sector. In terms of government policies (at the local, provincial, or national level) few (for Otavalo) or no (for Misahuallí) actions are taken to control tourism in these places. The advantage of this lack of government intervention is that control is in the hands of the local people. This may provide a good basis for sustainable development, because it is generally agreed that local level is the best position from where the needs of the local population can be monitored. The downside is that local participants do not always have the necessary means (in terms of money and knowledge) to invest in tourism projects. In Misahuallí, this is the reason for control being in the hands of a small group, mostly foreigners. Because there is no cooperation between the participants, tourism does not contribute to the improvement of the social, cultural, or economic situation of the whole community. In Otavalo, this situation is slightly different, for in this town the Indians are the ones that create and run the tourist market and therefore are in control of the situation. The money earned from the sales of handicrafts is indeed used to improve their social, cultural, and economic position. This, by lack of proper policy measures, does not occur at a collective level, but is limited to the advancement of the position of individual people.

The participation of the local population in processes of planning, control, and coordination of tourism development is essential in order to achieve a sustainable form of tourism (Hunter & Green, 1995). As stated before, tourism development has never been planned for Misahuallí. It has never been on the priority list of the Ministry of Tourism in Quito and the Department of Tourism has never acknowledged Misahuallí as an important tourist attraction. Rudimentary forms of coordination of tourism activities as facilitated by the tourist office disappeared altogether when the office closed down years ago. At the time of the research, CETUR was the only organization that kept contact with all participants and tried to stimulate people to participate in tourism. However, the real control over tourism in Misahuallí is in the hands of a small group of foreign hostel owners with financial power and with contacts with travel agencies in Quito and abroad. As control is not shared equally among the different actors in the tourism industry and as there is no cooperation (e.g., no shared funds), tourism in Misahuallí does not provide the conditions to enable the whole population to benefit. Thus, tourism as it is organized nowadays contributes to the well-being of only a few.

Opportunities for Sustainable Tourism in Otavalo and Misahuallí

The indigenous view towards opportunities and threats for the tourism industry in these communities is very different from a Western perspective on these issues. Western tourism experts most probably would recommend collective measures such as investments in the improvement of the local infrastructure. However, the indigenous people show a different point of view towards tourism opportunities and threats, which may be illustrated by some examples from the presented fieldwork. Most Indians interviewed exerted a rather individually oriented and short-term perspective on tourism, measuring its opportunities in terms of their own immediate situation or well-being. In Misahuallí the people involved in tourism were generally not satisfied with their social, their cultural, or, especially, their economic situation. The mestizos and Indians find their income to be low, especially during the low tourist season. They think that foreign participants and travel agents in Quito control the tourism industry and earn much more money than they do. Also, the harsh competition and envy among the mestizos are perceived unfavorably. As much of the discontent of the people in Misahuallí can be largely blamed on the small returns from tourism, it is striking that the Otavaleños also claim not to be satisfied with their present situation. After all, their social, cultural, and, especially, economic circumstances are far better than those of the Amazon Indians. This raises the question of which factors contribute to the overall discontent with tourism development among the indigenous population?

At first glance, the answer to the question seems rather straightforward, at least as far as the Misahuallí case is concerned. In Misahuallí, the main reason for discontent among the indigenous population is the fact that foreigners benefit more from tourism than the mestizos and Indians. The foreigners who settled in the community and established tourism businesses had more money at their disposal from the very beginning. They have used their money to promote their product in Quito and abroad and to invest in the improvement of their hostels in order to meet the needs and wishes of the Western tourists—of whom they had a better knowledge and understanding than the indigenous population. The mestizos always had little financial means and also lacked the knowledge of the needs and wishes (hot water, tarantula-free rooms, etc.) of the Western tourists. The Indians, largely confined to the low-paying agricultural sector, had even less money and, moreover, almost no chances of getting a loan from a bank. To overcome this financial problem, there are two options: either obtaining financial assistance from others (foreigners) or finding creative (new) ways of generating money themselves (e.g., marrying allegedly "rich" foreigners, i.e., tourists).

Because the Ecuadorian government has no funds to invest in tourism projects, except for the national parks, the first option boils down to foreign financial aid, which means that the local population will have no control over the future plans of tourism in Misahuallí. This scenario is described in terms of "culture dispossessed" by Butler and Hinch (1996). A good example of this loss of control to foreign aid agencies are the Galapagos Islands, which are now totally financed and controlled by UNESCO and other foreign organizations. On the other hand, there are possibilities for the local population to generate money themselves, besides marrying foreigners, which have shown a viable strategy for some individuals in Otavalo (cf. Meisch, 1995). They could, for instance, learn from the Otavaleños and start their own nature-based souvenir production. These products could be sold in the town, which could help attract more visitors. Another option for the mestizos and Indians would be to learn to speak a foreign language (preferably English). In this way, they would meet the need for English-speaking guides, which would increase their income and give them more control. Other opportunities for both Misahuallí and Otavalo would emanate from the improvement of the infrastructure, because there are only two roads in poor condition to reach Otavalo and Misahuallí from Quito. Furthermore, increasing the number of tours may keep visitors in both places for a longer period of time. As has been shown by many tourism experts, expanding the length of stay is a better strategy for enhancing the benefits from tourism than increasing the number of visitors. This implies that more effort has to be put into the tourist attraction system. For example, in Otavalo local traditional production of hand-woven textiles may have potential for organizing textile tours with stops at villages to observe the spinning, dyeing, and weaving process. Hence, the scope for developing indigenous tourism can be very broad; however, organization requires careful programming of itineraries with pre-arrangements made at stopping points and provision of good guides with proficiency in foreign languages (Inskeep, 1991). Presenting Otavalo as the "model" for successful tourism development to be adapted by people in Misahuallí still leaves the question why the Otavaleños are dissatisfied with their situation. To provide an answer, one has to dig deeper and not let oneself be blinded by the "success story" of tourism in Otavalo.

The problem with all the options mentioned above, however, is that they largely stem from analyses by Western experts based on experiences with tourism development in Western countries. These options, however promising they may seem, totally overlook cultural differences between developed and developing countries. In both Misahuallí and Otavalo, the population has specifically indicated that they do not want (or they even refuse) to learn another language, even if they do agree that this would improve their economic situation. Moreover, most people in Otavalo and Misahuallí are reluctant to change. The Indians in Misahuallí work in agriculture, as have their ancestors before them, and the whole idea of changing this pattern in favor of employment in the tourism sector does not appeal to them. And in Otavalo, most Indians (though they may be dissatisfied) think that things are at their best now. So they do not feel that changes for the better are possible. Besides, although there are indigenous people with new ideas in both places, no one seems to be able to take the initiative of implementing the ideas. Although a lot of people claim to resent the conservatism of their society (especially the conservative attitudes of the policy makers), the fact is that these people seldom initiate innovations themselves. This illustrates that no one seems to be prepared to make necessary sacrifices and put in the effort in order to improve his or her situation. This presents an interesting paradox. The indigenous people of Misahuallí and Otavalo claim to be dissatisfied, but at the same time they are not willing to change anything by taking advantage of tourism development. As several respondents put it: "Nothing has happened in the past twenty years, so why would anything change in the next twenty or more years?" Keeping in mind local resistance to change, it seems that a different approach is necessary. One has to look at the situation from the point of view of the local population, applying an actor-centric approach. Then the questions to be raised would be: In what way can the local population overcome their dissatisfaction with their present situation and improve their social, cultural, and economic situation? And is tourism the "remedy" to do so?

It is striking that the indigenous people from Otavalo and Misahuallí have quite similar views on the opportunities and threats emanating from tourism development, although the extent to which they participate in and benefit from tourism differs considerably. Their basic attitudes towards tourism are strongly oriented towards their individual benefits or losses, as is usually the case with small entrepreneurs, for their first concern is with their business, not with the situation of the community of which they are a part. Sustainability in their terms is the sustainability of their business. The Western tourism experts should keep this in mind. If they want to mobilize the support and participation of the local population in tourism planning and development, they need to point out two aspects of sustainable tourism development:

- they need to make clear what benefits the local indigenous participants can expect from a change in their business strategies towards more sustainable strategies;
- they need to generate an understanding for common investments in communal facilities and infrastructure to support individual business activities.

Only if the indigenous population feels that innovations make their business sustainable will they cooperate to implement measures that support a sustainable development of the community as a whole.

Conclusion

Many different theories have been developed and comparative studies have been made with reference to sustainable tourism development. Inskeep (1991), for example, thinks that integrated tourism planning may establish a comprehensive and long-term approach to achieve sustainable development. According to V. L. Smith and Eadington (1992), the answer may be found in the development of alternative tourism, a theory that has found many followers. All of these theories have one aspect in common: the conviction that tourism development is necessary in order to change the present situation that does not meet the requirements of sustainability. The present situation is characterized by a focus on the needs of the tourists, a focus that is reflected in many tourism theories and models that put the tourist in a central place. Recently, however, there has been a growing recognition that a balance has to be found in weighing the desires of visitors against the well-being of the host population. The local community needs to be involved in all forms of tourism development because, if the host community does not benefit from tourism, they will become alienated and reject tourism in all its forms (Pearce & Butler, 1993).

Models and concepts developed by Western researchers may look very efficient and solvent in theory, yet in practice unrealistic and impractical. This applies in particular to tourism in developing countries. Differences in culture and mentality, and practical matters such as finances and lack of knowledge and understanding, may create impediments with the implementation of Western ideas and plans regarding tourism development in a developing country. Therefore, local participation in and support of tourism development in such areas are a necessity in order to achieve sustainable development as intended from a Western perspective. This may imply measures that do not conform to the current definition of sustainability. It may require a change of attitudes among Western experts to accept that indigenous people exert different attitudes towards the concept of sustainability. After all, the concept of sustainability is a Western invention, which often does not correspond to the vision of the peoples in developing countries. This implies that a researcher should look at the matter from different angles to examine in what way such a concept could possibly be put into practice with due observance of both visions. In the end, participation by the indigenous population is a necessary criterion to help accomplish sustainable tourism development.

Tourism development does not yet contribute to the improvement of the socio-cultural and economic situation of the indigenous people of in Otavalo and Misahuallí. Otavalo seems to represent a model for a successful tourism development and many individuals have become quite wealthy because of their entrepreneurship in tourism. However, Otavalo still lacks a viable tourism policy that redistributes the wealth that is individually generated in a way that the community as a whole will benefit sustainably. In Misahuallí the indigenous population participates only marginally in tourism, while foreigners control the local tourism sector. In this situation, it makes no sense to develop tourism through outside intervention, for what is the use of financial aid without local involvement, know-how, and vision? There has to be a willingness to participate in the tourism sector first. Secondly, the local population should decide for themselves what opportunities and threats they have to consider and what reasonable ways there are to reach their goals, because it is the local community that knows their culture, attitudes, and capacity best. For a Western researcher, this conclusion may be difficult to accept, but the vision that indigenous peoples are not able to adapt and assimilate to a changing world is a vision of the past. Indigenous people always were and still are capable of decision making that suits their situation best. The Otavaleños may be the best example to illustrate this. Indigenous peoples are not prepared to change their culture and mentality towards an issue like tourism development that easily, just because a Western researcher considers adaptation to Western ideas by these native people to be better for them. They have their own ideas and wishes concerning particular developments and a perspective upon the tourism sector as well, which sometimes may be in flat contradiction with the Western definition of the concept of sustainability. Finally, there is a major actor in sustainable tourism development that is largely absent in Ecuador: the central government. Local initiatives will remain individually oriented and lacking impact on the community as a whole unless the government supports local development by means of a participatory approach. This government support should entail but not confine itself to tourism to prevent local indigenous communities from becoming totally dependent on the volatile tourism market.

Chapter 9

The (Missing) Gender Dimension: A Review of Tourism Literature on Latin America and the Caribbean

Anne-Marie Van Broeck

Introduction

This chapter focuses on gender issues in tourism as seen from the perspective of women. Based on an extensive review of the anthropological literature, the following questions will be raised. How do women participate in the production of tourism in general and in community-based tourism in particular? How, as hostesses, do they interact with others? What types of jobs are available to them in the tourism sector? How do women represent their culture and traditions? How are these aspects of gender linked to socially and culturally constructed gender roles and relationships? As will be shown in this chapter, women figure prominently in processes of production of *local* tourism products and *local* construction of tourism images, in particular images that radiate local "authenticity." Often, women are strategically used to add *couleur locale* to the tourism sector. This aspect will be highlighted in particular in the discussion of gender issues in Latin American and Caribbean tourism.

In order to fully understand aspects of gender and their role in tourism, three important perspectives must be taken into account (Kinnaird, Kothari, & Hall, 1994):

- Tourist activities and processes take place in "gendered" societies. The ways in which male and female identities are defined by the society to which the female hostess belong are important components.
- The economic, political, social, cultural, and environmental dimensions of societies that are involved in the development of tourism play a role in the way gender roles and relationships are defined and redefined through time. In turn, aspects of gender also influence these dimensions.
- Whenever ethnic, class, and gender relationships are discussed, power, (in)equality, and control also play a role, even in tourism.

In the limited number of anthropological studies on tourism in Latin America and the Caribbean, the specific position and participation of women has seldom been the central research focus. In this chapter, general information regarding gender aspects in the tourist industry will be presented to provide a "state of the art" overview. Gaps in the current knowledge regarding aspects of gender in the tourist industry will be discussed and a number of suggestions will be made for further research. The literature overview centers on the following themes:

- women and employment in the tourism industry;
- women as the erotic Other;
- women as the exotic Other.

Whenever possible, the findings presented in this chapter will be illustrated with examples from the literature or observations by the author.

Women and Employment in the Tourism Industry

Employment in tourism for women is by far the most closely studied topic in tourism-related gender studies. The main themes are the nature, conditions, and payment of "female" jobs, the reasons for gender differences, the effects of employment on the household, and the status of women in the home and in society. A number of researchers have investigated the employment of women in the large-scale tourism sector (Baldwin, 1997; Breathnach, Henry, Drea, & O'Flaherty, 1994; Chant, 1992, 1997; Devedzic, 1997; Hennessy, 1994; Leontidou, 1994; Purcell, 1997). In addition, the employment of women for small-scale projects has also received attention (Cabble I Rivera, 1997; Canoves, 1997; Castelberg-Kouma, 1991; Fairbairn-Dunlop, 1994; Garcia-Ramon, Canoves, & Valdovinos, 1995; Wilkinson & Pratiwi, 1995). On the basis of various case studies discussed in their book, Kinnaird and Hall (1994a) conclude that employment for women and men in tourism (as in other sectors of the economy) follows the historically constructed social practices and prejudices that relate to the roles of men and women. Differences in employment opportunity and types of jobs therefore articulate existing patriarchal power relations, and even reinforce them. They reflect the local and often transnational view of "women's" and "men's" work. "Women are recruited into work which is deemed to represent their traditional domestic responsibilities for which they will be inherently skilled" (Kinnaird et al., 1994, p. 16). This is even more evident in small-scale tourism where work is carried out in the home and is literally done in combination with household tasks. In addition to employment opportunities in the hotel industry, there are a number of other jobs in tourism; these include the production and sale of handicraft, and prostitution.

Work in Institutionalized Tourism

Most women employed in tourism work in the hotel industry. They are mainly responsible for the day-to-day cleaning of hotel rooms and catering tasks. By exception, they sometimes find a job in the bar or night club of a hotel. Very few women have a position at the management level. Still others find employment in the kitchen or behind the reception desk. In addition, women also hold positions in travel agencies and transport companies as salespersons, desk personnel, or air hostesses, or in catering. They seldom find employment as tour guides, pilots, or managers. The type of work they do manage to obtain is defined on the whole as "women's" work as it is seen as a continuation of the "natural" role of the house-wife. As a result, these jobs are regarded as requiring only low-skilled or unskilled labor. As in other economic sectors, such "women's work" is assigned low status and rewarded with a low salary. According to Enloe (1989):

> Since the eighteenth century, employers have tried to minimize the cost of employing workers in labor-intensive industries by defining most jobs as "unskilled" or "low-skilled" jobs, in other words, that workers naturally know how to do. Women in most societies are presumed to be naturally capable at cleaning, washing, cooking, and serving. Since tourism companies need pre-cisely those jobs done, they can keep their labor costs low if they can define those jobs as women's work. In the Caribbean, in the early 1980s, 75 per cent of tourism workers were women. (p. 34)

Women are often employed in temporary, seasonal, and part-time jobs, although there are also examples of permanent and full-time employment, probably in the star-rated sector in particular. The employment pattern follows and enforces the accepted cultural view that the work women do complements their primary responsibility—taking care of the family. A flexible work schedule—work in tour-ism often entails shifts—allows them to combine their work outside the home with their tasks as mothers. The income of women is also regarded merely as a supplement to their housekeeping money. After all, their primary responsibility is taking care of the household and the children. If necessary, a woman can pass these tasks on to other female members of her family, for instance, her daughters or mother (Norris & Wall, 1994). The income of women is merely regarded as a supplement to their housekeeping budget. A number of authors (e.g., Chant, 1997; Leontidou, 1994) have pointed out that women generally do not aspire to a professional career, but work because of economic necessity. Whatever the case may be, and given the other tasks that they are required to carry out, it remains difficult for women to embark on a career. Employment in the tourism sector at least provides them with an income. Even though this income is lim-ited, it gives women a certain degree of financial independence. The existing literature devotes very little attention to this factor and its consequences for these women. Chant's discussion of the situation in Mexico is an exception in this respect and will be discussed next.

Example: Mexico

Chant (1992, 1997) examined the tourism sector of Puerto Vallarta, Mexico. Although the region has played host to other types of industry in the past, only a relatively low proportion of women in general, let alone married women, found employment in these industries. Women were primarily entrusted with the task of taking care of the children and the household. The introduction of tourism to the region has brought about far-reaching changes. But in this sector, too, women are generally restricted to those jobs that strongly relate to their gender role: "Seg-ments of employment are distinctly feminized—especially those which represent an extension into the marketplace of skills generally acquired by women during gender socialization in the home. Typical jobs here include chambermaiding, laundry work and the preparation of food" (Chant, 1992, p. 97). Or as Chant states in another article:

> [D]istinctions between men's and women's sections are rather rigidly demarcated. While posts in receptions, offices and other areas requiring a secondary school education and/or vocational training seem relatively flexible in their recruitment pattern, among non-administrative workers, women are largely confined to housekeeping activities such as chambermaiding, linen-keeping and laundry work, whereas men are found across a much wider range of departments including portering, gardening, transport, and restaurant, kitchen and bar work. . . . The horizontal segregation between the male and female work-force . . . reflects (and in several respects reinforces) the traditional association of women with reproductive chores such as washing and bed-making, and that of men with "heavier" duties, "outside work" or work with a more "public' orientation." (Chant, 1997, pp. 138– 139)

This type of work requires no extra knowledge or skills in addition to those women already possess as a result of having to carry out care-taking tasks. Consequently, this type of work is regarded as low skilled in Puerto Vallarta too. In addition, women hold inferior positions with regard to status and reward. The chances of setting up a career in the female employment segments are slim, given that there are few opportunities for advancement (Chant, 1992). The fact that men are regarded as breadwinners in Puerto Vallarta, as they are everywhere else, reinforces the view that women's employment and their income are of only secondary importance. Nevertheless, the woman's income often makes up an important part of the total family income.

One characteristic of "women's" work that Chant refers to indirectly is its "private" nature. Men work in "public" spaces and often have more direct contact with tourists, while women work behind the scenes. This is strongly related to the idea of gendered space: which spaces are "private" (and thus "feminine") and which are not? In Latin American countries, the following saying is relevant in this respect: *hombre de la calle, mujer de la casa* (man out and about, woman at home). In practice, such spatial segregation is often a thing of the past, but it does, however, continue to play a role in the construction of value patterns and it influences the spaces or spheres in which female and male activities can be located.

The employment of women in the formal tourism sector also creates jobs for women who are asked to help carry out household tasks or take care of the children. Often, this extra help is recruited through family or social networks. A number of women in Puerto Vallarta prepare and sell meals for working women who do not have any time to cook themselves a meal. Some women, however, cannot rely on outside help. They end up doing two jobs, one paid and the other unpaid, and eventually have no time left for themselves.

The fact that women work and bring in income in this region also affords them a status that is more equal to that of their partners than in other parts of the country where women are less likely to participate in the workforce and where machismo is a very strong cultural force (Chant, 1992). This equality between men and women has resulted in the fact that tourism has broken through a number of "traditional" gender patterns and has, on occasion, caused family crises: "Some men cannot seem to cope with their wives' or partners' economic independence and may 'retaliate' by either dropping out of work or scaling down their contributions to household income. In addition, some husbands in this position even use their wives' earnings to play cards or to go out drinking with male friends" (Chant, 1997, p. 142). The question remains whether and to what extent gender roles shift through time, although the results of another study by Chant (1997) suggest that the daughters of working mothers join the workforce more quickly than daughters of nonworking women.

Another phenomenon that is linked to tourism in Mexico is migration to tourist areas. This type of migration tends to be gender specific. Given the fact that there is work for women in Puerto Vallarta, many families headed by women are now migrating to this coastal town. Such job opportunities, and the salary and financial independence they ensure, have afforded them the space not to have to commit themselves to a male partner. They have their own income, which allows them to take care of their family. Financial independence also influences the way women behave in a relationship. If a relationship is not working out, they can, and often do, break it off. Thus, financial independence leads to greater personal independence for women with respect to relationships (Chant, 1992, 1997). In addition, women who have migrated are strongly independent socially because they have moved away from their relations and family circle to come to Puerto Vallarta. As a result, they no longer feel socially pressured to get married or to conform to other socially expected behaviors. The social atmosphere is more liberal and relaxed than in many other conservative regions. Developments in tourism and migration have created greater freedom for women and have generally led to the social acceptance of unmarried mothers.

Work in Small-Scale Tourism

Small-scale tourist projects, such as bed & breakfast accommodation or small family hotels, are found mainly in rural regions and as part of agrotourism projects. Rural tourism (or agrotourism) evolved as an economic solution to problems caused by the stagnating agricultural industry. Farmhouse tourism is a specific form of rural tourism; tourists rent a (number of) room(s) on a working farm that is inhabited by the farmers. The tourists are closely involved with the daily running of the farm, but only work on the farm to a modest degree. After all, this is not the main attraction for tourists. The important aspects of rural tourism are staying "in the country," walking in rural areas, the peace and quiet, the animals, and the relationship with the host family. Renting rooms and offering other services related to tourism is of secondary importance if income generated by working the farm is merely supplemented by earnings generated from tourist projects, but becomes of primary importance when townspeople choose to live in the country and make agrotourism their profession (Garcia-Ramon et al., 1995).

If family farms are to survive in the regions (Catalonia and Galicia) examined by Garcia-Ramon et al. (1995), the active participation of women in agricultural production is a prerequisite. It is remarkable that women often take the initiative when it comes to starting a tourism-related enterprise (Garcia-Ramon et al., 1995). Without the participation of women, these rural families could not get involved in these new enterprises. It is the women who take on most of the tasks that are involved. After all, they cannot afford hired help to run their new business. Nevertheless, in exceptional cases, women call on or employ other women in their family to help out (Garcia-Ramon et al., 1995). However, the work done by the female head of the household is fundamental and indispensable. She views her tasks as a "natural" extension of the domestic duties that she already carries out for her family. But this time she carries them out for her "extended" family, which includes the tourists. The study by Garcia-Ramon et al. shows that women do not distinguish the work they do in agrotourism from everyday household tasks. These women are unaware of the change in the type of work they carry out: "When they prepared food, they cooked for the family as well as for the visitors. Cleaning and washing clothes were also combined. In effect, they perceive the work related to agrotourism to be an amplification or extension of domestic duties" (Garcia-Ramon et al., 1995, p. 274). By working in this sector, women are not breaking through the existing pattern of gender roles. On the contrary, it is this traditional role pattern that allows these women to work in this sector. Furthermore, this type of enterprise confirms and strengthens the traditional division on the basis of gender between domestic duties (including work generated by tourism) and work in agriculture.

Women appreciate their work in agrotourism because it allows them to earn money without having to leave the house. As a result, they can also continue to carry out everyday activities and fulfill any other traditional responsibilities they have. They can occupy themselves with their family, and if necessary, they can get involved in the family business. Tourism is seen as a complement to the traditional work that women do within the agricultural family unit. Another important aspect is the fact that the structure of the family remains intact. The work that women do in the tourist industry generates extra income for the family. As a result, their work in the family, in contrast to their "normal" domestic duties and contribution to agricultural activity, becomes more observable and is appreciated. The woman often feels proud of the contribution that she makes. However, the fact that this new activity is simply integrated into "unobservable" domestic duties promotes once more the invisibility of women's efforts, and does not lead to professionalization of the women themselves or the work they do. A job in agrotourism is not seen as a real profession by women or their families. This type of work does not require any specific formal qualifications and does not allow women to generate a complete income. The seasonality of the work also underlines its supplementary nature.

The women themselves clearly differentiate between generating income and holding down a job that ensures some kind of income. It is the latter category that is admired most in society. Work in tourism does not provide women with a salary (similarly, they are not paid when they help out on the farm or in the family business; see Canoves, 1997). With the income they generate, the women create a better standard of living for their family. Sometimes, extra income is invested in new accommodation. These enterprises do not afford women the opportunity to gain financial independence. They do not receive money to spend on themselves.

Two questions remain: To what extent do such projects promote women's development, economic independence, emancipation, and "empowerment"? How do the women themselves benefit? Part of the answer is given by Garcia-Ramon et al. (1995): "The time dedicated by women to agrotourism has resulted in a corresponding reduction in the time spent on agricultural activities. Overall, the total number of work hours for women has increased, although these hours are less physically demanding. More importantly, as the women expressed it, it is much cleaner work" (p. 275). Another important aspect is that this sector provides women with the opportunity to meet other people. The women rarely regard their in-house guests as constituting an invasion of privacy, but are more prone to emphasize the positive aspects of such meetings. Traditionally, these women would have lived their lives largely within the family group, so they certainly appreciate these new, more public, interactions. "With the operating of a lodging house, they feel more integrated into the outside world. Women focus more on this aspect of the venture than men, possibly because men (even in a rural setting) have always participated in the local public sphere" (Garcia-Ramon et al., 1995, p. 275).

Example: Colombia

To what extent can comparable conclusions be drawn with respect to *finca* (farmhouse) tourism in Colombia? The conclusions that will be discussed in this respect must be regarded as tentative as they are based on limited observation on the author's part (1996–1999) and on a small-scale survey (conducted in 1999). Still, in this example from Colombia, it is also clear that existing gender roles are confirmed and strengthened.

When Colombian coffee exports decreased because of competition from other coffee producers in the world market, numerous productive *fincas* tried to find a way out of the situation by supplementing or completely replacing their coffee production with income generated from tourism. Initially, these farmhouses had been kept available for the family of the owner, but now they became a commercial good. The *fincas* were adapted to a certain extent to offer room and board to paying guests. An important characteristic of the Colombian farmhouse tourism is that the owners usually do not live on their *fincas*, but in a nearby town. Although the owner has another profession, he visits the site regularly to check on the production process. The day-to-day running of the *finca* is in the hands of the *mayordomo*. (foreman) who lives locally and coordinates a number of other employees. During the harvest, extra workers are recruited. The wife of the owner is usually a housewife. She maintains contacts with customers who come to buy the agricultural products and oversees and checks the work done by the female workers who work on the *finca* and are "managed" by the *mayordomo*'s wife. These women take care of the maintenance and cleaning of the farm and prepare meals for the workers. In some exceptional cases, they help out during the planting. During the harvest, in particular, when the number of workers is larger, the number of women in the kitchen increases; they prepare the food for the workers. Tourism brings in extra work for female workers and for the *mayordomo*'s wife, in particular. Here, too, the work is a complement of women's domestic tasks. If there are many tourists, extra women are sometimes recruited to help out. The *mayordomo* manages the security of the *finca*, helps carry out the heavier work, and makes sure that all the tourists are satisfied. The *mayordomo* and his wife are the ones who have the most contact with the tourists, because they provide them with the necessary service. The couple receives more income from the owner during the tourist high season than at other times of the year. Sometimes the tourists directly contact the *mayordomo*'s wife to cook and clean for them.

The *mayordomo* has only limited contact with tourists; he might come by once in a while to see if everything is being provided for. The *mayordomo* sees it as his task to maintain the *finca* and, to a certain extent, to welcome the guests. His wife spends more time with the tourists. She usually takes part in all kinds of courses that are organized by the local federation of *finca* tourism. This illustrates that the tourist aspect of the *finca* is the domain of the woman, while her husband is concerned with guarding the production process.

For this study, it is important to analyze gender differences more closely in the light of class differences. Which gender roles are confirmed and strengthened for each of these women from different classes? What do women gain by participating in tourism? Does the *mayordomo*'s wife broaden her horizons through such contacts? The preliminary study of Colombian *finca* tourism shows that the *mayordomo*'s wife benefits from a financial perspective in particular. How is this extra income spent? It would be interesting to integrate into the present study an investigation of *fincas* whose owners receive guests into their homes and thus use their private domain to commercialize hospitality, and to compare these cases with others in which the private and public domain remain clearly separate.

Handicraft: Production and Sale

Tourists are usually interested in and eager to learn about the culture of a foreign country as reflected in its trades and handicraft. Objects that were originally produced for use in the home, such as textiles or ceramic objects, have now gained commercial value. This has created new employment opportunities in tourism, usually for the women who manufacture these products. Because these goods gain economic value, their manufacturers gain income. This can change their position within the family. After all, the development influences the ratio of the man's earnings to the woman's income, and their respective financial contributions to the running of the household. This can affect other aspects of family structure too, such as decision making on major family purchases or matters related to the education of their children. Furthermore, it is possible that the women's position in society changes as a result, although this is rare.

Let us consider the Kuna women from Panama as an example. Initially, their participation in tourism grew from trading the *mola*, a textile product that is typically worn by this ethnic group as part of their standard clothing. The *mola* is produced by the Kuna women. An increase in the production and sale of this product has led Kuna women to gain greater economic importance. This has given them greater independence and consequently more power in the household (Swain, 1978, 1989). In Kuna society in general, however, traditional gender roles have remained intact. It is still the Kuna men who take decisions regarding, for example, the group's interactions with the outside world, including the world of tourism. However, Swain (1989) suggests that local employment in tourism can bring about a gradual change in the pattern of gender roles.

Other studies have also pointed out that economic autonomy does not automatically lead to a greater influence on societal processes on the part of women:

All of them note that, in spite of potential increases in economic standing that women may attain due to employment in tourism, strong cultural barriers, the lack of government initiatives and the lack of organization among the women workers themselves inhibit women from aspiring to leadership roles both in the political and community sense. (Norris & Wall, 1994, p. 65)

But even within the tourist industry, women often fail to make progress: "Lack of organization among women workers, either through unionization, access to political power or government initiatives, prevented women from 'getting ahead' in the tourism industry" (Norris & Wall, 1994, p. 69). Whereas most work in the tourism sector is described as temporary, seasonal, and low skilled, handicraft has an exceptional status. This type of production is regarded as requiring certain skills, and this work is carried out on a more permanent and full-time basis than in many other domains of the tourism sector.

An increase in demand for handicraft products can bring about certain changes in the production process, which may be an advantage or disadvantage for the manufacturers. Sometimes, cooperative ventures are started, such as that initiated by some Kuna (Swain, 1989). In a number of cases, mass production calls for other methods and, as a result, workers with specific characteristics (e.g., younger men and women). On the other hand, the product can change too. As a result of the commercialization of the *mola*, for example, its designs and the production techniques used in its manufacture were adapted: the *mola* that is manufactured for the tourist industry is often of a lower quality than the traditional *mola*. However, the biggest problem is that different Kuna women report that they now have less time to manufacture the "traditional" *mola* because they have to work hard to manufacture the *mola* for tourists. In this way, tourism has also brought about changes in the way these women dress. The sale of these products is not necessarily in the hands of the women that manufacture them. At local markets, the Kuna women sell their own products, but it is the men who sell them in tourist towns and tourist areas. This phenomenon is linked directly to other specific gender role patterns that determine the cultural space for men and women.

The commercialization of handicraft in San Cristóbal (Mexico), on the other hand, is almost completely controlled by the women who produce as well as sell their products (Van den Berghe, 1994). Likewise, they are in full control of this new source of income. Thousands of women and their families in the region generate income from tourism. For the 200–300 women in San Juan Chamula or San Cristóbal who regularly sell their own work and that of others, the income that is generated is substantial, although they have a very low profit margin. In addition, about 300–400 Indians, primarily Chamula women and girls (95%), offer their wares in the streets (Van den Berghe, 1994). Van den Berghe (1994) puts it as follows: "While no one, to my knowledge, has yet become rich, for many families the tourist trade has made the difference between subsistence and starvation" (p. 144).

The tourist trade has elevated women to an economic level comparable to that of their husbands. In fact, given recent problems regarding employment, many men now can no longer take care of their family financially. The income of women from paid work has become of vital importance for a great number of families.

This phenomenon "upsets" existing gender relationships, an aspect that Van den Berghe neglects to discuss in greater detail. Women often deal with the opportunities offered by tourism in different ways. This is illustrated by the case study of Abbott Cone (1995) regarding two Maya women. Both women play an active role in the interaction with tourists and transcend the traditional behavioral patterns ascribed to Maya women. One woman designs textile products using traditional methods and designs. She makes friends with tourists and shares with them her extensive knowledge of Mayan culture. The other woman creates new forms. She identifies with tourists and, aided by her income from tourism, breaks with tradition in her work as well as her private life. The differences in attitude with regard to this traditional craft, gender relationships, ties to the community, and the personalities of these women lead to differences.

Women as the Erotic Other

For many tourists, sexual behavior is linked to tourism; hence, the four Ss of tourism are said to stand for *Sun, Sea, Sand,* and *Sex.* A fifth one may be added for Servility. Sex tourism is generally defined in the literature as a form of tourism in which commercial sex is the main goal. Oppermann (1999) believes that this type of 'ideal' sex tourist does not exist: "The 'ideal' sex tourist purposely takes a holiday to have sex, stays away from home at least 24 hours, meets the sex provider for the first time, has sexual intercourse as a result of direct monetary exchange, and obtains sexual gratification in encounters which last a relatively short time. However, this ideal type usually does not exist" (p. 261). He identifies six variables that are the basis for a categorization of sex tourists: the purpose of the trip, the monetary exchange, duration, the relationship, the sexual encounter, and who travels (Figure 9.1). Different combinations of these parameters give a more refined view of sex tourism, and ensure that sex tourism is not equated only with prosti-

–/–	Parameters	+/+
No intentions. Multiple purpose	Intentions to have sex with 'strangers' on holidays. Travel purpose	Full intentions. Sole purpose
No direct reimbursement	Monetary exchange	Direct monetary. Reimbursement
Years	Length of time spent 'together' by sex seeker and sex provider	Minutes
Long-term relationship	Seeker-provider relationship	First-time meeting
Voyeurism	Sexual Encounter	Intercourse
None	Who travels?	Sex seeker and sex provider

Figure 9.1. Sex tourism framework. Source: Oppermann (1999, p. 255).

tution. As such, sex tourism becomes behavior on a continuum rather than one specific type of behavior.

Many tourists do not travel with the specific goal in mind to engage in sexual encounters on vacation, but are open to offers nonetheless. Some authors (see Clift, 1994) claim that there is a difference between men and women in that men on vacation are looking for noncommittal sex, while women on holiday are seeking romance (Meisch, 1995, 1997; Pruitt & Lafond, 1995). On the basis of the broader definition of sex tourism referred to above, "romance tourism" can also be regarded as a variant.

In this section, the following elements of sex tourism in a broader sense will be considered with the focus on the women involved:

- the erotic woman as portrayed in tourist brochures to promote a particular destination;
- women involved in prostitution;
- the local female population whose partners or potential partners show a sexual interest in tourists.

Women and the Promotion of Tourist Destinations

The promotion of tourist destinations has, to a greater or lesser extent, an erotic dimension. In addition to sun, sea, and sand, promotional material often includes photographs of, or references to, beautiful women. The women are made into objects to such an extent that male tourists picture their holiday destination, even before their departure, as a place where they can find "exotic" sexuality (Sinclair, 1997a). "Tourism promotion in magazines and newspapers promises would-be vacationers more than sun, sea, and sand; they are also offered the fourth 's'—sex. Resorts are advertised under the labels of 'hedonism,' 'ecstacism,' and 'edenism' " (Baillie, 1980, pp. 19–20).

> Women are often used in the promotion of the exoticized nature of a place. Sexual imagery, when used to depict the desirability of places in such a way, says a great deal about the gendered nature of the marketing agents and their fantasies. Although the promotion of "Club 18–30"-holidays is a rare example of the encouragement of single people to travel, it is packaged with overt sexual overtones, which reinforces heterosexuality. As a result, the sexualized myths and fantasies extolled in the tourism promotion literature lead to the construction of these ideas in the hearts and minds of tourists. (Kinnaird & Hall, 1994b, p. 214)

The promotion of tourist destinations in developing countries plays on the "ideal" man–woman relationships: "Tourist brochures help to construct the myths and fantasies that are characteristic of certain key ideological features of Western culture which include representations of men and women which associate action, power and ownership with the former and passivity, availability and being owned with the latter" (Kinnaird et al., 1994, p. 13). But Western women no longer conform to this picture and can therefore no longer satisfy the wants of the Western man (Norris & Wall, 1994). These women are too feminist, too emancipated, and too strong. Men want women who will fulfill their every need, without making too many demands on them. The non-Western woman, in this respect, is an answer to their prayers. It is the Asian woman, in particular, that is presented in promotional material as subservient, gentle and pleasant in character, passive, and available. Latin-American women are presented as embodying fury and passion:

> Women in Latin America, Asia and Africa are explicitly praised for their specific feminine qualities. In publications and promotion material of the tourist industry, Latin American women are "passionate and fierce." Asian women are "affectionate, delicate, and submissive"; African women are assumed to be "obscure, mysterious, magic." Unnecessary to tell or demonstrate that these are lies, illusions; these illusions are created to sell a product, in this case black women to white men. (Translated from Peterson, 1989, p. 162)

In his book *Travel & the Single Male*, Cassirer (1992) provides a description of Brazilian women. Again, the picture that emerges is of active and sexually permissive women:

> In Brazil the women are not ashamed of their bodies and show as much as they can, be it on the beach, on the side-walk, or on the dance floor. Besides going topless on the beach, the Brazilian women will run, sing, flirt, and drink, and dance with you to death. . . . No place in the world has such beautiful, outgoing, and entertaining women who pray for a sunny day just to show off their bodies" (Cassirer, 1992, p. 102).

He makes an explicit comparison between Brazilian and Western women:

> What makes these women different is their lack of modesty. Our culture says that women should be generally modest, reserved, and sexually undemonstrative. Brazilian women, however, are not afraid to show off their bodies; in fact, they're proud! . . . These women are romantics, unashamed of their bodies, their feelings, or their sexual relations. (Cassirer, 1992, pp. 130–131)

At the same time he puts out a warning to Western men: "A poor Brazilian economy, a body-beautiful consciousness, and a 'one day at a time' perception of life make this a man's heaven. This doesn't mean that Brazilian women will obey your every command" (Cassirer, 1992, pp. 131–132).

With respect to Puerto Vallarta (Mexico), Cassirer (1992) points out that the Catholic faith determines, to a large extent, the role patterns of women in this culture. The middle-class working girls of Guadalajara, who make Puerto Vallarta their vacation spot, are not an easy prey for males. After all, Mexico is a Catholic country, and flirting and romance have to conform to rules that demand men to be patient. The Caribbean is also an "erotically tinted" destination. Momsen (1994) describes how promotion material for the islands presents images of women who are lightly clothed, in exotic locations. Furthermore, she refers to a description by Dagenais: "Popular representations of the region portray them as sexual objects and publicity props; the tourist industry presents them as sensual mulattos with endless free time to enjoy the beaches, and of course, the (male) visitors" (Dagenais, 1993, p. 83). The Dominican Republic is "sold" through its women:

Contrary to what it would be ethically proper to expect, advertising, which shows the country as a tourist destination, as a paradise, bases itself almost exclusively on allusions to the "beauty" of the Dominican women, to their charm etc. The women, almost naked, become another part of the country-side, another element in the package offered by travel agencies overseas and here, in the country itself, to the tourists who come from abroad. It is no exaggeration to say that in this type of publication, the sexual services of Dominican women have been codified. In late 1984, the newspaper "*Ultima Hora*," published in our capital, denounced the fact that the Italian tourist enterprise "Kristour" had paid to have an advertisement put in the magazine "*Playmen*" which said, literally, "We guarantee that you will have the personal accompaniment of a lady who will do everything to make your journey more pleasant." The agency collaborating with "Kristour" said, simply, that it had not been informed of this advertisement. The tourism secretary was totally silent about the case. (Cordero, 1986, p. 55)

Cuba is sometimes described as "a Cuban party including young women" (Jarray, 1999). This type of promotion invites much criticism: "At Cuba's 15th annual tourism convention, held in the beach resort of Varadero in 1994, Tourism minister Osmany Cienfuegos, . . . blamed foreign tour operators for projecting a distorted image of Cuba for their own propaganda: 'Our women are not a commodity,' he said" (Pattullo, 1996, p. 90).

The fact that tourists get only a limited view of the local population on the basis of promotional material, and during their stay, creates resentment on the part of the local population:

[L]ocal dislike of sexual relations between locals and tourists has less to do with sexual Puritanism . . . than with the realization that poor locals, whether men or women, are racially and economically exploited by tourists. Their availability is made more seductive by received images, laced with racism: the "exotic," easy "native" woman with a hibiscus behind her ear; or the beach boy whose sexual prowess has been defined by white culture. It is also resented that the only encounters that most tourists have with local people are either as waiters or beachboys. There are no representations of "ordinary" people in the tourists' experience. As one Barbadian advertising executive says: "Tourists only meet beach boys, therefore the idea of an Barbadian man is restricted to that image." (Pattullo, 1996, p. 87)

Tourism and Prostitution in Latin America and the Caribbean

More and more men and women in developing countries are turning to prostitution in an effort to escape poverty. The unemployment rate is often high in these countries and there are few jobs for unskilled (mainly female) workers (Figure 9.2). Prostitution is seen as one of only a few alternatives to make a living (for the Caribbean see Kempadoo, 1999). Various authors have reported that female and male prostitutes have different motives for entering prostitution. Women are often responsible for children or parents. Through prostitution, they generate a family income. For them, it is simply an economic necessity. Practical considerations also play a role in their decision, such as the fact that this type of work

Figure 9.2. Prostitutes in a bar in Puntarenas, Costa Rica.

allows for flexible scheduling, which facilitates the woman's caretaking tasks at home. Men are less likely to enter prostitution out of direct economic necessity. Instead, they hope to eventually be able to emigrate to Europe or the United States with a Western woman. There is also a sense of honor involved in "conquering" Western women. Momsen (1994) described this difference in motive as follows:

> In the case of male prostitution, the male drive for sexual power is matched by the female's quest for sexual adventure, although the West Indian male often hopes to use his tourist conquest as a ticket to North America. For the female prostitute whose aim is an income to support her children, her vulnerability makes her an easy prey to the unscrupulous male, whether local pimp or clients, local and visitor. (pp. 116–117)

Kinnaird et al. (1994) confirm this observation: "For women involvement in sex tourism is motivated by income generation which results in improved family welfare. Men's motivations are based on their desire to exercise sexual power over foreign women and, perhaps, forge a relationship that allows them to leave the islands altogether" (p. 26). Some women hope that they will marry a Western man and leave the country with him. A Cuban *jinetera* (the Cuban word for prostitute), 26 years old, admits to the following:

> I used to study medicine. But that was no fun. I had no money to go out and I had no expectations of my future. Now I spend all my time with tourists in hotel discos. I go dancing where the tourists are and drink what the tourists

drink.And although I don't have an official income, I have enough money to have a good time. My biggest wish is to marry a foreigner and leave this country. (Van Hattum, 1997, p. 9)

Lee (1991) claims that sex tourism and the many problems that women experience on the job market are in fact linked:

> The issue of sex tourism is related to problems which are fundamental to women's role in the workforce in an international context: women's lack of economic and educational opportunity, their neglect in rural development or land reform schemes, their subjugation within the family, their domestic burdens and family responsibilities, and their exploitation in new forms of factory work.The oppressive character of customary values and much family and employment legislation, together with women's location within the labor process generally, mean that prostitution becomes a means of survival in a patriarchal world. (p. 97)

Example: Dominican Republic

One of the most popular locations for sex tourists in the Caribbean is the Dominican Republic. The sex tourist industry was already booming on this island before regular tourism made an entrance but it grew dramatically once greater numbers of tourists came to the island. Recent estimates show that there are about 25,000 registered prostitutes on the island; in reality, this figure is thought to be four to six times as high: "While much sex tourism in the Caribbean, especially that between local men and women tourists, exists within an informal framework, more formal prostitution has become a matter for concern, especially in the Dominican Republic and Cuba" (Pattullo, 1996, p. 87). Next to professional prostitutes, the tourist high season attracts young women, including students, who enter prostitution for only a certain period of time.Around 10% of Dominican women from the lower social classes are said to work in prostitution. In addition, numerous women from the middle classes are in the same profession.They enter prostitution out of economic necessity. High unemployment rates and economic crises drive these women into prostitution (Cordero, 1986).Their social class strongly determines where they work; for example, there are closed houses, bars and cabaret shows (many run by foreigners), and there is streetwalking. In the lobbies of various large hotels in Santo Domingo, hundreds of women offer themselves to tourists.And in the streets near the hotels or on the beaches, sexual services are also offered to visitors. However, more commonly, a tourist will negotiate a temporary relationship with a Dominican woman, based on a predetermined price that covers the woman's living expenses during the man's stay.

Local Men and Female Tourists: The Reactions of Local Women

The literature on tourism has recently been focused more and more on the phenomenon of women who engage in sexual relationships with local men during their vacation (see Dahles, 1997; Leontidou, 1994; Meisch, 1995, 1997; Pattullo, 1996; Pruitt & LaFont, 1995). Detailed discussion of this issue has to be left for another occasion; instead, the focus will be on the reactions of local women to this phenomenon. They are confronted with local men who devote attention to female tourists in their own community. What does this mean to local women?

Women have been complaining about the disturbance of social life since local men were only paying attention to foreign women. This caused problems for the families and their well-being. Castelberg-Kouma (1991) makes the following comments (with respect to Greece): "This has an effect on the way women relate to their men in the sense that men can no longer guarantee the honor necessary to maintain a family. In this sense they negate women's roles and the values women learn to respect and admire in men" (pp. 210-211). The local women she interviewed "felt that this adversely affected their lives and relationships and clouded the acquisition of any material gains" (Castelberg-Kouma, 1991, p. 197).

Tourism brings about changes to sexual and moral codes of behavior, but these changes are often limited to the male population. There seems to be a double moral standard at play, because women are by no means free to explore their own sexuality. Strict codes for sexual behavior remained unchanged for local women. The gap between local men and women becomes even wider as a result (Koussis, 1989). Tourism seems to impose a new, different image of the local women, yet this is mere imagery. Earlier, it was pointed out that tourists view Latin American women as passionate creatures, and yet, in real life, these women's sexual behavior is often determined by cultural values, including the importance of virginity, and Catholicism.

In Latin America and the Caribbean, there is a growing army of local men to satisfy the demand generated by female tourists. By all accounts, the local women are not happy with this development. Meisch (1997) studied a number of relationships between local male guides and female tourists on treks through the Andes (Peru). She refers, indirectly, to comments made by the wife of one of the guides: "On one trek I was the company guide, the wife and two children of John, the local guide, came to the trailhead to see the group off. This can be viewed as wifely affection, but also as territorial: this man is married and here we are, his wife and children, bidding him a fond farewell" (Meisch, 1997, p. 6). Without going into detail, Meisch also mentions the fact that the marriages of a number of male guides broke down.

Various authors (e.g., Antrobus, 1990; Pattullo, 1996) have described the phenomenon of the "Caribbean beach boy" and Caribbean sex tourism: "The impact of their behavior on their own community, however, was disruptive. Firstly, relationships between women tourists and locals were resented by local women and provoked tensions between partners" (Pattullo, 1996, pp. 89-90). Pattullo also points out that class differences and the associated behavioral codes can have a dramatic effect on gender relations: "these encounters reverse more conventional gender roles and also confuse race and class roles. Within Caribbean societies, a lower-class male would never be invited by a middle-class woman for a drink in a hotel, but women tourists do not observe (or care about) such prescriptions" (Pattullo, 1996, p. 89). Finally, Momsen also refers to the impact of male sexual behavior: "West Indian men often have many sexual partners and, in the era of AIDS, interaction with tourists contributes to the rapid spread of the disease and to even more unstable relationships for West Indian women" (Momsen, 1994, p. 117).

Sex Tourism and Mobility

As was said earlier, tourism causes internal, employment-related migration. In the Dominican Republic seasonal migrations involve women leaving the rural and inland regions to move to tourist locations to work as prostitutes. The tourism sector stimulates migration in a similar way: "the presence of these industries, products and tourists from the rich Western countries in the Third World has created other images among poor black women: the illusion of a rich white man who takes vacations and enjoys life from home, and who seems to want a relationship with a prostitute whom he promises everything, even the moon" (translated from Peterson, 1989, p. 162).

There is also a link between sex tourism and the international trade in women. A number of authors claim that interest in a particular destination can stem from familiarity with prostitutes that originate from that foreign country. A more important and more embarrassing problem is the trade in women that is encouraged through sex tourism. Women will leave their country with male tourists who promise them a lasting relationship (and even marriage) or work. Upon their arrival, however, these women are forced to work as prostitutes. The German embassy in the Dominican Republic warns that many Dominican women are misled by foreigners who promise to take them to Europe to work as dancers, models, or singers, but who actually want them to work as prostitutes. One person at least is known to recruit girls locally and to inform men in Europe of the "possibilities" in the Dominican Republic with respect to prostitution. Pattullo (1996) also discusses trade in women: "There is also evidence of traffic in prostitutes, notable from the Dominican Republic, to other islands and to Europe, and some participation of organized crime in prostitution networks" (p. 87). Cordero (1986) also links tourism to trade in women:

> It seems to me that international traffic in women originates from a conception which is very racist and imperialist. There is the myth of the sexual power of the Caribbean women who are made available to males from the First World, who cannot afford to buy tickets to the "paradise of the homosexuals and the prostitutes," as one North American travel agency has recently named the Dominican Republic. This is offering the possibility of sexual pleasure much more cheaply to the men at home. (p. 56)

Muroi and Sasaki (1997), therefore, are right saying: "Prostitution spread from the tourist destination countries to tourist origin countries" (p. 212).

Women as the Exotic Other

The interest and fascination for the "authentic" Other has existed for much longer than mass tourism. This interest has existed through the ages but increased dramatically in the 19th century to generate exotism: "The exotic was found in historical regressions into the past, and in a removal (imaginary or otherwise) through space and time to a faraway destination" (De Boeck, 1997, p. 10). That which the Western world thought it had lost was projected onto a faraway, objectivized, "authentic" Other, our ancestor (De Boeck, 1997, p. 10).

Since MacCannell (1973) introduced his theory about the "quest for authenticity," the search for and discovery of authenticity in travel experiences has been a point of discussion in tourism studies. According to MacCannell, modern-day people lead an "empty" life in a "nonauthentic" society. Modern people are worried about the nonauthenticity of their experiences and feel increasingly estranged from, and less involved in, their work, the community, their town, and the family that was once "theirs" (MacCannell, 1976). Modern people wish to fill this emptiness by seeking authenticity and authentic experiences, such as meetings with "authentic" Others while traveling, for example. This quest is said to be a prominent motif in modern tourism. MacCannell's conclusion is not accepted by the majority of researchers; rather, it has helped launch a debate—the authenticity debate—that focuses on finding out what it is that tourists are really looking for (see Cohen, 1979, 1988).

Whatever the case may be, it would seem that, with respect to modern tourists, there is a strong link between the "authentic," the "premodern," the "traditional," and the "exotic." The idea exists that authenticity is somehow stronger in "primitive communities" that have remained untouched by modernity, in an as yet "unspoiled" natural environment. It is in ethnic tourism in particular that tourists seek contact with this exotic Other, want to "take part" in the real life of the "primitives," or at least observe how authentic life is experienced (MacCannell, 1973, p. 594). Tourists want to see "unspoiled natives," not "tourees": "The touree is the native when he begins to interact with the tourist and modify his behavior accordingly. The touree is the native-turned-actor—whether consciously or unconsciously— while the tourist is the spectator" (Van den Berghe & Keyes, 1984, p. 347).

Portrayal of the Other

The tourism sector plays on the desire for exotica and authenticity—and this is certainly the case with respect to the developing countries. In words and images, destinations and local populations are described as pure, untouched, and original. De Boeck (1997) states that: "It is remarkable that the way in which modern Western photographers portray the Other does not deviate much from the exotic, colonial portrayal of the Other in olden days. As such, they manage to preserve the fiction of a primitive mentality" (pp. 11–12). This observation obviously applies to promotional material and postcards used in tourism as well:

> The postcard is a quintessentially touristic consumable, interchangeable as a marker of touristic experience with a beaded souvenir. Many of the images on postcards sold in native communities were also perfect analogues for the ethnologists' reconstructed representations of the past, showing Native Americans dressed in "traditional" dress, archetypically posed in canoes or looking out across an empty landscape. (Philips, 1995, p. 112)

Silver (1993) links tourism literature and publicity to Orientalism. After all, it is not the tourist industry that has created images of the authentic, non-Western Other in travel brochures. Orientalism, the ideological discourse that discusses differences between "West" and "East," has existed for a considerable time and provides the background against which touristic images of the Other can be understood and interpreted.

> Within the context of orientalism, marketed images of indigenous people tend to portray predominantly what Westerners have historically imagined the Other to be like. Although some representations of the Other may be ethnographically accurate, they also exaggerate many of the distinctions that anthropologists have made between industrialized societies and tribal cultures. In an important sense, then, tourist marketing reveals more about what tour operators think of a Western need to experience authentic and primitive natives than about the natives themselves. (Silver, 1993, pp. 303-304)

When reality (and images of reality) fit known markers and stereotypes, this is regarded as proof of authenticity. Authenticity is strongly determined by such stereotypes: "Authenticity is a label attached to the visited cultures in terms of stereotyped images and expectations held by the members of tourist-sending society. . . . Authenticity is thus a projection of tourists' own beliefs, expectations, preferences, stereotyped images, and consciousness onto toured objects, particularly onto toured Others" (Wang, 1999, p. 355).

How is the local population portrayed in tourist brochures and on postcards? It would seem that the local population is portrayed only infrequently in tourist brochures. A study by Dann (1996) shows that 60.1% of all images are of tourists only. Some 24.3% of pictures include no people at all. Only 6.7% portray the local population only, and the remaining 8.9% of pictures show tourists interacting with locals, particularly in a "hotel context," as entertainers or as salesmen. Marshment (1997) distinguishes two categories of tourist publicity in which the local population is portrayed. On the one hand, there are photographs of people in "traditional" costumes. These can be national/regional costumes, formal or festive costumes, or clothing that is worn for traditional dancing. On the other hand, people are often portrayed in their work environment. Here, it is the profession rather than the clothing that represents local culture. Usually, these images are of professions that are regarded as "typical" for that country's culture: tea pickers, fishermen, or monks. There are also pictures of people who work in less typical professions, as potters. Sometimes the local population is portrayed doing tourism-related jobs, such as selling products on the beach or entertaining tourists: "Locals occupying service roles are overwhelmingly waiters (serving drinks more often than food) followed by shopkeepers or market stall-holders selling traditional food or craft products such as carpets and pottery. Finally, there are the entertainers, such as musicians or dancers. Only as dancers, in 'traditional' costume, are women more common than men" (Marshment, 1997, p. 26). On the whole, people are pictured individually or in groups with members of the same gender. With the exception of mother-child tableaus, pictures rarely portray the family life or social life of the local population.

It would seem, therefore, that many scenes from daily life are not portrayed, which again contributes to the image of the authentic, untouched by Western forces, colonialism, nationalism, industrialization, and even tourism itself.

> Tourist marketing seeks not only to present a pastoral myth, but in so doing it also obscures the inherent realities of many tourism destinations. In its effort to foster an appeal for the Third World, the tourism industry markets travel as a form of escape in which host countries must necessarily be viewed

by tourists as devoid of problems. Therefore, advertisements rarely empha-size, or even mention, that most native peoples live amidst wretched pov-erty. (Silver, 1993, pp. 303– 304)

Marshment (1997) claims that there is such a thing as a "gendered" aesthetic:

> The "mystery" of her demure femininity is being employed, not to offer an exotic sexuality to a male spectator, but rather to offer an aestheticized experience of "the other" to an ungendered Western spectator . . . used . . . to connote a geographical and cultural "otherness." To represent the beautiful and to render the "other" as a pleasurable, com-fortable experience. In the context of ethnic "otherness," native women do not signify anything radically different from what is signified by native men, because of the ways in which British culture has constructed both gender and race along parallel oppositions of the "natural" and "emotional" against the "masculine" and "white" norms of civilization and reason. But the aes-thetic, it seems, . . . is still associated with femininity rather than with mas-culinity. In addition, women from even the most exotically different cul-tures may be considered as embodying a less potential threat than might similarly "exotic" men. . . . The ideologies, which associate women with physical beauty and docility, are employed in taming the disturbing poten-tial of the "other" embodied in these images of "primitive" manhood. (Marshment, 1997, p. 26)

So the women portrayed are not portrayed here with an erotic or sexual conno-tation:

> [L]ocal people smiling to the camera. Some of these are photographs of men but the overwhelming majority are young women or girls. Often they wear some kind of "national" costume, and are always beautiful. None, however, are overtly sexual images: they are mostly head-and-shoulder shots of demurely clothed women, with smiles that are reassuring rather than inviting. The po-tential sexuality of the image of a young woman is articulated to offer, not sex itself, but beauty, friendliness and difference. (Marshment, 1997, p. 26)

Silver (1993, pp. 310– 311) points out possible if limited resistance on the part of "natives" with respect to the way tourism regards them. Natives are hardly pas-sive in accepting marketed images about them, but often they have no choice but to present themselves according to the romanticized imagery, as they have little influence on Western travel agents who control the marketing of tourist images.

Reconstructed Ethnicity

Tourists want a glance of "real, authentic life," but usually get to see a "staged authenticity" (MacCannell, 1992), a staged performance or, in the worst case, a diluted version of what was once a cultural custom. In this way, the tourist indus-try creates "traditions" for the consumer. A number of authors claim that such commercialization is destroying the authenticity of local products and of human relationships, given that these products will lose their original meaning for the local population. What was once an "authentic" ritual is now staged and promoted as a product that can be bought. Others doubt this. After all, there are plenty of counterexamples that would seem to prove that the original meaning of cultural customs is not lost as a result of commercialization, but that commercialization in fact assigns new, additional meanings to such customs. Moreover, staging does not lead to a deterioration of the product. Sometimes, the original meaning of customs is lost over time and only rediscovered as a result of the fact that tourists become interested in it (Cohen, 1988). The local population is not a passive victim of the commercialization of their traditions either. They are actors that construct new meanings and new identities. MacCannell (1984) speaks of reconstructed ethnicity in this respect. "The term reconstructed ethnicity is used here to refer to those kinds of ethnic identities which have emerged in response to pressures from tourism" (MacCannell, 1984, p. 377).

Crain (1996) demonstrates how women in Quito (Ecuador) play the game and develop strategies to exploit interest in their culture.

> This analysis illuminates native women's calculated enactment of their identities in a manner which resonated with dominant stereotypes regarding "Indianness" circulating in metropolitan Quito. . . . The agency of native women, who, while drawn into unequal relations not of their own choosing, were not passive subjects but actively reshaped hierarchical relations to their advantage. They accomplished this via a self-conscious representation of their gender and ethnic identities in the urban setting, a new self-fashioning designed to win them favors and extend their employment opportunities in the urban marketplace. (Crain, 1996, p. 126)

These women are well aware of the image tourists (and well-to-do locals) have of the indigenous and manipulate them accordingly. Crain refers to this mechanism as "reversed orientalism."

Crain's case study undermines MacCannell's hypotheses regarding the fact that the impact of the ethnic identity of the local population is less dramatic in institutionalized tourism and in commercial settings. Encroachment on the local identity is more probable when tourists try to meet the Other in an "authentic" setting on their own initiative (MacCannell, 1984). In Quito, the women learned from "service encounters" in institutionalized tourism to realize their importance as an ethnic group. Eventually, they learned to play with it, reconstructing a new ethnicity.

> Reconstructed Ethnicity is fully dependent on the earlier stages in the construction of ethnicity. But it represents an end to the dialogue, a final freezing of ethnic imagery which is both artificial and deterministic. The new reconstructed ethnic forms are produced once almost all the groups in the world are located in a global network of interactions and they begin to use their former colorful ways both as commodities to be bought and sold, and as rhetorical weaponry in their dealing with one another, suddenly, it is not just ethnicity anymore, but it is understood as rhetoric, as symbolic expression with a purpose of a use-value in a larger system. (MacCannell, 1984, p. 385)

MacCannell (1984) describes the negative effects of a reconstructed identity for the local population in terms of the internalization of the "authentic" ethnic identity as created for tourist requirements. This internalization of the role of a living tourist attraction may affect every detail of local life.

Summary

Gender, seen as "a system of culturally constructed identities, expressed in ideologies of masculinity and femininity, interacting with socially structured relationships in divisions of labor and leisure, sexuality, and power between women and men" (Swain, 1995, pp. 258–259), is an often ignored dimension in tourism studies. This is the case with respect to studying the Latin American countries and the Caribbean. With respect to employment opportunities for women, tourism does not differ from other economic sectors. Some sectors are clearly oriented towards female employees, at the bottom of the hierarchical ladder of status and income. Such work is usually an extension of care tasks in the household. Nevertheless, the work and the income it generates can cause a number of gender patterns to be broken, as the study of Mexico has shown. Although participation in small-scale projects is often more actively encouraged, its impact seems to be smaller than expected. Above all, women are invisible. However, this observation cannot be generalized to all situations. It is the small-scale accommodation sector in particular that seems to afford women the room to maneuver into a better social position. Nevertheless, it seems that employment in the tourist industry in itself does not necessarily change traditions and accepted gender roles and relations, certainly not outside of the household.

The case study on Colombia demonstrated the importance of taking into account gender and socioeconomic aspects. *Finca* tourism extends the domestic tasks of women in different positions on the social ladder. Social class to a large extent determines the way tasks are divided between women who work in tourism.

It cannot be ignored that "cultural identities and social relations between men and women" (Swain, 1995, p. 247), when considering different types of sex tourism, for the purpose of which women are portrayed as the "erotic" Other. An interesting research topic in this respect is the local woman and her reaction to relationships between local men and tourists: How does this influence her sexuality, identity, and chances of marriage? What view of authenticity do women evoke? How do men and women deal with the commercialization of their culture and which gender-related differences distinguish them? Do men and women create a different reconstructed identity? These are just some of the questions that can be asked with respect to the exotic Other.

In order to better understand and explain gender-bound roles in Latin America and the Caribbean, an in-depth analysis has to be conducted of different cultural elements, such as religion (e.g., the importance of virginity in many Catholic countries), machismo, the "live today" attitude, the ideology of *hombre de la calle*, *mujer de la casa*, and the importance of the family (and, in contrast, the *madresolterisme*, i.e., unwed motherhood, and families headed by women). In addition, specific cultural contexts need to be distinguished, because the different Latin American and Caribbean countries cannot be regarded in the same light. The examples of different local communities involved in tourism as provided in this chapter illustrate the earlier made point that the participation of women in tourism—as provider of services and images—is of great significance for the way tourist products are constructed. More research is necessary to explore the ways in which women shape and are shaped by tourism.

Chapter 10

Future Prospects and Perspectives of Latin American and Caribbean Tourism Policies

Lou Keune and Heidi Dahles

Tourism is an important growth sector in Latin America and the Caribbean. In numbers of tourists, the growth of this sector in this region is even above world average. Although average expenditure by these tourists lags behind world average, the total amount of expenditure has risen sharply. It is certain that this growth will continue for the time being, probably at an even faster rate; witness the sharp increase in tourism needs in OECD countries and in rapidly developing countries such as China. It is to be noted, however, that, for the time being, tourism is concentrated in a few countries and regions, particularly Mexico, the Caribbean, and some South American countries—especially Argentina. Some countries, such as Costa Rica, are clearly catching up. It is also a fact that tourism is increasing, at least gradually, in most countries of the region.

The Need for Development

These opportunities for growth are warmly welcomed in the region. As will have become clear from Chapter 2, the countries in Latin America and the Caribbean are still characterized by an average level of human development that is clearly lower than the levels in the OECD countries. And within the region, even within countries, there are great differences. Some countries or sections of the population approach or even surpass the average level of, for example, the United States, while others are close to the level of the least developed countries. The social inequalities are making themselves felt in many different areas; for example, property and profession, town and countryside, gender and ethnicity. In general, there is an enormous need for income and employment, and the region is characterized by a structural balance of trade and balance of payment deficits. Moreover, there are serious ecological problems, so serious that in some instances the survival of large sections of the population and the continued existence of nature are fundamentally threatened. No wonder that, from the point of view of human development, tourism is highly valued, because it is expected that domestic currency, employment (both directly in the tourism industry and indirectly in sectors such as food supply, transportation, and other necessities), and total income will be improved structurally and that social inequalities can be lessened. Additionally, some people presume that tourism can have an emancipatory function, for example, through the demonstration effect, which, from the point of view of class, gender, and ethnicity, may be of invaluable importance (see Chapter 9). Finally, some people even presume that tourism can contribute not only to the preservation of nature, but also to combating the damage already done to the environment and to taking measures aimed at preventing such damage (see Chapter 4). Such a contribution would have to stem from, first, an overall improvement of the economy, which would result in more means being available for these aims. Second, tourist visits to certain natural areas could generate direct income; for example, by charging admission fees or by special levies on other local expenditure by tourists, such as lodgings.

This positive outlook on the possible contribution tourism can make to human and environmental development is not only founded on tourists' needs, which have mushroomed worldwide. As all contributions in this book show, Latin America and the Caribbean also have something to offer to these tourists. The best known, of course, is the wealth of opportunities the region offers to tourists looking for rest and relaxation in the setting of a sunny climate, beautiful scenery, and wonderful beaches. In addition, the region offers many potential and real opportunities in many other areas. It still boasts many superb areas of natural beauty, an increasing number of which are being protected. Besides, there is a variety of cultural hot spots, such as fine ancient cities with wonderful architecture and museums, and linguistic, musical, and other attractions. Many archaeological monuments are scattered over the entire region. But there are also many possibilities for meeting other cultures, such as the culturally interesting Indian peoples. Highly specific attractions are also developing, such as the so-called "romance" tourism, political tourism, and drugs (see Chapters 5 and 9). In sum, Latin America and the Caribbean have much to offer modern tourists with all their varied needs and interests.

Two main categories of tourism have been developing. The first and biggest of these is mass tourism, which is focusing on specific locations offering rest, comfort, consumption, and relaxation. The second is alternative tourism, which is varied and small scale, and characterized by tourists taking private initiative (and even looking for adventure). This latter kind of tourism is becoming increasingly popular (see Chapters 3 and 4), not only because some segments of mass tourism are reaching saturation point, but also because new tourists are arriving who are interested in the alternative attractions. It is this kind of tourism that is also linked to what is called sustainable tourism, which aims to protect and develop the existing human, environmental, natural, and cultural elements. It is assumed that this type of tourism also offers more opportunities for the participation of the local population in the development and the profits of tourism (such as employment and income).

Impact on the Environment

In terms of the way in which tourism is currently developing, however, there are some significant drawbacks that raise the question whether tourism causes more problems than it solves. The most important ones here concern nature and the environment. Disregarding the environmental impact of international air traffic, the direct impact on the environment in the region itself will be the focus here, of which Chapters 3 and 4 give several examples. First, there is the major issue of waste disposal. In fact, waste that is predominantly produced by mass tourism is disposed of in nature on a large scale, particularly in rivers and the sea. The Caribbean has many examples of this, but also in and around nature reserves, this problem is acquiring dimensions that are absolutely unacceptable. Unfortunately, Latin America and the Caribbean are not regions that either take an interest in or have structural arrangements for waste disposal. Second, tourism is often of a kind that causes immediate damage, such as damage to mangrove forests by pleasure crafts, hunting in nature reserves, or the sacrifice of nature reserves to the infrastructure, such as airfields, roads, harbors, and large hotel facilities. There are even examples of tourism, referred to as "ecotourism," which in actual fact entail an increasing exploitation of nature. Chapter 3, therefore, raises the question whether ecotourism should be preferred to mass tourism at all. As mass tourism allows far-going measures of concentration and control, Chapter 3 suggests that mass-related resort development in many instances deserves preference against ecotourism, which implies small-scale and dispersed, and therefore difficult to control and regulate, forms of tourism developments.

Economic Effects

In economic terms, the relevance of tourism can be questioned. Tourism may be at the expense of other kinds of production (see, for example, Chapter 3); for instance, agricultural land that is used for tourism facilities. This issue is particularly poignant where, because of tourism, the price of land is pushed to a level that is way beyond the means of other producers like farmers and craftsmen. In a wider sense, this is the problem of the possible inflationary effects of tourism: it stimulates price rises, including those of basic necessities. These effects are getting stronger as tourist facilities make greater demands on the land. Drinking water may become scarce (because groundwater levels drop, demand increases, or available water supplies are more easily accessible to the tourist sector as it has the facilities or is given preferential treatment). In such a situation, local agriculture and forestry may suffer badly. And it is a moot point whether the labor force, whose conditions of existence are threatened, will be able to find new employment in the tourism sector.

Employment

In general, tourism does indeed generate new employment. Examples of new enterprises and jobs emerging with increasing numbers of tourism in local communities can be found in the case studies on Costa Rica (Chapter 5), El Salvador (Chapter 6), Belize (Chapter 7), and Ecuador (Chapter 8). Chapter 9 shows that quite a number of women, in particular, find conditions of employment in tourism that often are better than those in the traditional sectors. Employment in sectors adjacent to tourism, such as food supply, transportation, and nature conservation, may also receive extra impetus. However, the importance of tourism should certainly not be overestimated, not only because tourism displaces employment in other sectors, as was shown above, but also because in practice many jobs are held not by locals but by outsiders, even by foreigners. Several chapters point this out. Local people usually only have limited career perspectives. This phenomenon is manifest not only in mass tourism, but also in alternative tourism, where foreigners sometimes hold the most important positions. This phenomenon is partly due to the lack of well-educated and experienced staff. In addition (see Chapters 5 and 7), foreigners have easier access to international networks that draw in tourists. A cultural element may also play a role here: many tourists find it easier to trust and/or communicate with staff with the same cultural background. All this is not to deny, however, that tourism can boost local employment considerably.

Income

Chapter 2 indicates that quite a number of studies report very limited effects of tourism on income. This is mainly due to the problem of leakage: a large, if not the largest, share of tourist expenditure flows to nonlocals is drained away abroad. To start with, there are the costs of international transportation and of the tour operators. Next, many of the inputs that are needed in the tourism sector (such as investments and consumables) have to be imported. Also, large shares of local expenditure may disappear to foreign countries; for example, in payment of interest on loans, transfer of profit, and salaries of foreign personnel. All this is not to deny that tourism, in theory and in practice, may contribute considerably to improving local income. Various studies confirm this point. In theory, tourism could thus also contribute to diminishing income inequalities. However, there are few indications that this is in fact the case, one of the reasons being that in the new tourism sectors property and power relations are created that, almost by tradition, cause inequality in Latin America and the Caribbean.

External Dependency

A third economic aspect concerns external dependency as a result of tourism. In general, this sector is also dominated by big international enterprises (Chapter 2). In this sense, local communities remain strongly dependent on the strategic interests of such enterprises. This may lead to, for example, considerable limitations to the possibilities of local and national governments to develop their own policies, not to mention the fact that it is impossible for the local population to participate fully. In addition, these countries are becoming increasingly dependent on the developments on the world tourism market, as regards both the possibilities for expenditure in the tourists' countries of origin and the, at times, fast-changing preferences of these tourists. For the time being, this is a genuine growth market, which means that in the short term sales potential will increase. In the medium and long term, however, problems of a cyclical nature may arise. The so-called Asia crisis of 1997, for example, clearly slowed down the growth of international tourism for a short time. Such possible negative aspects can be felt more strongly in two situations: where tourism is such a dominating sector that it resembles a monoculture; when tourism primarily originates from one country (so-called relational dependence). Both situations apply, for example, to the Caribbean, where a small ripple on the tourist demand side (e.g., fear of violence) may have considerable consequences regarding income on the supply side. All these potential economic drawbacks will, generally, be more manifest in small countries or societies than in large countries.

Gender

As Chapter 9 shows, tourism may have a positive influence on the position of women. Examples are the sharply increasing demand for female personnel in mass tourism, the production and sale of souvenirs, and the activities of particularly women in alternative tourism (such as the management of lodgings and the sale of food). The potentially emancipatory effect of tourism has already been pointed out. However, there are drawbacks as well. It appears, for example, that, in its promotional campaigns, the tourism industry uses constructions of women's images that not only are unrealistic, but also harm the position and self-respect of women. This risk is even greater if women's images are eroticized: prostitution and the trade in women go hand in hand with the expansion of tourism. In those images, there may also be instances of ethnification that harm women's self-images; for example, by laying too much emphasis on traditional costumes and women's professions that are representative of only a small part of the female population.

Ethnification

In general, ethnification may constitute a big problem, for both women and men (see Chapters 3, 5, 7, and 8). This not only presents itself in cases where particular ethnical images are used in publicity campaigns. The tourist may reduce the inhabitants of certain regions to objects, for example, of surprise and, as a result of feelings of superiority, contempt. There are also many instances of tourist behavior showing the tourist's lack of understanding of the local community and an attitude to life (e.g., as regards consumerism and sexuality, and through drunkenness and noisiness) that goes against the culture of the local community and has disruptive effects. Another problem may be that tourism is accompanied by certain types of ethnic discrimination; for example, when certain native groups carry the burden of tourism but have no share in the profits thereof or are even confronted with deteriorating means of existence (such as traditional agriculture and hunting). However, there are also instances of the reverse.

Foreign Assistance

In theory, there are ample opportunities for Latin America and the Caribbean to take advantage of the fast-growing tourism world market. It may be clear, however, that leaving this market to laissez-faire–laissez-aller powers entails great risks. First, this world market has too little contact with the many potential tourist attractions in the region. Second, the risk is great that the potential drawbacks of tourism surpass the potential profits. Various strategic questions arise that need to be answered. One of these questions is whether there is a willingness to improve the sales potential in a responsible manner. In quite a few situations, the tourism sector cannot be developed without financial, technical (e.g., in the field of education), and structural assistance from abroad.

Sustainable Tourism

A second strategic question concerns the need for sustainable tourism. As may be clear from Chapter 6, the question of sustainability forces itself to the fore not only with respect to ecology, but also with respect to other dimensions (e.g., the economy, type of society, gender, ethnicity, and culture). Particularly, mass tourism entails great damage to ecology. However, the question is whether it is all that sensible to defend alternative tourism. As Chapters 3, 4, 5, and 8 have shown, there are undoubtedly huge problems attached to mass tourism. But there are also drawbacks to alternative tourism, even to the type of alternative tourism that is presented under the banner of ecotourism, for not all ecotourism deserves that label. Moreover, it is increasingly difficult to check abuse in the fast-growing number of places where small-scale tourism takes place. And even in alternative tourism, numbers are growing. In Costa Rica, for example, it appears to be very difficult, if not impossible, to set limits to the numbers of visitors to nature reserves. The plea for paying more attention to mass tourism (Chapter 3) is of major importance, not only because alternative tourism will not be able to deal with the expected increase in numbers of tourists, but also because in the mass tourism locations there are more opportunities for sustainable development, in particular as far as the use of materials or waste disposal are concerned.

The Role of Governments

Of great strategic importance is the answer to the question whether governments—at the local, national, and international levels—should play a bigger role in the field of tourism. A negative answer forces itself upon us, because Latin America and the Caribbean in particular have seen many instances of bad governance—or at least of the absence of good governance. In such situations, a stronger role of governments may intensify the drawbacks of tourism. It cannot be denied, however, that leaving the sector to the mercy of the powers of the "free" market could turn out to be irresponsible. From all the chapters in this book it is evident that governments are badly needed—governments that are active not only in developing sound conditions for the expansion of tourism sales potential, but also in embedding that sector in conditions and interests that offer guarantees for sustainable development in the broadest sense of the word.

The Issue of Local Participation and the Role of the Community

At the local level participation in tourism developments in closely related to power relations within the community and between communities. Unequal distribution of power and uneven flows of information can maneuver members of the community, even whole communities, in a disadvantaged position, when decisions are taken about tourism developments or initiatives are taken to establish tourism-related businesses. In the most extreme cases, like in the Guanacaste area in Costa Rica as mentioned in Chapter 4, state power is used to further the interest of developers to the detriment of ecotourism projects, stifling environment-friendly and grass-roots approaches to development. Here, tourism policies favor external over local interests and, in the process, jeopardize the "green" reputation of the country as a whole. Involving the community and allowing its members to make informed decisions about the course of tourism development requires access to appropriate information within that community. As Richards and Hall (2000c) point out: "The flow of information is crucial, since the concept of bottom-up development presupposes that all sections of the community are adequately informed about the nature and consequences of tourism development. This is also necessary for the sustainable tourism development of future generations" (p. 299).

Long-standing participation in regional and even international trade networks offers advantages for communities to acquire information about changing markets, trends, and tastes. Such skills prove to be of great value when a community enters the tourist market, as is shown for the case of Otavalo in Ecuador, which has become the center of folkloric tourism in Ecuador, and through the export of its textiles and people has come to represent South American culture worldwide. This case contrasts with another Ecuadorian community, Misahuallí in the Amazon rainforest, which lacks the experience to operate in an international market and to understand the fluctuations and dynamics of tourism. The members of this community are controlled by the whims of this volatile sector instead of controlling it themselves. Confronted with the disadvantages of tourism participation they are reluctant to take an active stance towards tourism developments; instead, they largely reject it.

Within communities access to relevant information and skills to apply this information to the benefit of local business initiatives are unequally distributed in terms of differences of class, gender, and ethnicity. Generally, the business of tourism consists predominantly of small and medium enterprises. At a community level small-scale entrepreneurs form an important element in the local economy, as most of the case studies in this volume have shown. The role of entrepreneurs in terms of risk-taking and innovative impulses for the creation of new products is of crucial importance. This innovative impact of small-scale local entrepreneurship is illustrated in the case studies in this volume in various ways: in the accommodation sector (*cabinas* and ecolodges in Costa Rica, *finca* tourism in Colombia, agrotourism in El Salvador among cashew-growing farmers); in souvenir production (like Otavalo textiles); in attraction-building processes (like boat tours organized by a Belizean guide, jungle tours in the rainforest of Costa Rica and the Ecuadorian Amazon area, or the enticement offered by reggae, drugs, and rastamen in the Caribbean); in the restaurant sector (like the establishment of traveler restaurants in Cahuita, Costa Rica, and San Ignacio, Belize, which offer not only tourist menus but also information about local attractions and Internet access).

In contrast to popular wisdom, it is not only the large-scale resort tourism that is dominated by foreign investors. Strikingly, the most successful local entrepreneurs turn out to be foreigners in the communities studied by the contributors to this volume. Some of these foreigners stayed after decolonization (Belize), others came and hung on with the wave of hippie travelers that were looking for "alternative" destinations in the 1970s (the Caribbean coast of Costa Rica and other Caribbean areas), and again others kept on coming back after a first visit and eventually settled down (like Western women getting married to local men as reported from Costa Rica). The predominance of foreigners, in particular Westerners, in local tourism-related business life is closely related to their advantage in accessing and processing relevant information about the tourism market; or as Chapter 7 illustrates, to the composition and volume of their "capital." Compared with the native locals, foreigners possess more economic capital (money), social capital (networks connecting them to their country of origin and related sources of information and market data), and cultural capital (proficiency in languages, which is a crucial advantage in the tourism business, general knowledge of the tourism market, and the tastes of Western tourists). However, in contrast to the foreign investors in the large-scale, mass tourist resorts, "local" foreigners do contribute to the community's economy, because their life is intertwined with community life. They themselves have become "locals," although distinguished from others by their origin and ethnicity (as illustrated that they are classified as foreigners by the local community even after decades of living and working in a community). They generate income and employment, and they also consume and reinvest their income in the local community. Basically, the foreigners' economic activities turn out to be very beneficial to the local community. On the downside, however, the foreigners' economic successes may arouse jealousy, social tensions (as in Cahuita, Costa Rica, where the expansion of foreigners' small-scale accommodations into hotels is strongly objected to by other locals, as is shown in Chapter 5), and even conflict that escalates into physical violence (as in San Ignacio, Belize, where the competition between a foreign and a local entrepreneur generated life-threatening assaults on both sides as described in Chapter 7).

The predominance of foreign actors in local tourism development raises the question of how to stimulate a more equal participation in tourism development at the community level. Obviously, financial subsidies alone are insufficient to guarantee involvement of all actors in the community, particularly when flows of social and cultural "capital" are uneven. In this respect, the national governments could play a significant role in facilitating structural support in terms of (tourism) education, credit facilities, and other producer services required by local small-scale businesses. In the case of Latin American countries, the failure of governments to either adequately facilitate local tourism developments (e.g., Costa Rica, Cuba) or view community-based tourism as an economic sector of any importance at all (e.g., Belize, El Salvador, Ecuador, Jamaica) represents a serious obstacle in the realization of more sustainable forms of tourism. One potential solution to problems of participation and empowerment may be the intervention of the so-called "third sector": NGOs, local associations, and community groups. This third sector may compensate some of the structural deficiencies that local communities possess vis-à-vis the global tourism market. It has contacts with national and international funding agencies, possesses networks that extend far beyond national boundaries, and provides access to sources of knowledge that may redress some of the power imbalances that hamper local participation in tourism developments. The feasibility study in a yet touristically undeveloped area in El Salvador (Chapter 6) offers solutions to the problem of community participation in tourism planning. From the vantage point of NGO involvement in initiating sustainable forms of tourism, a number of scenarios are designed in Chapter 6 for the local community to explore. These scenarios include options for "no tourism development" as well as "mass tourist development." It is the community that should decide which path to take. This approach encourages a wide range of participants in decision-making processes representing all relevant stakeholders in the community. The decision-making process within the community will be supported by information about tourism provided by an NGO. This approach empowers local communities in the sense that it enables them to take their fate into their own hands. After all, as Chapter 8 illustrates, one possible outcome of local participation in tourism developments is almost never considered by tourism researchers and planners; that is, the decision not to develop any tourism at all. In some cases, however, this very decision may be the only sustainable option for a local community.

Contributors

Carin de Bont studied Management at a Technical College in Eindhoven. Although fascinated with technique, she was also interested in tourism. After graduation, she enrolled in Leisure Studies at Tilburg University. She graduated in 1997 and has worked as a system engineer ever since.

Maryse Brouwer went to the United States after high school as part of an exchange program. She studied Leisure Studies at Tilburg University, where she graduated in 1996. For her graduation project she conducted fieldwork in San Carlos Lempa, El Salvador, which resulted in a feasibility study for a small-scale sustainable tourism project. At present, she works in El Salvador for a development organization with the purpose of introducing sustainable tourism projects in two different regions of the country.

Heidi Dahles received her Ph.D. in Cultural Anthropology from the University of Nijmegen, the Netherlands. She worked in the field of tourism and leisure studies at Tilburg University and was affiliated as a senior fellow at the International Institute for Asian Studies in 1998. At present she is associate professor in the Department of Organizational Anthropology, Vrije Universiteit Amsterdam. She is a member of the editorial board of *Pacific Tourism Review, The Journal of Sustainable Tourism*, and *Tourism Studies*. Her current research interests include business culture in Southeast Asia.

Bea Groen is a social geographer and planner. She did research on the use of alternative energies in developing countries; wrote for different magazines on the theme of women and development; worked for engineering companies on the design of offices; traveled extensively in Central America and camped in the Costarican jungle. Currently she works as a marketeer at Networkconsultants and as a freelance writer.

Wendy Janssen graduated from the Department of leisure Studies at Tilburg University in 1997. Since her graduation she has worked as a consultant at ANWB (the Dutch Traffic Association) and as a lecturer of recreation marketing.

Lou Keune earned his master's degree in Economics in 1961 and his Ph.D. in Social Sciences in 1969. He participated in a large number of research, educational, and development projects in Latin America and the Netherlands. He published about community development in Colombia, development education in Europe, development assistance, the decline of the textile industry in Tilburg, action research, popular movements in Central America, traditional seed production systems in Central America, survival strategies during the civil war in El Salvador, and production of bananas in Costa Rica. He is currently working at the Faculty of Social Sciences, Tilburg University, the Netherlands.

Jan Philipsen studied Geography at the Catholic University of Nijmegen and has worked at the Department of Environmental Sciences of Wageningen University since 1987. Currently he develops and conducts research programs in the field of sustainable planning and management of recreation and tourism in natural environments and acts as a senior lecturer in (inter)national training programs in the field of leisure and tourism management in the Department of Spatial Analysis and Recreation & Tourism of Wagingen University.

Jorinde Sorée studied Cultural Anthropology at the University of Amsterdam. She graduated in 1998. Currently she is working as a researcher for and producer of documentaries.

Anne-Marie Van Broeck holds a Ph.D. in Anthropology. She currently lives in Cozumel (Mexico), where she teaches tourism at the Universidad de Quintana Roo. Prior to this position, she taught Anthropology at the Universidad de Antioquia (Medellin, Colombia), and in the School of Tourism Business Administration of the Colegio Mayor de Antioquia. She is an executive member of the commission for Anthropology of Tourism of IUAES (International Union of Anthropological and Ethnological Sciences) and member of the editorial committee of *Estudios y Perspectivas de Turismo* and of *Annals of Tourism Research* en Español.

René van der Duim studied Tourism at the Netherlands Institute of Tourism and Transport Studies in Breda and Sociology at the University of Tilburg. He was a lecturer in Tourism and Leisure Studies in Breda and worked nine years as a staff member of the Association for Outdoor Recreation. Since 1991 he has been a lecturer/researcher at Wageningen University, Department of Spatial Analysis and Recreation & Tourism. Current research projects focus on sustainable tourism in Costa Rica and Kenya.

Anne Marie van Schaardenburgh graduated from Tilburg University in 1996, where she was a project assistant for developing research and courses on "Third World Tourism." Since her graduation she has been involved in several projects in the field of leisure and tourism.

Suzette Volker studied Cultural Anthropology at the University of Amsterdam, where she graduated in 1998. Since her graduation she has been working as a photographer.

Jan Vugts graduated in Development Economics from Tilburg University in 1996. His thesis focused on the "unsustainability of the banana production in Costa Rica." After graduation he was coordinator of the interurban cooperation between the towns of Tilburg and Matagalpa (SSTN) (1996-1998). Currently he is the president of this cooperation. He is also involved in a number of freelance activities in the field of development cooperation. Recently he joined the North–South Federation as a part-time staff member. He published extensively on Central American developmental issues.

Bibliography

Abbott Cone, C. (1995). Crafting selves: The lives of two Mayan women. *Annals of Tourism Research, 22*(2), 314-327.

Antrobus, P. (1990). *Gender issues in tourism.* Paper presented to the CTRC. Conference on tourism and socio-cultural change in the Caribbean, June 25-28.

Archer, B., & Cooper, Ch. (1994). The positive and negative impacts of tourism. In W. Theobald (Ed.), *Global tourism. The next decade* (pp. 73-91). Oxford: Butterworth-Heinemann.

Baez, A. L. (1996). Learning from the experience in the Monteverde Cloud Forest, Costa Rica. In M. F. Price (Ed.), *People and tourism in fragile environments* (pp. 109-122). Chichester, England: Wiley.

Baillie, J. G. (1980). Recent international travel trends in Canada. *Canadian Geographer, 24*(1), 13-21.

Baldwin, J. (1997). Textual conflict in the mobile American racial gaze: Geographies of resistance to servitude within tourist space in Antigua, West Indies. In *Gender/Tourism/Fun? Proceedings of the International Conference* (pp. 212-236). University of California, Davis, October 24-26.

Barker, D., & Miller, D. (1995). Farming on the fringe: Small-scale agriculture on the edge of the Cockpit Country. In D. Barker & F. M. McGregor (Eds.), *Environment and development in the Caribbean* (pp. 271-292). University of the West Indies, Jamaica: The Press.

Belize Tourism Board. (1995). *Belize tourism statistics.* Belize City: Author.

Bermudez, F. (1995). Lecture at the Second Ecolodge Forum and Field Seminar, Ecotourism Society, October 22-29, Puntarenas, Costa Rica.

Bien, A. (1995). Lecture at the Second Ecolodge Forum and Field Seminar, Ecotourism Society, October 22-29, Puntarenas, Costa Rica.

Blanco, S., & Lipperts, M. (1995). *Groen Goud? De rol van de lokale bevolking binnen toerisme in Manuel Antonio en Quepos.* Unpublished M.A. thesis, Wageningen Agricultural University.

Boissevain, J. F. (1974). *Friends of friends. Networks, manipulators and coalitions.* Oxford: Blackwell.

Boo, E. (1990). *Ecotourism: The potentials and pitfalls.* Washington, DC: World Wildlife Fund.

Bourdieu, P. (1977). *Outline of a theory of practice.* Cambridge: Cambridge University Press.

Bramwell, W., Henry, I., Jackson, G., Prat, A., Richards, G., & van der Straaten, J. (1998). *Sustainable tourism management: Principles and practice* (2nd ed.). Tilburg: Tilburg University Press.

Breathnach, P., Henry, M., Drea, S., & O'Flaherty, M. (1994). Gender in Irish tourism employment. In V. Kinnaird & D. Hall (Eds.), *Tourism: A gender analysis* (pp. 52-73). Chichester, England: Wiley.

Britton, S. (1989). Tourism, dependency and development. A mode of analysis. In S. Tej Vir, H. L. Theuns, & F. M. Go (Eds.), *Towards appropriate tourism: The case of developing countries* (pp. 93-116). Frankfurt: Peter Lang Verlag.

Brohman, J. (1996). New directions in tourism for Third World development. *Annals of*

Tourism Research, 23(1), 50-70.

Brouwer, M. (1996). *"Para Salir Adelante," een onderzoek naar de haalbaarheid van duurzame toeristische ontwikkeling in de sector San Carlos Lempa, El Salvador.* Unpublished MA thesis, Tilburg University.

Buckley, R. (1994). A framework for ecotourism [Research Note]. *Annals of Tourism Research, 21*(3), 661-669.

Butler, R. W. (1991). Tourism, environment and sustainable development. *Environmental Conservation, 18*(3), 201-209.

Butler, R., & Hinch, T. (Eds.). (1996). *Tourism and indigenous peoples.* London: International Thomson Press.

Caalders, J. (1997). Managing the transition from agriculture to tourism: Analysis of tourism networks in Auvergne. *Managing Leisure, 1*(1), 127-142.

Caalders, J., & Philipsen, J. (1998). Innovatie in toerisme: naar een strategie voor tijd-ruimte specifieke ontwikkeling. *Vrijetijdstudies, 16*(4), 29-147.

Caalders, J., van der Duim, V. R., van der Boon, G., & Quesada Rivel, H. (1999). *Tourism and biodiversity. Impacts and perpsectives on interventions in the Netherlands and Costa Rica.* Wageningen: Bureau Buiten, Wageningen University.

Cabble I Rivera, A. (1997). Some comments on starting to conceptualize farm tourism activity using feminist theories. In *Gender/Tourism/Fun? Proceedings of the International Conference* (pp. 19-29). University of California, Davis, October 24-26.

Canoves, G. (1997). The multi-adaptive rural women: Is tourism the solution? In *Gender/Tourism/Fun? Proceedings of the International Conference* (pp. 31-41). University of California, Davis, October 24-26.

Carley, R. (1998). *Kuba. Architektur aus vier Jahrhunderten.* Leipzig: Seemann.

Carrière, J. (1991). The crisis in Costa Rica. In D. Goodman & M. Redclift (Eds.), *Environment and development in Latin America. The politics of sustainability* (pp. 191-204). Manchester: Manchester University Press.

Cassirer, B. (1992). *Travel & the single male.* Channel Island, CA: TSM Publishing.

Castelberg-Kouma, M. (1991). Greek women and tourism. Women's co-operatives as an alternative form of organization. In N. Redclift & M. T. Sinclair (Eds.), *Working women. International perspectives on labour and gender ideology* (pp. 197-212). London: Routledge.

Cater, E. (1995). Environmental contradictions in sustainable tourism. *The Geographic Journal, 161*(1), 21-28.

Central Intelligence Agency. (1998). *The world factbook 1997.* Washington, DC: Author..

Central Intelligence Agency. (2001). *The world factbook 2000.* Washington, DC: Author.

Central Statistical Office. (1995). *Abstracts of statistics—1995.* Belmopan: Ministry of Economic Development.

Cernea, M. (1991). *Putting people first: Sociological variables in rural development* (2nd ed.). New York: Oxford University Press.

Chamberlain, F. (1995). Lecture at the Second Ecolodge Forum and Field Seminar, Ecotourism Society, Puntarenas, Costa Rica, October 22-29.

Chant, S. (1992). Tourism in Latin America: Perspectives from Mexico and Costa Rica. In D. Harrison (Ed.), *Tourism and the less developed countries* (pp. 85-101). Chichester, England: Wiley.

Chant, S. (1997). Gender and tourism employment in Mexico and the Philippines. In M. T. Sinclair (Ed.), *Gender, work and tourism* (pp. 120-179). London: Routledge.

Clift, S. (1994). Romance and sex on holidays abroad. A study of magazine representations. *Travel, Lifestyles and Health* (Working paper, No 4). Canterbury: Christ Church College.

Cohen, E. (1979). A phenomenology of tourist experiences. *Sociology, 1*, 179-201.

Cohen, E. (1988). Authenticity and commoditization in tourism. *Annals of Tourism Research, 15*(3), 371-386.

Cordero, M. (1986). Women and tourism in the Dominican Republic. In *Third world people and tourism. Approaches to a dialogue* (pp. 52-57). Germany: Ecumenical Coalition on Third World Tourism (ECTWT).

CORSATUR. (1997). *Estadisticas turisticas de El Salvador 1997*. Division de planificacion, borrador.

Crain, M. M. (1996). Negotiating identities in Quito's cultural borderlands. Native women's performance for the Ecuadorean tourist market. In D. Howes (Ed.), *Cross-cultural consumption. Global markets, local realities* (pp. 125-137). London: Routledge.

Cramer, M., & van Lierop, M. (1995). *Round the world in five experiences, motives of tourists in Monteverde and Manuel Antonio, Costa Rica*. Unpublished M.A. thesis, Wageningen Agricultural University.

Cukier, J. (1996). Tourism employment in Bali: Trends and implications. In R. Butler & T. Hinch (Eds.), *Tourism and indigenous peoples* (pp. 49-75). London: International Thomson Press.

Dagenais, H. (1993). Women in Guadeloupe: The paradoxes of reality. In J. Momsen (Ed.), *Women and change in the Caribbean; a pan-Caribbean perspective* (pp. 83-108). London: James Currey.

Dahles, H. (1997). The new gigolo. Globalization, tourism and changing gender identities. *Focaal. Tijdschrift voor Antropologie, 30/31*, 121-137.

Dahles, H. (1998). Tourism, government policy and petty entrepreneurs in Indonesia. *South East Asia Research, 6*(1), 73-98.

Dahles, H. (1999). Tourism and small entrepreneurs in developing countries: A theoretical perspective. In H. Dahles & K. Bras (Eds.), *Tourism and small entrepreneurs. Development, national policy and entrepreneurial culture: Indonesian cases* (pp. 1-19). New York: Cognizant Communication Corporation.

Dahles, H., & Bras, K. (Eds.). (1999). *Tourism and small entrepreneurs. Development, national policy and entrepreneurial culture: Indonesian cases*. New York: Cognizant Communication Corporation.

Dahles, H., & van der Duim, R. (Eds.). (1994). Themanummer, casestudies in het toerisme [Special issue]. *Vrijetijd en Samenleving, 1/2*.

Dahles, H., & Van Meijl, T. (Eds.). (2001). Local perspectives on global tourism in Southeast Asia and the Pacific region. *Pacific Tourism Review, 4*(2/3), 53-148.

Dann, G. (1996). The people of tourist brochures. In T. Selwyn (Ed.), *The tourist image. Myths and myth making in tourism* (pp. 61-81). Chichester, England: Wiley.

Debbage, K. G. (1990). Oligopoly and the resort cycle in the Bahamas. *Annals of Tourism Research, 17*, 513-527.

De Boeck, F. (1997). Beeld, tegenbeeld, evenbeeld. Exotisme, fotografie en antropologie in de (post-)koloniale ontmoeting in Afrika. In *Exotisme. Culturele studies* (pp. 9-18). Leuven: KUL, Cultureel Centrum Leuven.

Demeritte, K. (1998). Measuring the impact of foreign capital flows in the Bahamian tourism industry. *Social and Economic Studies, 47*(2-3), 89-118.

Devedzic, M. (1997). Tourist region heterogeneity and gender: The case of the Yugoslav seaside. In *Gender/Tourism/Fun? Proceedings of the International Conference* (pp. 237-243). University of California, Davis, October 24-26.

Dubesset, E. (1995). Le tourisme à Cuba: une indistrie en pleine expansion. *Cahiers d'Outre-Mer, 48*, 189-192.

Dulude, J. (2000, July 14). Much 'protected' land unpaid. *Tico Times* (http://www.ticotimes.net/).

Dwyer, L., & Forsyth, P. (1998). Economic significance of cruise tourism. *Annals of Tour-*

ism Research, 25(2), 393-415.

Eadington, W., & Milton, R. (1991). Economics and tourism. *Annals of Tourism Research, 18*(1), 41-56.

Easton, S. T. (1998). Is tourism just another commodity? Links between commodity trade and tourism. *Journal of Economic Integration, 13*(3), 522-543.

Echeverría, J., Hanrahan, M., & Solórzano, R. (1995). Valuation of non-priced amenities provided by the biological resources within the Monteverde Cloud Forest Preserve, Costa Rica. *Ecological Economics, 13*, 43-52.

Echtner, Ch. M. (1995). Entrepreneurial training in developing countries. *Annals of Tourism Research, 22*(1), 119-134.

Economic Commission for Latin America and the Caribbean. (1998). *Economic survey of Latin America and the Caribbean 1997-1998.* Santiago de Chile: United Nations.

Engelenburg, H., & van Duijvenbode, A. (Eds.). (1995). *The role of non-governmental development organisations in the development of sustainable tourism.* Utrecht-Lanzarote: Profound, Advisors in Development.

Enloe, C. (1989). *Bananas, beaches & bases. Making feminist sense of international politics.* London: Pandora.

Espino, M. D. (1993). Tourism in Cuba: A development strategy for the 1990s? *Cuban Studies, 23*, 49-70.

Fairbairn-Dunlop, P. (1994). Gender, culture and tourism development in Western Samoa. In: V. Kinnaird & D. Hall (Eds.), *Tourism: A gender analysis.* Chichester, England: Wiley.

Garcia-Ramon, M.-D., Canoves, G., & Valdovinos, N. (1995). Farm tourism, gender and the environment in Spain. *Annals of Tourism Research, 22*(2), 267-282.

Go, F. M. (1997). Entrepreneurs and the tourism industry in developing countries. In H. Dahles (Ed.), *Tourism, small entrepreneurs, and sustainable development. Cases from developing countries* (pp. 5-22). Tilburg: ATLAS.

Goodrich, J. N. (1994). Health tourism. In M. Uysal (Ed.), *Global tourist behaviour* (pp. 227-238). Binghampton, England: Binghampton International Business Press.

Groen, B. (1996). Vakantie in eco-Costa Rica. *América Ventana, 241*, 40-42.

Hagenaars, D. (1995). *De maatschappelijke discussie over toeristische ontwikkkeling en milieu in Costa Rica.* Unpublished M.A. thesis, University of Amsterdam.

Hall, D. R. (1995). Tourism development in Cuba. In D. Harrison (Ed.), *Tourism to less developed countries: The social consequences* (2nd ed., pp. 102-120). Chichester, England: Wiley.

Hall, J.A., & Braithwaite, R. (1990). Caribbean cruise tourism. *Tourism Management, 11*(4), 339-347.

Harrison, D. (1992). *Tourism & the less developed countries.* Chichester, England: Wiley.

Harrison, D. (1994). Tourism, capitalism and development in less developed countries. In L. Sklair (Ed.), *Capitalism and development* (pp. 232-257). London: Routledge.

Harrison, L. C., & Husbands, W. (Eds.). (1996). *Practicing responsible tourism.* New York: Wiley.

Hennessy, S. (1994). Female employment in tourism development in south-west England. In V. Kinnaird & D. Hall (Eds.), *Tourism: A gender analysis* (pp. 35-51). Chichester, England: Wiley.

Heykers, J., & Verkooijen, R. (1997). *Costa Rica, Puur natuur of zon-zee-strand?* Unpublished M.A. thesis, Wageningen Agricultural University.

Holder, J. S. (1979). *Caribbean tourism, policies and impacts.* Barbados: Caribbean Tourism Research and Development Centre.

Honey, M. (1999). *Ecotourism and sustainable development. Who owns paradise?* Washington, DC: Island Press.

Hunter, C., & Green, H. (1995). *Tourism and the environment: A sustainable relation-*

ship? London: Routledge.

Hudson, B. (1996). Paradise lost:A planner's view of Jamaican tourist development. *Caribbean Quarterly, 42*, 22-31.

Hummel, J. (1992). *Ecotourism:The role of sustainable tourism development in nature conservation and local socio-economic development in protected areas of developing countries:A few conditions and some preliminary links with the Attraction System concept.* Paper voor VVS congress "Internationalisation and Leisure research," December 10-13,Tilburg University.

Inter-American Development Bank. (1999). *Facing up inequality in Latin America—economic and social progress in Latin America—1998-1999 report.* Washington, DC:John Hopkins University Press.

International Monetary Fund. (1990). *International financial statistics yearbook.* Washington, DC:Author.

International Monetary Fund. (1995). *International financial statistics yearbook.* Washington, DC:Author.

International Monetary Fund. (1998). *International financial statistics yearbook.* Washington, DC:Author.

Inman, C. (1998). *Impacts on developing countries of changing production and consumption patterns in developed countries:The case of ecotourism in Costa Rica* [Draft report]. San José, Costa Rica: INCAE.

Inskeep, E. (1991). *Tourism planning, an integrated and sustainable development approach.* New York:Van Nostrand Reinhold.

Jafari, J. (1989). Sociocultural dimensions of tourism.An English language literature review. In J. Bustrzanowski (Ed.), *Tourism as a factor of change:A sociocultural study* (pp. 17-60).Vienna: Economic Coordination Centre for Research and Documentation in Social Sciences.

Jarray, I. (1999, February 1). Cuba contaminé par les "vices capitalistes." *Le Figaro.*

Kempadoo, K. (Ed.). (1999). *Sun, sex and gold. Tourism and sex work in the Caribbean.* Lanham, Boulder: Rowman & Littlefield Publishers.

Key, C. J. (1993). *From fishing to tourism. The case of Placencia, Belize.* Louisville: Published privately.

Kinnaird, V., & Hall, D. (Eds.). (1994a). *Tourism:A gender analysis.* Chichester, England: Wiley.

Kinnaird,V., & Hall, D. (1994b). Conclusion:The way forward. In V. Kinnaird & D. Hall (Eds.), *Tourism:A gender analysis* (pp. 210-216). Chichester, England:Wiley.

Kinnaird,V., Kothari, U., & Hall, D. (1994).Tourism: Gender perspectives. In V. Kinnaird & D. Hall (Eds.), *Tourism:A gender analysis* (pp. 1-34). Chichester, England:Wiley.

Koussis, M. (1989).Tourism and the family in a rural Cretan community.*Annals of Tourism Research, 16*(3), 318-332.

Laarman, J. G., & Perdue, R. R. (1989). Science tourism in Costa Rica. *Annals of Tourism Research, 16*(2), 205-215.

Landau, S., & Sparratt, D. (1994, November). Cuba's economic slide. *Multinational Monitor*,7-12.

Langen, B. (1996). Internationaal toerisme op Cuba. *Tijdschrift Derde Wereld, 15*(1), 49-58.

Lee, W. (1991). Prostitution and tourism in South-East Asia. In: N. Redclift & M. T. Sinclair (Eds.), *Working women. International perspectives on labour and gender ideology* (pp. 79-103). London: Routledge.

Leiper, N. (1990).Tourist attraction systems.*Annals of Tourism Research, 17*(2), 367-384.

Leontidou, L. (1994). Gender dimensions of tourism in Greece: Employment, subcultures and restructuring. In V. Kinnaird & D. Hall (Eds.), *Tourism:A gender analysis* (pp. 74-

105). Chichester, England: Wiley.

Lindberg, K., & Hawkins, D. E. (1993). *Ecotourism: A guide for planners & managers.* North Bennington: The Ecotourism Society.

Luft, A., & Wegter, I. (1990). *Reishandboek Costa Rica.* Rijswijk: Elmar Reishandboeken.

Lumsdon, L. M., & Swift, J. S. (1998). Ecotourism at a crossroad: The case of Costa Rica. *Journal of Sustainable Tourism, 6*(2), 155-172.

MacCannell, D. (1973). Staged authenticity: Arrangements of social space in tourist settings. *American Journal of Sociology, 79,* 589-603.

MacCannell, D. (1976). *The tourist: A new theory of the leisure class.* New York: Schocken Books, Inc.

MacCannell, D. (1984). Reconstructed ethnicity. Tourism and cultural identity in Third World communities. *Annals of Tourism Research, 11,* 375-391.

MacCannell, D. (1992). *Empty meeting grounds: The tourist papers.* London: Routledge.

Marshment, M. (1997). Gender takes a holiday: Representations in holiday brochures. In M. T. Sinclair (Ed.), *Gender, work and tourism* (pp. 16-34). London: Routledge.

Mazumdar, D. (1989). *Government interventions and urban labour markets in developing countries* [EDI working papers]. Washington, DC: World Bank.

McElroy, J. L., & de Albuquerque, K. (1998). Tourism penetration index in small Caribbean islands. *Annals of Tourism Research, 25*(1), 145-168.

McIntyre, G. (1993). *Sustainable tourism development: Guide local for planners.* Madrid: World Tourism Organization.

Meisch, L. A. (1995). Gringas and Otavaleños. Changing tourist relations. *Annals of Tourism Research, 22*(2), 441-462.

Meisch, L. A. (1997). Sex and romance on the trail in the Andes. In *Gender/Tourism/Fun? Proceedings of the International Conference* (pp. 24-26). University of California, Davis, October 24-26.

Menkhaus, S., & Lober, D. J. (1996). International ecotourism and the valuation of tropical rainforest in Costa Rica. *Journal of Environmental Management, 47,* 1-10.

Midgley, J. (with Hall, A., Hardiman, M., & Narine, D.). (1986). *Community participation, social development and the state.* London/New York: Methuen.

Moberg, M. (1993). *Citrus, strategy and class. The politics of development in southern Belize.* Iowa City: University of Iowa Press.

Momsen, J. H. (1994). Tourism, gender and development in the Caribbean. In V. Kinnaird & D. Hall (Eds.), *Tourism: A gender analysis* (pp. 106-120). Chichester, England: Wiley.

Mowforth, M., & Munt, I. (1998). *Tourism and sustainability—new tourism in the Third World.* London: Routledge.

Muroi, H., & Sasaki, N. (1997). Tourism and prostitution in Japan. In M. T. Sinclair (Ed.), *Gender, work and tourism* (pp. 180-219). London: Routledge.

Murphy, P. E. (1985). *Tourism. A community approach.* London: Routledge.

Norris, J., & Wall, G. (1994). Gender and tourism. In C. P. Cooper & A. Lockwood (Eds.), *Progress in tourism, recreation and hospitality management* (Vol. 6). Chichester, England: Wiley.

Oppermann, M. (1999). Sex tourism. *Annals of Tourism Research, 26*(2), 251-266.

Pariser, H. S. (1992). *Adventure guide to Costa Rica.* Ashborne: Moorland Publishing.

Pashby, Ch. (2000, June 16). Ministry: Tourism growth OK. *Tico Times* (http://www.ticotimes.net/).

Pattullo, P. (1996). *Last resorts. The cost of tourism in the Caribbean.* London: Cassell.

Paul, S. (1987). *Community participation in development projects. The World bank experience* [World Bank discussion paper No. 6]. Washington, DC: The World Bank.

Pearce, D. (1992). *Tourist organizations.* New York: Longman.

Pearce, D., & Butler, R. (1993). *Tourism research. Critiques and challenges.* London:

Routledge.

Peterson, G. (1989). *Nosotras, las putas*. Madrid: Talasa.

Philips, R. B. (1995). Why not tourist art? Significant silences in Native American museum representations. In G. Prakash (Ed.), *After colonialism. Imperial histories and postcolonial displacements* (pp. 98-125). Princeton: Princeton University Press.

Place, S. (1991). Nature tourism and rural development in Tortuguero. *Annals of Tourism Research, 18*(2), 186-201.

Pronk, J., & Haq, M. (1992). *Sustainable development. From concept to action*. Den Haag: Ministerie van Ontwikkelingssamenwerking.

Pruitt, D., & Lafont, S. (1995). For love and money: Romance tourism in Jamaica. *Annals of Tourism Research, 22*(2), 422-462.

Purcell, K. (1997). Women's employment in UK tourism: Gender roles and labour markets. In M. T. Sinclair (Ed.), *Gender, work and tourism* (pp. 35-39). London: Routledge.

Rachowiecki, R. (1997). *Costa Rica*. Hawthorn, Australia: Lonely Planet Publications

Richards, G., & Hall, D. (Eds.). (2000a). *Tourism and sustainable community development*. London: Routledge.

Richards, G., & Hall, D. (2000b). The community: A sustainable concept in tourism development? In G. Richards & D. Hall (Eds.), *Tourism and sustainable community development* (pp. 1-13). London: Routledge.

Richards, G., & Hall, D. (Eds.). (2000c). Conclusions. In G. Richards & D. Hall (Eds.), *Tourism and sustainable community development* (pp. 297-306). London: Routledge.

Richter, L. (1994). Exploring the political role of gender in tourism research. In W. Theobald (Ed.), *Global tourism. The next decade* (pp. 146-157). Oxford: Butterworth-Heinemann.

Roessingh, C. (1998). *De Belizaanse Garifuna. De contouren van een etnische gemeenschap in Midden-Amerika*. Amsterdam: Thela Thesis.

Rovinski, Y. (1991). Private reserves, parks and ecotourism in Costa Rica. In T. Whelan (Ed.), *Nature tourism. Managing for the environment* (pp. 39-57). Washington, DC: Island Press.

Salazar, M. A. G. (1995). Lecture at the Second Ecolodge Forum and Field Seminar, Ecotourism Society, October 22-29, Puntarenas, Costa Rica.

Scheepmaker, M. (1998). Stille palmplantage organiseert agro-ecotoerisme. *Vice Versa, 1*, 26-27.

Schlüter, R. G. (1994). Tourism development: A Latin American perspective. In W. Theobald (Ed.), *Global tourism. The next decade* (pp. 146-260). Oxford: Butterworth-Heinemann.

Seward, S. B., & Spinrad, B. K. (1982). *Tourism in the Caribbean, the economic impact*. Ottawa, Canada: International Development Research Centre.

Shaw, G., & Williams, A. M. (1994). *Critical issues in tourism. A geographical perspective*. Oxford and Cambridge: Blackwell.

Shoman, A. (1994). *13 chapters on a history of Belize*. Belize City: Angelus Press Ltd.

Silver, I. (1993). Marketing authenticity in Third World countries. *Annals of Tourism Research, 20*(2), 302-218.

Sinclair, M. T. (1991). Women, work and skill: Economic theories and feminist perspectives. In N. Redclift & M. T. Sinclair (Eds.), *Working women. International perspectives on labour and gender ideology* (pp. 1-24). London: Routledge.

Sinclair, M. T. (Ed.). (1997a). *Gender, work and tourism*. London: Routledge.

Sinclair, M. T. (1997b). Issues and theories of gender and work in tourism. In M. T. Sinclair (Ed.), *Gender, work and tourism* (pp. 1-15). London: Routledge.

Sinclair, M. T. (1997c). Gendered work in tourism: Comparative perspectives. In M. T. Sinclair (Ed.), *Gender, work and tourism* (pp. 220-234). London: Routledge.

Sinclair, M. T. (1998). Tourism and economic development: A survey. *The Journal of Development Studies, 34*(5), 1-51.

Smith, D. C. (1995). Implementing a national park system for Jamaica: PARC Project. In D. Barker & F. M. McGregor (Eds.), *Environment and development in the Caribbean* (pp. 249- 258). University of the West Indies, Jamaica: The Press.

Smith, V. L. (Ed.). (1989). *Hosts and guests. The anthropology of tourism* (2nd ed.). Philadelphia, PA: University of Philadelphia Press.

Smith, V. L., & Eadington, W. R. (Eds.). (1992). *Tourism alternatives. Potentials and problems in the development of tourism.* Philadelphia, PA: University of Pennsylvania Press.

Sorée, J., & Volker, S. (1998). *Wanted or unwanted. Casestudie van ondernemerschap in de toeristenindustrie in Belize.* Unpublished M.A. thesis, University of Amsterdam.

Stone, M. C. (1991). *Caribbean nation, Central American state: Ethnicity and race. A national formation in Belize, 1798-1900.* Michigan: U.M.I. Dissertation Services.

Swain, M. (1978). Cuna women and ethnic tourism: A way to persist and an avenue to change. In V. L. Smith (Ed.), *Hosts and guests. The anthropology of tourism* (pp. 71-81). Oxford: Blackwell.

Swain, M. (1989). Gender roles in indigenous tourism: Kuna Mola, Kuna Yala and cultural survival. In V. L. Smith (Ed.), *Hosts and guests: An anthropology of tourism* (2nd ed., pp. 83-104). Philadelphia, PA: University of Pennsylvania Press.

Swain, M. B. (Ed.). (1995). Gender in tourism. *Annals of Tourism Research, 22*(2), 247- 266.

Taylor, F. F. (1993). *To hell with Paradise. A history of the Jamaica tourist industry.* Pittsburg: University of Pittsburgh Press.

Telfer, D. J., & G. Wall (1996). Linkages between tourism and food production. *Annals of Tourism Research, 23*(3), 635-653.

Theuns, H. L. (1989). *Toerisme in ontwikkelingslanden.* Tilburg: Tilburg University Press.

Thomas, C. Y. (1988). *The poor and the powerless. Economic policy and change in the Caribbean.* London: Latin America Bureau.

Tosun, C. (2000). Limits to community participation in the tourism development process of developing countries. *Tourism Management, 21*(6), 613-633.

UCLA. (1976). *Statistical abstract of Latin America.* Los Angeles: University of Califronia, Latin American Center Publications.

UCLA. (1984). *Statistical abstract of Latin America.* Los Angeles: University of Califronia, Latin American Center Publications.

UCLA. (1996). *Statistical abstract of Latin America.* Los Angeles: University of Califronia, Latin American Center Publications.

UCLA. (1999). *Statistical abstract of Latin America.* Los Angeles: University of Califronia, Latin American Center Publications.

United Nations Development Programme. (1990). *Human development report.* New York/ Oxford: Oxford University Press.

United Nations Development Programme. (1992). *Human development report.* New York/ Oxford: Oxford University Press.

United Nations Development Programme. (1998). *Human development report.* New York/ Oxford: Oxford University Press.

United Nations Development Programme. (2000). *Human development report.* New York/ Oxford: Oxford University Press.

United Nations Environment Programme. (1997). *Global environment outlook.* New York/ Oxford: Oxford University Press.

United Nations Organization. (1979). *Demographic yearbook.* New York: Author.

United Nations Organization. (1984). *Demographic yearbook.* New York: Author.

United Nations Organization. (1990). *International standard industrial classification of all economic activities.* New York: Author.

United Nations Organization. (1994). *Demographic yearbook.* New York: Author.

United Nations Organization. (1997). *Demographic yearbook.* New York:Author.

Urry,J. (1990). *The tourist gaze.* London: SAGE Publications.

Urry,J. (1991).Tourism, travel and the modern subject. *Vrijetijd en Samenleving, 9*(3/4), 87-98.

Urry,J. (1992).The tourist gaze and the 'environment.' *Theory, Culture & Society, 9*(1), 1-26.

Urry,J. (1995). *Consuming places.* London: Routledge.

Valentine, P. S. (1992). Nature-based tourism. In: B.Weiler & C. M. Hall (Eds.), *Special interest tourism* (pp. 105-127). London: Belhaven Press.

Van Berkel, P. (1994). *Toerisme en sociaal-culturele verandering in Puerto Viejo, Costa Rica.* Unpublished M.A. thesis, Rijksuniversiteit Leiden.

Van den Berghe,P.(1994). *The quest for the Other.Ethnic tourism in San Cristóbal, Mexico.* Seattle: University of Washington Press.

Van den Berghe, P. L., & Keyes, C. F. (1984). Introduction.Tourism and re-created ethnicity. *Annals of Tourism Research, 11*, 343-352.

Van der Duim, V. R. (1993). Ecotoerisme: een nieuwe natuurbeschermer? In *Paperboek Nederlands-Vlaamse Vrijetijdsstudiedagen* (pp. 24-33). Den Haag/Amersfoort: Vereniging voor de Vrijetijdssector/Hogeschool Midden-Nederland.

Van der Duim,V. R. (1997).The role of small entrepreneurs in the development of sustainable tourism in Costa Rica. In H. Dahles (Ed.), *Tourism, small entrepreneurs, and sustainable development. Cases from developing countries* (pp. 35-48).Tilburg:ATLAS.

Van der Duim,V. R., & Philipsen,J.(1995). Recreatie, toerisme en natuurbescherming tussen romantiek, ecologie en commercie. *Vrijetijd en Samenleving, 13*(2), 21-41.

Van der Duim, V. R., & Philipsen, J. (1996). Hoe eco is Costa Rica's ecotoerisme? *Derde Wereld, 15*(1), 59-71.

Van der Heyden,A., &Vierboom, M. (1997). *Tourist in Costa Rica.* Unpublished M.A. thesis, Tilburg University.

Van Hattum,W.(1997).Jineteros bepalen toekomst van socialisme in Cuba.*América Ventana, 247*, 9-11.

Van Hout,A. (1984).Toerisme in de derde wereld. *Derde Wereld, 3*, 50-67.

Van Iperen,A. (1996). *De lege etalage. Cuba na de revolutie.* Amsterdam-Antwerpen:Atlas.

Van Leiden, G. (1995). *The economic importance of tourism in Costa Rica.* Unpublished M.A. thesis,Wageningen Agricultrual University.

Van Schaardenburgh,A. (1996). *Local participation in tourism development.A study in Cahuita, Costa Rica.* Unpublished M.A. thesis, University of Tilburg.

Van Wijk, J. (2000). *Costa Rica: Going for the green? The use of environmental impact assessment with special attention to golf course development* [Report 3].Wageningen: Wageningen University, Socio-Spatial Analysis & Recreation and Tourism.

Vargas Leiton, J. L. (1995). Lecture at the Second Ecolodge Forum and Field Seminar, Ecotourism Society, October 22-29, Puntarenas, Costa Rica.

Vasquez, C. (1992). *Investigacion sobre motivaciones del turismo receptivo en El Salvador* (37h/11). San Salvador, El Salvador.

Vellas, F., & Becherel, L. (1995). *International tourism: An economic perspective.* Basingstone: Macmillan.

Verschoor, G. (1997). *Tacos, Tiendas and Mezcal.An actor-network perspective on small scale entrepreneurial projects in Western Mexico.* Unpublished Dissertation,Wageningen Agricultural University.

Wall, G., & Long,V. (1996). Balinese homestays:An indigenous response to tourism opportunities. In R. Butler & T. Hinch (Eds.), *Tourism and indigenous peoples* (pp. 27-48). London: InternationalThomson Business Press.

Wang, N. (1999). Rethinking authenticity in tourism experience. *Annals of Tourism Re-*

search, 26(2), 349-370.

Weaver, D. B. (1998). *Ecotourism in the less developed world.* London: CAB International.

Wheatcroft, S. (1994). *Aviation and tourism policies: Balancing the benefits.* London: Routledge.

Whelan, T. (1991). *Nature tourism. Managing for the environment.* Washington, DC: Island Press.

Wilkinson, P. (1992). Tourism. The curse of the nineties? Belize. An experiment to integrate tourism and the environment. *Community Development Journal, 27*(4), 386-395.

Wilkinson, P. F. (1997). *Tourism policy & planning: Case studies from the Commonwealth Caribbean.* New York: Cognizant Communication Corporation.

Wilkinson, P. F., & Pratiwi, W. (1995). Gender and tourism in an Indonesian village. *Annals of Tourism Research, 22*(2), 283-299.

Wilson, A. (1992). *The culture of nature.* Cambridge/Oxford: Blackwell.

Wilson, D. (1996). Glimpses of Caribbean tourism and the question of sustainability in Barbados and St. Lucia. In L. Briguglio, R. Butler, D. Harrison, & W. Leal Filho (Eds.), *Sustainable tourism in islands and small states.* New York: Pinter.

Wood, R. E. (1993). Tourism, culture and the sociology of development. In M. Hitchcock, V. T. King, & M. J. G. Parnwell (Eds.), *Tourism in South-East Asia* (pp. 48-70). London/New York: Routledge.

Wood, R. E. (2000). Caribbean cruise tourism—globalization at sea. *Annals of Tourism Research, 27*(2), 345-370.

World Bank. (1969). *Annual report 1969.* Washington, DC: Author.

World Bank. (1986). *The BAHAMAS, economic report.* Washington, DC: Author.

World Tourism Organization. (1992). *Yearbook of tourism statistics.* Madrid: Author.

World Tourism Organization. (1994). *National and regional tourism planning methodologies.* London: Routledge.

World Tourism Organization. (1995). *Yearbook of tourism statistics.* Madrid: Author.

World Tourism Organization. (1996). *Yearbook of tourism statistics.* Madrid: Author.

World Tourism Organization. (1997). *Yearbook of tourism statistics.* Madrid: Author.

World Tourism Organization. (1999). *Yearbook of tourism statistics.* Madrid: Author.

World Tourism Organization. (2000). *Yearbook of tourism statistics.* Madrid: Author.

World Tourism Organization. (2001). *Yearbook of tourism statistics.* Madrid: Author.

Index

Books in the
TOURISM
DYNAMICS SERIES

PUBLISHED BY COGNIZANT COMMUNICATIONS

www.cognizantcommunication.com